THE DOG
ENCYCLOPEDIA

ESTHER J.J. VERHOEF-VERHALLEN

THE DOG ENCYCLOPEDIA

A FIREFLY BOOK

A FIREFLY BOOK

Published by Firefly Books Ltd. 1997
Copyright © 1996, 1997 by Rebo Productions Ltd.

Published in the United States in 1997 by
Fierfly Books (U.S.) Ltd.
P.O. Box 1338, Ellicot Station
Buffalo, New York 14205

Second printing

Cataloguing in Publication Data

Verhoef-Verhallen, Ester J.J.
     The dog encyclopedia

Includes index.
ISBN 1-55209-155-4

1. Dog breeds - Encyclopedias.   2. Dogs - Encyclopedias.
I.Title

SF422.V47	19971636.7'1'03	C97-930886-0

Cover design: Ton Wienbelt, The Netherlands
Production: TextCase, The Netherlands
Translation: Stephen Challacombe for First Edition Translation Ltd., Great Britain
Editing for the North American edition: Irene Cumming Kleeberg
Typsetting: Hof&Land Typografie, The Netherlands

Printed in Slovenia.

Contents

Foreword

This book is designed to concentrate on the practical considerations of buying, owning, and caring for a dog. Because there are many specific books giving information on the histories and origins of the various breeds of dogs this book has been created, rather, to deal with those basic questions concerning each breed which are most often raised with both breed societies and professional dog breeders. From these breed descriptions you should be able to judge whether or not a dog you are considering will meet your own personal circumstances. At the same time, the photographs throughout the book will give an opportunity to consider that most basic of questions: what does the dog actually look like?

The classification system used is the one that is used by the International Cynological Federation (FCI), a system which differs only slightly from the systems of other organizations, such as the Canadian Kennel Club and the American Kennel Club. More important, however, for the reader who is considering the purchase of a dog, this book discusses the suitability of the dog for country or urban living, the size of the dog, its exercise needs, and whether or not it gets along well with other animals and children. Detailed discussion of each dog's grooming needs is also included.

Esther J. J. Verhoef-Verhallen

Introduction

A pedigree dog is more than just another dog

Almost everyone who is looking for a pedigree dog will be influenced initially by the basic appearance of the breed, and there is nothing wrong with that provided you remember that each breed of dog has its own specific character. Many breeds have existed for centuries and have been used for a very wide range of purposes, mainly to work for humans and to make our jobs easier, or even to take over the job entirely. Originally, of course, the outward appearance of the dog was of little significance, although it seems that it was realized fairly early that certain types and colors of coat and the build of a dog were better suited to certain tasks than other colors and builds. It was not just coincidence that led to uniformity among dogs doing the same work in the same part of the world. Those early standardized dogs are not far removed from today's pedigree animal.

Today, particularly in the West, most dogs no longer perform the tasks for which they were originally bred. For the most part, however, with relatively few exceptions, dogs have adapted perfectly to their new role as pets.

Grooming to keep the coat in condition is an important part of keeping a dog

Dog owners must realize that a dog's primitive instincts are carried in the genes through the generations. Centuries of selective breeding cannot be eradicated in a few decades. Remember this fact when you are deciding on your choice of breed. It is often said that the look of a particular dog is something to which you will become accustomed, but its character may be harder to adapt to. The dog's character has to please you throughout its life and for that reason, careful and correct choice is very important. The purchase and care of a pedigree dog should be a rewarding and pleasurable experience for both the dog and the family of which it will form part.

The purchase of a pedigree dog

Take time to decide right

Clearly the decision to buy a pedigree dog is not one to be made lightly on the spur of the moment. The dog which you choose will probably be a part of your family for more than ten years, with you every day and every night. It will be as much a part of your family as your own relatives and it must be considered as such. You must realize that a dog will make a significant impression upon your daily life. Since there are both good and bad dog breeders find out as much as you can before rushing off to buy a dog.

Consider first your reason for acquiring a dog. Do you hope to make money by breeding and selling puppies? Are you planning to enter your dog in dog shows, hoping to move it higher and higher in the dog world? Or are you just seeking a family pet? If you are only looking for a good family pet a dog with what would be considered a small imperfection in color or coat will be much cheaper to buy than one of the more 'perfect' dogs, but do not expect to walk away with the prizes at a dog show, or to breed a future champion. Such a dog, though, might be a perfect family member.

If you are looking for a hunting dog, then seek out a breeder who specializes in hunting dogs. You are then more likely to obtain a puppy which will hunt well than if you buy a dog of the same breed with only show championships in its pedigree. The opposite is also true, of course.

If it is possible, first make contact with the society which promotes the welfare of the particular breed you have become interested in. Visit and talk with a number of breeders and enthusiasts and join the breed association so that you will receive newsletters. These newsletters usually come out about twice a year and are full of useful information. Whatever you do, consider the entire purchase of your dog carefully and never buy a dog from puppy farms, traders, pet shops, or from a market. It is impossible to know from these sources whether the dog is healthy, the appearance and character of its parents, and, most importantly, how it has been handled during the crucial imprinting phase of its development. Such a puppy may well be much cheaper but the apparent gain can be wiped out after several months of heavy veterinarian's bills with a sickly animal.

Should your choice be an uncommon breed, it will be very difficult to find the best breeder. The national breeds' registration organization should be able to assist your search. Occasionally an unusual breed will have to be imported. If so make sure that any papers are in order and ask your national organization if they know of anyone with previous experience of importing the breed in question. Don't be afraid that an unusual breed will be more expensive than a popular one. In some cases, in fact, the dog can be cheaper, since the breeder of a relatively unknown breed has greater difficulty in finding good homes for the offspring.

Dog or bitch

Both dogs and bitches have their advantages and disadvantages. Dogs are generally more uniform in character than bitches because the bitches suffer from hormone changes when they are in heat. This usually happens about twice each year, making them eager to be with dogs (and the dogs eager to be with them) and causing them to leave spots on the carpet. There are various ways of making this less of a problem including letting the bitch wear special diapers, having the veterinarian give her a special shot to prevent ovulation, or having her spayed.
Dogs are usually more independent by nature and less gentle. This is especially noticeable with the more dominant breeds such as the Rottweiler. The difference between the sexes is generally far less pronounced with the more gentle breeds, but there are countless exceptions to this rule.
The choice between dog or bitch is a personal one. For those interested in the

more dominant breeds but who have little experience in bringing up dogs, a bitch will be a better choice. Ask the breeder for advice. He or she spends every day with the dogs and knows their characters like none other. A good breeder will agree to select from the litter the puppy that is most suitable for your wishes and situation. Although this book provides guidelines to the characters of different breeds remember that these are general character traits of the average member of the breed. Within specific lines of breeding of the same breed, character can vary widely. Above all, every dog is unique, even dogs from the same litter.

Older dog or puppy?

The majority of people will choose a puppy in preference to an older dog as a puppy is comparatively easy to train. Most people enjoy watching a young dog grow up. In spite of this, an older dog can be an ideal choice. The mature dog has already developed its character and has finished growing. Normally, they have had at least rudimentary training and are housebroken. The exuberance of puppy-hood is behind them and they adapt readily to the new circumstances. It is possible to develop as equally strong a bond with an older dog as with a puppy.

Many breed associations have a special department to find new owners for fully grown or almost fully grown dogs that, for some reason or other, need a new home. The breed association will be perfectly honest about the reason why a new home needs to be found. If you don't feel strongly about acquiring a puppy, then contact the organization for your preferred breed. There will be no obligation for asking.

Training

Socializing

Various scientific studies have shown that the influences and experiences which a puppy undergoes during the first twelve to fourteen weeks of its life are the most formative in its upbringing. This period is known as the imprinting phase and if during this time a dog learns that strangers, children, cats, and busy urban traffic mean it no harm, it will then react in a stable way to them throughout its life.

The opposite of this is equally true: a puppy which has spent the entire period of fourteen weeks in a kennel with its mother and the other members of the litter for company, apart from the one human who looks after them, finds it difficult to adapt to human society later when it is more mature. The way in which these experiences occur has an enormous influence upon the young dog. If the puppy is attacked by a cat during this period, it is likely that it will react badly towards cats for the rest of its life, and no one can really fail to understand why.

It is clearly best to buy a puppy from a breeder who can prove to you that sufficient time and energy are spent in ensuring the puppies are well socialized. When a puppy is seven to twelve weeks old, you will be able to take it home. Now it is your responsibility to complete what the good breeder has begun.

Consistent and logical

Consistent handling in its upbringing is essential with every dog, irrespective of the breed. This means, for example, that a dog is only told what a "good dog" it is when it has been a good dog by obeying a command. This may seem obvious but it some that people find it difficult to remain consistent and logical in daily life. If you want your dog to lie down, only show you are pleased with it when it has done so. When people leave a dog, they often say "stay in your basket" to it. Since it is impossible to verify whether the dog actually does so, it is better not to give such an order.

If you decide not to allow the dog on to the sofa, then it must never be permitted, even when it is sick. If the dog is feeling sick and you want it near you for comfort, place an old mattress or bed pad on the floor rather than letting the dog up onto the sofa.

The same applies if you do not want your dog to jump up enthusiastically to greet people; never permit it, not even on occasions when you find it fun as you happen to be wearing old clothes. A dog cannot understand the subtle difference that makes certain behavior acceptable at one time and not so on another and it will become confused and unhappy.

Remaining consistent as a dog grows up is of course difficult, particularly in a large family in which everyone has his or her own idea about the best way of bringing up a dog. It is highly confusing for a dog not to know where it stands. Some breeds are so sensitive to this that they end up either trying to dominate or by being much too submissive. Do not permit the family to adopt flexible rules. Before a dog joins the family, every member must know what the rules for the dog are and understand the importance of sticking rigidly to them.

Punishment

Only punish a dog immediately if it does something wrong, never when the mischief happened some time ago. Imagine that, in your absence, the dog has played havoc with the contents of your home. When you discover this on returning home, you punish the dog, verbally or physically. It may seem obvious to you that the dog is at fault and you may think from the expression on the dog's face that it knows this. Nothing could be less true. Most dogs will have forgotten entirely what they have done but will react to your manner and either become submissive or try to escape. The only lesson the dog will learn is that punishment is associated with your returning home and consequently it will anxiously anticipate what will happen when you enter the room. Depending upon the breed, a dog may become aggressive or very nervous and submissive. It will lose trust in its fickle and unpredictable pack leader – you.
If your dog misbehaves whenever you are away, then it is best to put it in a kennel outdoors or restrict it to a room where it can do no harm. This ensures that it will always be a "good dog" on your return. Most dogs grow out of the destructive urge once out of puppy-hood but a few continue because they get insufficient exercise or attention. Sometimes it is the result of pure boredom. It is essential to punish the dog immediately for any misbehaviour during the early days of its upbringing. Perhaps you call your dog to you and eventually it comes to you after much dithering. Since it has obeyed your command, the dog now deserves a reward. Unfortunately, dogs are often punished by owners for failing to come quickly enough. The likely consequence will be that the dog learns to associate

your orders with punishment and will most certainly have no desire to react quickly the next time. This book does not, of course, extend to a full explanation of the training and upbringing of a dog. You are advised to consult one of the many excellent books on this subject.If you have no experience in the training and upbringing of a dog, it is a good idea to join a puppy course – with the puppy of course! In this way your puppy's education can be well guided. Keep in mind always that every dog is different and that there are considerable differences between and within breeds. Ensure that the instructors are familiar with the characteristics of your dog's breed.

Association with dogs, other pets, and children

How well the dog mixes with dogs, other pets, and with children is partially dependent upon the individual dog and its breed and partially upon its imprinting and socializing. Breeds once kept in packs need to be sociable and there is a high risk they will display disturbed behavior towards other dogs, pets, and children unless they are properly socialized from birth.

The character descriptions in this book are generalized; they assume that a dog will have enjoyed good socializing and be well brought up. A word of caution is appropriate though. However lovable and patient a dog is with children, it should never be left unsupervised with children.

Association is very important. These Dobermans leave the poultry alone because they have been correctly socialized in their upbringing

It is important for children to understand that a dog must be left in peace when in its basket or while it is eating. Teach your children never to approach the dog but to call it to them instead in order to establish the correct hierarchy.

Caring for your dog

Ears, claws, and teeth

Every type of dog's coat has specific requirements for its care. These specific points are dealt with in the sections on the breeds. To clean the ears, it is important never to use cotton swabs since these will only push any dirt further into the ear. Use instead a recognized brand of ear cleaner. Let the drops enter the ears and massage them. Afterwards clean away surface dirt with a tissue.

Some dogs have excessive hair in the ears which should be removed regularly to avoid infection. Avoid removing too much at once but also do not clip one hair at a time because this will be painful for the dog. Sometimes too much hair grows between the pads of the feet. In this case the best method to care for this is to cut the hair growing between the pads. Curved scissors are the safest to use. Keep the curve facing away from the dog's foot so that you will not cut a pad.

Keep your dog's claws short. When a dog walks regularly on hard or rough ground, its claws will wear themselves down but some dogs have very quick-growing claws and in such cases the claws must be clipped. In order to keep your dog well groomed and cared for it is important to get it used to this ritual when young. An older and stronger dog which is not accustomed to it will try to resist, so that

regular grooming could become a major problem. If you find it unpleasant to do these jobs yourself, take your dog to a professional salon where they trim and groom dogs. They can explain and demonstrate to you the best way to do the more difficult tasks so that you may then be able to cope with them yourself.

General care also includes care of the teeth, although provided that your dog is fed with hard biscuit and regularly has a good quality bone to chew on, the teeth should require little attention. Dogs which on the contrary are mainly fed soft food and seldom if ever get the chance to use their teeth are far more likely to develop tartar with all the wretchedness this causes. Check regularly to see if your dog is developing tartar scale because prevention is always better than cure.

The coat

Some coats, especially the long-haired varieties, require intensive grooming. This can mean at least an hour a day of

The excess of hair between the pads of the feet must be regularly trimmed back.

brushing and combing. Teach your dog to stand or lie on a table with a hard surface for this ritual. This will prevent you from getting backache and make it easier to do the job thoroughly. Brush dogs with long hair at least once a week. This is not an unnecessary luxury even for smooth-haired breeds. During grooming you may notice things that would otherwise be overlooked such as small wounds, ticks, and other parasites. To shampoo a dog, use only a recognized brand of dog shampoo that will not affect the skin's natural oils. Never leave a wet dog out-doors, or in a cold draughty place. Make sure your dog is fully dry before letting it out of the house.

With a number of breeds it is necessary to have the coat trimmed regularly. This may be a simple task which can be learned from the breeder, but more usually it is a complex job best left to the professionals in the grooming salon. These salons know the right way to deal with the coats of most breeds. If your dog is unusual, it is best to take an illustration of the right style of trimming for your breed with you to the professional. A visit to such a salon is an excellent idea if you intend to show your dog. The correct trimming style can usually be obtained from the breed assoc-iation or from your dog's breeder.

Exercise

A breed to suit you

On warm sunny days or lovely autumn ones people often think how nice it would be to take a dog for a walk with them to play in the woods, or on the beach. Walking the dog has been rather over-romanticized. Once a dog is established in the home, it usually falls to just one person to "take the dog out." When it is howling a hurricane, raining, or freezing, the eagerness to walk the dog is no longer considered so romantic! A year consists of 365 days, on every one of which a dog will need to be exercised a minimum of three times, preferably four, whatever the weather. There are breeds that require considerable exercise. In these cases four times is certainly not sufficient – it may be necessary to bicycle with a dog of this type to make sure it gets the exercise it needs. It is clear then that choosing a breed which – so far as exercise is concerned – suits the life-style of your family is essential. If you are sporty, enjoy cycling, or run for pleasure, then highly active dogs make perfect companions. If these are not things you enjoy, choose a less active breed.

Dog sports

Sports for dogs, such as games of catch and baseball and agility skill trials have become increasingly popular. Certain breeds –specifically the sheepdogs– enjoy this form of exercise tremendously. Other less developed breeds can also participate in training classes for these sports. The important point is that both you and your dog should enjoy the activity. This does not have to be a competitive activity, although competition can become addictive if you discover that you and your dog form a good team.

Another well-known sporting activity is defence or security classes for highly trained dogs. Only certain breeds are permitted to participate or are considered for the mandatory training. Competing forms a key part of this activity and is taken very seriously. Often the organizers will insist that your dog has gained diplomas for obedience classes before they will accept it. This is understandable in view of the role dogs play in such competitions where they grab hold of "suspects" wearing protective suits with their teeth to "arrest" them. It is essential for the dogs to be strictly controlled. A brave and intelligent dog is essential, but it is of equal importance for the dog to be equable and good-natured. Considerable effort, patience, and dedication are also demanded from the owner. With appropriate training your dog will be no less trustworthy than before the course, and probably more so. The notion, which some people have, that these dogs become unreliable is baseless. This is an extremely disciplined activity in which there is no room for initiative on the part of the dog, on or off the training ground. This sport becomes a way of life to many of the human participants rather than just an interest. This is equally true of hunting. The bond between you has to be good if you go hunting with your dog. The dog must be well under control. Consequently, not every breed is suitable to be used as a hunting dog. In the group of hunting dogs there are numerous sections, each of which has a breed regarded to be the best in its category. Hunting need not necessarily include hunting wild game and killing it. Drag hunts use dummies bearing a scent for the dogs to follow. This can be an exciting multi-faceted sport for both you and your dog.

Dog racing is the best known way for a greyhound to really stretch its legs, although in some countries coursing is permitted. Both sports are generally restricted to greyhounds or dogs of the same group.

In mild climates it is rather difficult to exercise sledge dogs so many owners take their dogs to higher, and colder places where snow can be usually guaranteed. The dogs can then carry out the work for which they were originally bred, although generally not in competitive circumstances. In countries with little or no snow the practice sledge on wheels forms a means of training and exercising the dogs.

Showing dogs is an art in itself. First and foremost, your dog must be an outstanding specimen of its breed. Secondly, its coat must be faultless. That is unfortunately not the end of it. Not every dog, however beautiful, is prepared to stand as the centre of attention, and not every owner knows how best to accentuate his dog's best points. Every national breed registration organization runs courses on showing dogs and preparing them.

This summary of sporting activities for dogs is far from comprehensive. Taking part in a sport with your dog is an enjoyable way for both of you to be active together. You will understand your dog better from it and it will know you better. The bond between you will be strengthened. It is important that both of you should enjoy the activity. If your dog is not suited for a particular activity, this does not devalue its other qualities.

Adapted exercise

Many of the fast-growing breeds require adapted exercise in the first year of their life. With these breeds it is inadvisable to walk or play too much with the dog during its growing phase because the joints, bones, and limbs would be too highly stressed, leading to problems later in life. Hip displacement, knee, and back problems are in part inherited disorders,

but the wrong upbringing can cause harm. At the same time, these breeds will not be happy to be wrapped in cotton wool! Take them for a short walk, twice per day. Movement straight ahead at a tempo suitable for the dog is a good way to develop the muscles. Running next to a bicycle is ideal for many breeds as exercise.

After the dog is fully grown, the distance can be gradually increased. A winter break is quite acceptable in this routine but do not then begin straight away in the spring with long distances. The dog also needs to regain its condition. Not everyone will be able to find a safe place to exercise their dog alongside a bicycle, although there are probably more opportunities in your area than may at first be apparent. The chosen track must enable you to bicycle safely with the dog alongside away from other traffic.

1. Sheepdogs and cattle herders

Sheepdogs and other herding dogs

Australian Shepherd

COUNTRY OF ORIGIN
United States.

SPECIAL SKILLS
Sheepdog.

SIZE
The shoulder-height is 50 – 57cm
(19½ – 22½in) for dogs and 45 – 52cm
(17¾ – 20½in) for bitches.

COAT
The coat consists of medium to long hair with pronounced or loose waves and a dense under-coat. The Australian Shepherd's colorings can be blue-black marbled, red marbled (liver-colored), or plain black or brown, possibly with tan markings and some white.

CARE REQUIRED
Relatively little grooming is needed of the coat most of the time. When the dog is shedding, the under layer of the coat is shed, requiring a good combing to remove loose hairs.

CHARACTER
This intelligent, astute, eager to learn dog is level-headed, vigilant, alert, active, and tough. It is very loyal, has ample stamina, and bonds closely with the family.

TRAINING
Training is easy because the Australian Shepherd learns so quickly and eagerly but it should not be condemned to only three outings a day. In addition to a fairly high level of regular exercise, this breed also requires to be kept occupied. It is sensible to involve it in agility skills training, catch, or obedience competitions – for which it is ideally suited.

Long-haired Border Collie

SOCIAL BEHAVIOR
Provided that it has been well socialized, Australian Shepherds cause no problems with other dogs and pets.
They are also generally good with children but can be a bit shy with strangers.

EXERCISE
This dog needs lots of exercise, but almost more important it needs to be kept occupied to keep it happy. Perhaps the best homes for these dogs are with sporty people who are able to spend time every day doing things that both the dogs and the people enjoy.

Australian Shepherd

Head of an Australian Shepherd

Bearded Collie

COUNTRY OF ORIGIN
Scotland.

SPECIAL SKILLS
Sheepdog and family pet.

SIZE
The shoulder-height is 53 – 56cm (20¾ – 22in) for dogs and 51 – 53cm (20 – 20¾in) for bitches.

COAT
The undercoat is dense and woolly; the outer coat is straight, tough, long, and rough. Permitted colors are black, blue, slate-colored, reddish-brown, all shades of grey with white markings on the nose, chest, legs, and feet or neck. The white markings are not permitted beyond the shoulder.

Bearded Collie

CARE REQUIRED
The Bearded Collie requires a great deal of grooming. The hair must be brushed and combed a couple of times each week to avoid tangles. Remove excessive hair between the pads and keep the inside of the ears clean. The hair of a Bearded Collie should be parted along the back.

CHARACTER
The Bearded Collie is a high spirited, cheerful, and clever dog that is eager to learn, lovable, gentle, sociable and companionable, extremely independent, and active. A Bearded Collie belongs to the family and should not be banished outdoors to a kennel.

TRAINING
The Bearded Collie is an intelligent dog who learns quickly. Treating it severely during training does not work; you can achieve better results by a playful, soft-handed approach. Give it ample praise and plenty of cheerful commands and avoid pressuring it, because that spoils its receptive and friendly disposition.

SOCIAL BEHAVIOR
These dogs get on well with children, household pets, and other dogs. Even strangers are normally greeted exuberantly.

EXERCISE
The Bearded Collie is a dog which will adapt itself to the situation it finds itself in but you can give it no greater pleasure than to take it on long country walks. Bearded Collies have no tendency to run away (in common with most dogs in this group); on the contrary they stay close by you. This breed usually performs well in obedience trials and agility competitions.

SPECIAL POINTS
Because of its gentle nature the Bearded Collie is ideal for those with little experience of bringing up a dog; with its great adaptability it fits into a family just as happily in town as in the country. Bear in mind that the coat requires extensive grooming.

Bearded Collie

Clipped harlequin-coated Beauceron

Unclipped Beauceron

Beauceron

COUNTRY OF ORIGIN
France.

SPECIAL SKILLS
Herding dog and family pet.

SIZE
The shoulder-height is 65 – 70cm (25½ – 27½in) for dogs and 63 – 68cm (24¾ – 26¾in) for bitches. The weight can vary from 30 to 40 kg (66 to 88 lb).

COAT
The short, tough, and smooth coat has both a dense and soft undercoat. There are two recognized colors: black with brand marks and black-grey brindle. The latter color is fairly rare.

CARE REQUIRED
The coat of the Beauceron does not require a great deal of attention. An occasional grooming with more attention during the time when the dog is shedding is sufficient.

CHARACTER
This dog is clever, attentive, active, intelligent, sometimes stubborn, and loyal to its owner and the family. It has considerable stamina and is very watchful.

TRAINING
A consistent and loving upbringing with plenty of exercise and ample contact with its owner are indispensable for the well-balanced development of a young Beauceron. If it is denied this it can become neurotic or aggressive. The dog should get to know in a positive way many different people, animals, things, and situations when it is still a puppy.

SOCIAL BEHAVIOR
A Beauceron that has been well socialized and brought up gets on fine under normal circumstances with children, and that also ensures that other dogs and pets will present no problems.

EXERCISE
This breed is not satisfied with a circuit of the block three times a day. Take it for regular long walks during which it can run free off the leash and play. If both of you seem to enjoy it, enrol it for a course to train in catch or to compete in agility skills classes, although in competition it is likely to be less successful than other more suitable breeds.

Head of a Laeken Belgian Shepherd

Belgian Shepherd

Laeken Belgian Shepherd

• Laeken Belgian Shepherd

COUNTRY OF ORIGIN
Belgium.

SPECIAL SKILLS
Historically a cattle-driving dog, today a guard-dog and family pet.

SIZE
The shoulder-height is about 62cm (24½in) for dogs and 58cm (22¾in) for bitches. The breed standard permits variation in height of 2cm (¾in) shorter and 4cm (1½in) taller.

COAT
The coat is rough-haired and a drab sandy color with darker streaks around the nose and tail.

CARE REQUIRED
This rough-haired dog needs to be trimmed about twice each year, depending upon the quality of the coat. Dead and excessive hair should be removed. Resist suggestions to have your dog close trimmed as this ruins the coat for several years. In addition to the occasional light trim, use a coarse-toothed comb for grooming. The Laeken Belgian Shepherd can manage perfectly well in an outdoor kennel provided it receives sufficient attention and exercise.

CHARACTER
This breed is attentive, tough, and brave, eager to work, a good guard-dog, has great stamina, and is lively, intelligent, dominant, and bonds with its family.

TRAINING
For the right owner the Laeken Belgian Shepherd is not difficult to bring up. This breed requires a well-balanced and confident handler. These dogs are usually very intelligent and eager to learn. They like a lot of variety in their training sessions.

SOCIAL BEHAVIOR
Generally these sheepdogs get on with children but they can be rather dominant towards other dogs. Provided they are correctly socialized with cats and other pets, these should present no problems.

EXERCISE
This breed demands a significant level of exercise. These are dogs which must be taken out regularly and thoroughly exercised to burn off their surplus energy.

• Mechelen Belgian Shepherd

COUNTRY OF ORIGIN
Belgium.

Mechelen Belgian Shepherd

SPECIAL SKILLS
Historically a cattle-driving dog, today this dog is a guard-dog, defence dog, and family pet.

SIZE
The shoulder-height is about 62cm (24½in) for dogs and 58cm (22¾in) for bitches. The breed standard permits both sexes to be 2cm (¾in) shorter and 4cm (1½in) taller.

COAT
The coat is short-haired, drab sandy-colored with black tips to the hairs and a black muzzle.

CARE REQUIRED
The Mechelen Belgian Shepherd's coat does not require much in the way of grooming. The occasional brushing, particularly during shedding, is sufficient. This dog is quite happy in an outdoor kennel provided it gets sufficient exercise and attention.

CHARACTER
This breed is attentive, brave, tough, a good guard dog, intelligent, eager to work, has considerable stamina, bonds with its own people, is dominant, and can be temperamental.

TRAINING
The dog learns relatively quickly. Its potentially dominant character demands a firm, confident handler.

SOCIAL BEHAVIOR
This breed usually gets on with children. Provided it has been correctly socialized, contact with other pets should present no problems. Some are rather aggressive to their own kind.

EXERCISE
This breed is ideally suited to defence dog and security-training and performs well in such competitions. It is important to take the dog for long walks to burn off its excess energy or find other ways of providing it with exercise. Most Mechelen Belgian Shepherds enjoy playing ball games, swimming, retrieving, and running alongside a bicycle.

• *Tervueren and Gnendael Belgian Shepherds*

COUNTRY OF ORIGIN
Belgium.

SPECIAL SKILLS
Historically herding dogs, now family pets.

SIZE
The shoulder-height is about 62cm (24½in) for dogs and 58cm (22¾in)for bitches. The breed standard permits both sexes to be 2cm (¾in) shorter and 4cm (1½in) taller.

Mechelen Belgian Shepherd, study of the head

Gnendael Belgian Shepherd

COAT

This breed has a long-haired coat with an under-coat. Gnendael Belgian Shepherds are black with perhaps some white on the chest and feet. Tervueren Shepherds are red, mixed brown-grey, and every variety of brown to grey, with a black muzzle.

Gnendael Belgian Shepherd

CARE REQUIRED

Do not brush or comb these dogs too much since this can damage the under layer of the coat. During shedding use a coarse-toothed comb to make the coat more respectable in appearance.

CHARACTER

These dogs are energetic, alert, intelligent, eager to work, very lively, and attentive. Both breeds like to be close to their owner in the home.

TRAINING

Both breeds need to have their confidence strengthened as puppies. Take them to new places and let them, under control, become acquainted with different people and animals. Make sure these meetings are positive in nature. They learn quickly and react well to the voice of the handler. Hitting and screaming are both unnecessary and likely to have an adverse effect. A gentle but determined hand works wonders with them. They are suitable for various types of sports, particularly agility competitions, and catch.

SOCIAL BEHAVIOR

These breeds get on well with their own kind, cats, and other pets especially if they originally met them when young. If children treat them well, they present no problem with children. They tend to be rather shy with strangers.

EXERCISE

When both breeds get sufficient outdoor exercise, they are calm. Most examples of the breed greatly enjoy retrieving and playing with balls.

Bergamsco

COUNTRY OF ORIGIN
Italy.

SPECIAL SKILLS
Sheepdog, guard-dog, and family pet.

SIZE
The dogs weigh 32 – 38kg (70½ – 83½lb) with a shoulder-height of 60cm (23½in). The bitches weigh 26 – 32kg (57 – 70½lb) with a shoulder-height of 56cm (22½in).
The breed standard permits both sexes to be 2cm (¾in) shorter.

Fully-grown Bergamsco bitch

COAT
The Bergamsco has a thick under layer to its coat and has a tendency for the outer layer to become felt-like; the hair on the head and shoulders is free from this problem. The coat is plain grey or speckled grey, plain black, or greyish-yellow with fawn markings. White markings are per-

Tervueren Belgian Shepherd

Young Bergamsco male

missible provided they do not represent more than 20 per cent of the area of the coat.

CARE REQUIRED
During its first year the Bergamsco needs only combing. Thereafter, the coat will start to felt-up and to prevent this you will need to pluck bunches of hair out by hand. The hair on the head must be combed. A bath now and then does no harm but it is best given in the summer since it can take more than a day for the coat to dry.

CHARACTER
Intelligent and extremely eager to work, independent, well-balanced and calm, brave and alert, friendly, and bonds very closely with its human family.

TRAINING
Bergamsco is not a difficult breed to bring up and to train. If these dogs are socialized when young and are treated consistently and clearly they will form a strong part of the family.

SOCIAL BEHAVIOR
Provided they have been correctly socialized, they get on well with other pets. This breed is generally fine with children; indeed it has a tendency to protect them against being pestered by other children. They make first-class guard-dogs and an extremely unpleasant surprise for anyone who should break into your house. They are rather reserved with those whom they do not know.

EXERCISE
These are dogs which require plenty of exercise, best done with regular walks. Within a large enough, well-fenced area the Bergamsco will happily take care of its own exercise. They are still used daily to herd livestock, making them true working dogs. They do not belong in a small apartment.

Maremma Sheepdog

COUNTRY OF ORIGIN
Italy.

SPECIAL SKILLS
Family pet and guard-dog for herds.

SIZE
The shoulder-height is 63 – 73cm (24¾ – 28¾in) for dogs and 60 – 68cm (23½ – 26¾in) for bitches.

COAT
The coat is long-haired and wiry with a dense under layer. Colors of white with markings of ivory, light yellow, or pale orange are permitted by breed standards.

CARE REQUIRED
This breed requires regular thorough grooming with both brush and comb to remove all dead

Maremma Sheepdog

and loose hairs. This is especially important when it is shedding.

CHARACTER
This dog is friendly and loyal, sober, determined, brave, intelligent, dignified, well-balanced, and a very good guard-dog without being a constant barker. It is correctly described as affectionate but not dependent.

TRAINING
This breed is not one to follow your every command slavishly and certainly not if it cannot see the point to it.
Its education and training require mutual respect in handling and voice, and above all consistency.

SOCIAL BEHAVIOR
This breed gets on well with other dogs and pets, and in general is patient and forgiving with

children. They can be slightly reserved with strangers but not strongly so. Someone with no right to be on your property gets no chance to step on to it.

EXERCISE
This breed needs space, mentally as well as physically. Do not condemn this dog to a walk-around three times a day.

Long and alternating walks are necessary for this breed. It must indulge itself freely from time to time. When it gets enough freedom and space, it will be quiet in the house.

Maremma Sheepdog

Border Collie

COUNTRY OF ORIGIN
England.

SPECIAL SKILLS
Sheepdog and cattle-herder.

SIZE
The shoulder-height is 53 – 55cm (20¾ – 21½in) for dogs; bitches are slightly smaller.

COAT
The thick undercoat is medium length and shiny. All colors are permissible but white should not be predominant. Black and white coats are the most usual.

Border Collie

CARE REQUIRED
The Border Collie's coat does not require much attention. Weekly brushing will keep it in good condition.

CHARACTER
This dog is very eager to work, intelligent and astute, a quick learner, attentive, lively, and alert. It forms a very close bond with his handler and family. It is also determined and brave.

TRAINING
The Border Collie is famous throughout the world for its tremendous intelligence and its desire to please. These dogs quickly learn new commands and almost all of them have a natural aptitude for herding sheep.

Border Collie, study of the head

SOCIAL BEHAVIOR
Provided it gets sufficient activity to keep it occupied and ample exercise, the Border Collie will get along quite happily with other dogs and pets and children. If there is insufficient activity then it will find work to do, which could be herding your children!

EXERCISE
The idle Border Collie will become extremely badly behaved and even aggressive. Physical exercise alone is not sufficient for this breed. They want to work and must do so, with body and mind as one, carrying out different tasks. It is not surprising that at competitive level in various sports – agility skills, obedience, and sheepdog trials – Border Collies are represented among the top in the sport. They are perfectionists with a permanent will to please. In brief, this breed lives for serving you day in day out.

SPECIAL REMARKS
• This breed is fine in a kennel provided it has daily activity and sees plenty of its handler.
• For those who wish to reach high levels in dog sports, the Border Collie is a gift from heaven. Farmers, for whom the dogs perform the work for which they were bred, are also happy with them. They are not ideal pets.

Briard

COUNTRY OF ORIGIN
France.

SPECIAL SKILLS
Herding dog, guard-dog, and family pet.

SIZE
The shoulder height is 62 - 68cm (24½ - 26¾in) for dogs and 56 - 64cm (22 - 25¼in) for bitches.

COAT
The Briard has a long wavy coat of rather dry hair and a light undercoat. All plain colors are permitted with the exception of white and chestnut. The most usual colors are black and fawn.

CARE REQUIRED
Briards require weekly grooming with brush and comb. The inside of the ears must be kept clean and any excessive hair in the ears should also be removed. This is also true of the excessive hair which grows between the pads of their feet.

Untrimmed Briards

CHARACTER
Intelligent and prepared to work, tough, brave, alert, loyal, slightly dominant, and totally unsuitable for a life in a kennel.
The Briard has no sense of humor, so do not tease it.

TRAINING
Training of the Briard must be consistent, with much patience and love combined with a firm hand. Severe, unjust training will have the same result as none at all. With poor handling and training the Briard becomes withdrawn and even aggressive.
They are happiest in the home as part of the family.

SOCIAL BEHAVIOR
With the right handler the Briard blossoms as a first-class pet who can happily coexist with other pets.

They can be slightly aggressive towards other dogs. Strangers are viewed with suspicion.

EXERCISE
This breed needs reasonable amounts of exercise. This can be a simple country walk but swimming and running alongside a bicycle are also excellent forms of exercise for them. They are ideally suited to defence dog/police dog trials.

SPECIAL REMARKS
In countries outside France the Briard will be a novelty who will protect you and your family; however, this is definitely not the dog for everyone.

Cao da Serra de Aires (Serra de Aires Mountain dog)

COUNTRY OF ORIGIN
Portugal.

SPECIAL SKILLS
All-round herding dog, guard-dog, and family pet.

SIZE
The shoulder-height is 45 - 55cm (17¾ - 21½in) for dogs and 42 - 52cm (16½ - 20½in) for bitches.

COAT
The coat is long and smooth or with a slight wave; there is no under layer to the coat. The most usual color is black, but grey, yellow, and brown are also to be found, preferably with tan markings.
A few white hairs are permissible but patches of white hairs are not, except for a white patch on the chest.

CARE REQUIRED
Check regularly for tangles but do not brush the coat too much as it will affect the texture.

Cao da Serra de Aires

Trim any excess hair between the pads of the feet. It is said that this breed should be shampooed as little as possible.

CHARACTER

This high spirited, animated, and intelligent dog is eager to work, very loyal and bonds with its own people, is sober, alert, easily learns, but is also stubborn, and dominant.

TRAINING

The Cao da Serra de Aires demands an extremely consistent and well-balanced training. It learns quickly and easily, but can exhibit stubbornness and dominance. It requires a confident handler.

SOCIAL BEHAVIOR

These dogs mix well with other dogs, and live happily alongside other pets, provided they have been correctly socialized. They are usually patient with children but the dogs in particular can be possessive of their territory. This breed tends to be reserved with strangers and makes a good watchdog.

EXERCISE

The Cao da Serra de Aires has an extreme stamina.

If it gets enough exercise, it will be calm in the house. This breed achieves very well in agility.

German Shepherd

COUNTRY OF ORIGIN

Germany.

SPECIAL SKILLS

Family pet, suitable for a number of other purposes.

SIZE

The shoulder-height is 60 - 65cm (23½ - 25½in) for dogs and 55 - 60 cm (21½ - 23 ½in) for bitches.

Cao da Serra de Aires

Head of a German Shepherd

German Shepherd

COAT

The German Shepherd can have three kinds of coat: coarse straight-haired, long coarse straight-haired, and wavy long-haired. The last of these three is less desirable. The coat can be black, iron-grey, ash-colored, or can be one of these colors with regular brown, or yellow-to-light-brown markings. An upper layer of black is very common.

CARE REQUIRED

The coat requires relatively little attention. During shedding the use of a special comb will help to remove dead and loose hairs.

CHARACTER

This very intelligent and eager pupil is an obedient, sociable, and friendly dog that is temperamental, attentive, alert, protective, brave, self-assured, independent, and unconditionally loyal towards its handler and family.

TRAINING

Throughout the world these dogs are used as guide dogs, avalanche rescue dogs, tracking dogs, watchdogs, defence dogs, and police dogs. In some of these roles, the German Shepherd is almost the only breed used. In obedience competitions they stand head and shoulders above over breeds. It is eager to learn from you, intelligent and quick to get the hang of things. Work principally with your voice. The great majority of the breed worship their handler and have an enormous need for contact with him. If you do not have the time to devote to it, do not purchase a German Shepherd. In its country of origin, the German Shepherd is still used for herding livestock.

SOCIAL BEHAVIOR

German Shepherds get on well with their own kind, other animals, and children provided they have been correctly socialized, but unwanted visitors are stopped. They are territorial by nature – which means that they have no tendency whatever to run away.

EXERCISE

People who keep German Shepherds frequently overlook the fact that they are eager to work for their handler. It is not sufficient for them to be companions in the home with nothing else to occupy them. Join a breed group or other organization so that you can participate together in agility, obedience, defence and police trials, tracking, or whatever else is available, in order to keep your dog both physically and mentally fit. For all large dogs, and that includes the German Shepherd, all their energy is needed during the growing stage for healthy bones, joints, and muscles. Damage which cannot be put right can be done by over-exercising or inadequate diet.

German Shepherd

They can happily live in an outdoor kennel provided they get sufficient exercise and regular attention.

SPECIAL POINTS
The German Shepherd is the only breed for which there is a world-wide umbrella organization engaged in matters relating to the breed. Based in Germany, the WUSV has more than half a million members in sixty countries.

Dutch Shepherd

COUNTRY OF ORIGIN
The Netherlands.

SPECIAL SKILLS
Sheepdog and family pet.

SIZE
The shoulder-height is 57 - 62cm (22½ - 24½in) for dogs and 55 - 60cm (21¾ - 23½in) for bitches.

COAT
There are three different types of coat for the Dutch Shepherd: short-haired (silver and gold streaks), rough-haired (blue-grey pepper-and-salt-colored, or silver and gold streaked), and long-haired (silver and gold streaked).
With all varieties, dogs for the show ring should not display too much white on their chest and feet.

CARE REQUIRED
Both short- and long-haired coats require regular grooming with brush and comb to remove dead and loose hairs. The rough-haired coat should never be brushed, although combing is fine in moderation.

Always use a coarse comb. Have the coat plucked by a professional twice a year. The hair can be clipped in a few places as a finishing touch and the excessive hair in the ears should be removed.

Short-haired Dutch Shepherds

CHARACTER

This affectionate dog is eager to learn, intelligent and obedient, sober, very loyal to its handler and family, incorruptible, active, lively, and alert.

TRAINING

Dutch Shepherds are happy to be all-round dogs. They can and will learn new commands quickly.

In certain branches of sport such as agility, catch, and obedience competitions, they can eclipse their rivals. The short-haired type is the most usual sort for defence/ police dog trials.

SOCIAL BEHAVIOR

Dutch Shepherds enjoy the company of their own kind and get along fine with other animals. Provided children let the dogs have some peace when they want it, the dogs can also be good friends for children. Unwanted visitors are stopped in their tracks, while known family friends will be greeted enthusiastically.

Rough-haired Dutch Shepherds

EXERCISE
It is good for this breed to let it regularly run beside a bicycle, or take it into the woods or open countryside where it can run to its heart's content. Because Dutch Shepherds want to work, run them through a regular drill at least twice per week to keep them both physically and mentally fit.

Komondor

COUNTRY OF ORIGIN
Hungary.

SPECIAL SKILLS
Guard-dog for herds of sheep or cattle.

SIZE
The shoulder-height is a minimum of 65cm (25½in) for dogs and a minimum of 60cm (23½in) for bitches.
It is generally preferred to see heights much taller than this. There is no maximum height.

COAT
The coat is the most important distinguishing feature of this breed. It consists of felt-like strands which form and become longer over the

years. It can take up to three years for the final coat of the Komondor to be formed. The coat is always white.

CARE REQUIRED
This breed should never be brushed or combed since the felting of the coat is a desirable feature. The felt is formed because the soft undercoat is not shed but catches in the tougher, and longer, outer hair. To encourage development of the felt strands, they can be teased by hand. Bathing is best left until summer, since it can take several days for the dog's coat to dry.

CHARACTER
These are independent, dominant, and very alert dogs that are brave, incorruptible, determined, social, very loyal to their handler and family, sober, well-balanced, and calm. They are said to be able to judge if a person is "up to no good".

TRAINING
The Komondor is a dog whose natural instincts are still close to nature and it will often rely upon its own instinct – and be right. Its training must be consistent and based upon mutual respect. The Komondor has an uncomplicated character and, once he understands your rules, will not overstep them. Despite its honest nature, the Komondor needs a confident handler. Because it

Komondor

Damp and chilly or even cold weather will not harm this breed as it is so well protected by its impenetrable coat.

Kuvasz

COUNTRY OF ORIGIN
Hungary.

SPECIAL SKILLS
Family pet and guard-dog.

SIZE
The shoulder-height is 71 - 75cm (28 - 29½in) for dogs and 66 - 70cm (26 - 27½in) for bitches. Dogs weight 40 - 52kg (88 - 114½lb), while bitches are somewhat lighter.

COAT
The hair is short on the head and the front of the legs, longer on the rest of the body. The texture is coarse and the hair is wavy, with a soft under-coat. The coat is always plain white.

CARE REQUIRED
The Kuvasz has a very thick coat which protects it from all kinds of weather.

When shedding this breed loses great amounts of hair so it is sensible to brush it thoroughly and regularly, and especially when it is shedding.

Kuvasz

will only obey an order if it makes sense to it, it is not suitable for obedience courses and similar activities.

SOCIAL BEHAVIOR
The Komondor will get along fine with other animals and with children provided they are part of your household and family. It will protect your children from being pestered by other children.

Strangers are instinctively mistrusted and unwanted visitors get no chance to step on to your property. Regular visitors will be treated as part of the family.

EXERCISE
It is possible to keep this breed in an urban environment although the country is more to its liking. If the Komondor is kept outdoors, it will naturally meet its own needs for exercise. This dog can be extremely lazy and will sleep and rest for hour upon hour.

CHARACTER
This is a good watchdog, which is intelligent, barks only when necessary, very independent,

brave, dominant, honest, well-balanced, determined, and loyal to the family. The Kuvasz is affectionate but not dependent.

TRAINING
This breed requires a balanced and consistent training and upbringing.
Since the Kuvasz flourishes with a confident owner, it is not a good dog for a beginner. At the same time, a too severe owner is wrong for this breed. This dog will learn best in a pleasant environment which provides scope for its own initiative.

SOCIAL BEHAVIOR
The Kuvasz can be rather dominant towards its own kind, but if it is properly socialized with other animals when young, there will normally be no problems with it towards these animals. Its high pain threshold and stable nature make it tolerant with children but given its independent initiative and large size, it is best not to leave it to look after the children.

It is important to know that the Kuvasz will protect people and animals who belong to its family which means it will protect your children from their friends if play becomes a little rough.

EXERCISE
Since the Kuvasz will patrol and inspect its borders a number of times every day, it keeps itself in good condition. If you do not have a lot of space, it will be necessary to take it out regularly because the Kuvasz needs a feeling of space for its mental well-being as much as the exercise.

Mudi

COUNTRY OF ORIGIN
Hungary.

SPECIAL SKILLS
Hunting dog (principally for large wild game), herding dog, guard-dog, and family pet.

SIZE
The shoulder height is 35 - 47cm
(13¾ - 18½in).

Head of a Kuvasz

COAT
The hairs of the coat are fairly long, thick, and curly or wavy. The length of the hair varies on different parts of the body.

Mudis are colored black or white or a combination of the two.

CARE REQUIRED
Mudis are very easy to care for. A regular combing is sufficient to keep the coat in good condition.

CHARACTER
This watchful and animated dog is alert and

Head of a Mudi

brave, it barks gladly, learns willingly, is intelligent, slightly independent, and sober.
The Mudi has a strong urge to protect the family to which it belongs.
Within the family it also has the tendency to bond with one particular person.

TRAINING
If you keep in mind that Mudis like to feel independent, they are usually not difficult to train.

SOCIAL BEHAVIOR
The Mudi usually gets on well with other dogs and animals, and with children. They are excellent guard-dogs and will protect the entire family without being unduly suspicious of strangers. When circumstances demand courage, the Mudi will display it.

EXERCISE
This breed adapts to any form of exercise. They are suitable for various sporting activities such as agility training and catch.

Mudi

Old English Sheepdog

COUNTRY OF ORIGIN
England.

SPECIAL SKILLS
Sheepdog and family pet.

SIZE
The shoulder-height is a minimum of 60cm (23½in) for dogs and 56cm (22in) for bitches.

COAT
The coat is luxuriant, rough, tough, and long, with a waterproof under-layer. Permitted colors are blue or different shades of grey. The head, neck, front quarters, and belly are white, with or without markings. White patches in the blue on the back are not permissible.

CARE REQUIRED

These dogs require regular grooming: brush them thoroughly at least once a week, not overlooking the places where tangles form. When a dog is shedding it is possible to collect a half or even an entire garbage bag of hair.

Keep the inside of its ears clean and remove both dirt and hair. The claws must be kept short so clip them regularly.

Excessive hair between the pads of the feet should also be trimmed. For successful showing, the rear of the dog must be higher than the shoulders and this is sometimes accentuated for the show ring.

Sometimes these dogs are trimmed, which, however unpopular with some purists, is better than a mass of tangled hair although it does seem strange that anyone would buy a long-haired dog and then have it clipped.

Old English Sheepdog

CHARACTER

Intelligent, with considerable adaptability, amiable, social, not particularly alert, boisterous, uncomplicated nature, and likes to be part of the family.

TRAINING

This breed needs gentle and consistent handling during training. It wants to please you and rarely displays dominant behavior, making it suitable for people with little experience with dogs. Because grooming forms so important a part of the general care for this breed, it is important to start brushing it when it is as young as possible.

This prevents grooming degenerating into a wrestling match when it is much larger and stronger.

SOCIAL BEHAVIOR

The Old English Sheepdog gets on exceptionally well with other animals, dogs, and children. Visitors too will be greeted warmly.

EXERCISE

This breed needs a fair amount of exercise but it will not misbehave if you miss a day if you are exceptionally busy.

Most of the breed are crazy about playing with a ball and are well represented as competitors in various sports.

Old English Sheepdog groomed ready for a show

Picardy Shepherd

Picardy Shepherd

COUNTRY OF ORIGIN
France.

SPECIAL SKILLS
Watchdog, sheepdog, and family pet.

Picardy Shepherds

SIZE
The shoulder-height is 60 - 65cm
(23½- 25½in) for dogs and 55 - 60cm
(21½ - 23½in) for bitches.

COAT
This dog's coat consists of coarse and wiry medium-length hair. The colors are grey, grey-black, blue-grey, red-grey, and light or darker fawn. A small white patch on the feet is not desirable but is permissible.

CARE REQUIRED
The Picardy Shepherd requires regular grooming with both brush and comb. The coat should never be trimmed.

CHARACTER
Energetic, intelligent, alert, loyal, amiable with children, and a little stubborn.

Usually they are quite detached from strangers. They like to bark and do so frequently. This can be a problem if you live surrounded by other people.

Head of a Picardy Shepherd

To really please this dog, enroll it for an agility skills course or obedience training.

These dogs do not do well in competition, because they find it almost impossible to perform consistently.

Polish Lowland Sheepdog

Polish Lowland Sheepdog

TRAINING
The Picardy Shepherd must be properly socialized when young if it is to grow up as a well-balanced dog. Training this breed, which is full of character, is not an easy matter since they can be willful and also are sometimes subject to fits of bad humor.
If you decide on this breed, then you must learn to accept these moods; try hard not to break the dog's will because this can really harm its character.

These dogs are very sensitive to the voice and it is necessary to tread carefully as you first begin to train them. Cheerfully given commands generally work best.

SOCIAL BEHAVIOR
Contact with other animals and children is not generally a problem. However, the Picardy Shepherd wants lots of attention from its handler and is not happy to share it with other dogs.

EXERCISE
This breed of dog requires lots of exercise. Running alongside a bicycle, swimming, and walking are all ideal ways to channel this dog's energy in a positive direction.

COUNTRY OF ORIGIN
Poland.

SPECIAL SKILLS
Sheepdog and family pet.

SIZE
The shoulder-height is 45 - 50cm (17¾ - 19½in) for dogs and 42 - 47cm (16½ - 18½in) for bitches.

Dogs weigh about 20kg (44lb), while bitches are in the region of 18kg (39½lb).

COAT
This breed has a long, wire-haired coat with a soft under-layer.
All colors are permitted – the most usual being white with grey or black, or plain grey.

CARE REQUIRED
The coat needs to be groomed thoroughly with a brush once a week to prevent tangles.

CHARACTER
This animated, happy, and alert dog has a good memory, is obedient and intelligent, affectionate, and slightly lacking in confidence with strangers.

TRAINING

This breed is easy to educate. The dog learns quickly and is happy to do things for its handler.

SOCIAL BEHAVIOR

The Polish Lowland Sheepdog is a breed that is excellent with children, dogs, and other pets. Visitors will be announced at the top of its voice.

EXERCISE

This dog's origins are as a working dog. Previously it watched over the herds and flocks on the extensive Polish plains and it remains a herding dog in heart and mind. It is definitely not a town dog which will be content with three little outings per day.

Its brain needs stimulating with changes of scenery and something to do. Join a dog group where it can join in agility training, or catch which are both activities it will relish. This dog, too, enjoys chasing Frisbees.

Polish Lowland Sheepdog

Thirteen-year-old Hungarian Puli

Hungarian Puli

Hungarian Puli

COUNTRY OF ORIGIN

Hungary.

SPECIAL SKILLS

Sheepdog or family pet.

SIZE

The desired shoulder height is 40 - 44cm (15½ -17¼in) for dogs and 37 - 41cm (14½ - 16¼in) for bitches. The weight is 10 - 15kg (22 - 33lb).

COAT

The coat of the Puli is its trademark. These dogs are richly covered in long cords of felted hair. The Puli is usually black, but white, broken white, and black with apricot are also known.

CARE REQUIRED

The Puli's distinctive coat does not fully develop until the third year. The soft under layer does not fall out but becomes felt on the outer, and harder, hairs. If required, the felted strands are teased to encourage the development of the felt strands or cords.

An advantage of this coat is that the Puli does not shed, but there is the disadvantage that all manner of dirt and small objects can become caught up in the hairs. Wash the Puli in the summer because the long coat will take several days to dry fully.

CHARACTER

This intelligent dog learns easily, is full of character, animated, a good watchdog, and loyal to the family.

This breed is very adaptable to the circumstances surrounding it although it can be somewhat independent. A Puli will rarely run away.

TRAINING

This breed requires a very consistent approach to training which needs to take place within the first year.

They do not like boring drills, preferring a challenge. Vary the training routine constantly and include plenty of play. This breed usually learns quickly.

SOCIAL BEHAVIOR

They normally get on well with their own kind, other animals, and children. They have the tendency to bond closely with one member of the family.

EXERCISE

This breed is in its element if it can romp and play and with its unusual coat it is delightful to watch. If you enjoy it, you could enrol both of you for agility skills or ball courses.
This breed also enjoys playing with Frisbees. The Hungarian Puli usually does well in all these activities.

Hungarian Pumi

Hungarian Pumi

Hungarian Pumi

COUNTRY OF ORIGIN
Hungary.

SPECIAL SKILLS
Sheepdog or companion.

SIZE
The desired shoulder height is 35 - 44cm (13¾ - 17¼in).

COAT
The coat consists of medium length hair in tufts. In some places the hairs are shorter and rougher; in others they are longer and tangled. The coat has a rather unkempt look about it. The most common colors are slate-grey and other tints of grey; black and white also exist, but patches are not permissible.

CARE REQUIRED
The Pumi requires relatively little grooming. Brush the coat right through about once a week and remove excessive hair from inside the ears. For showing, the Pumi need special grooming.

CHARACTER
Attentive, alert, likes to bark, dapper, energetic, temperamental, intelligent, learns readily, and sober.

TRAINING
This is not a difficult breed to train. They are intelligent enough to grasp what you mean quickly.
If you live surrounded by neighbors, it is sensible to teach the dog that after a couple of barks it must be quiet.

SOCIAL BEHAVIOR

The Pumi can be shy and rather mistrustful of strangers. A well brought up Pumi will cause no problems with children provided they do not pester it.

EXERCISE

This is an outdoors dog and at its best living on a farm where it will find work enough to do for itself, such as guarding the entrance and keeping the livestock together.

If it is to live in an urban environment then you must find replacement activities to keep it occupied. These dogs do well in playing catch, chasing Frisbees, and in agility skills classes.

SPECIAL POINTS

This dog is happiest where there is sufficient work for it to do for its family. It is really not a town dog.

Pyrenean Sheepdog

Pyrenean Sheepdog

COUNTRY OF ORIGIN
France.

SPECIAL SKILLS
All-round herding dog and family pet.

SIZE
The shoulder height is 40 - 50cm (15¾ - 19½in) for dogs and 38 - 48cm (15 - 18¾in) for bitches.

Pyrenean Sheepdog

COAT
The coat consists of fairly long, or at least medium length hair with either a strong curl or lighter wave which can be sand colored, with or without black hairs, streaky grey, or black with white markings.

CARE REQUIRED
These dogs need little attention to their coats. The breed is supposed to look natural and rather rustic and the coat is of such a texture that at most a quarter of an hour a week with a brush is sufficient to groom it properly.

Do not forget to remove excessive hair regularly from inside the ear. Wash its short beard from time to time.

CHARACTER
This is an intelligent dog that is ready to work, alert and quick, vigilant, animated, with good scenting powers, and which is loving with children. The Pyrenean Sheepdog enjoys an outdoor life.

TRAINING
Requires consistent, strict and honest training that is not too tough. It is ready to work and can and will learn.
The Pyrenean Sheepdog who is condemned to its basket with nothing to look forward to other than a trot around the block three times a day will become troublesome. This dog is ideally suited for training as a rescue dog and also does well in activities such as catch, chasing Frisbees, and agility classes.

SOCIAL BEHAVIOR
This breed gets on well with families, including the children. There is also no problem with other pets provided it has had good experiences with

them as a young dog. They are somewhat cautious with strangers.

Wolf grey Saarloos Wolfhound, study of the head

EXERCISE
It is advisable to spend at least an hour each day in activity with the dog. Walking is fine, so are dog sports.

Saarloos Wolfhound

COUNTRY OF ORIGIN
The Netherlands.

SPECIAL SKILLS
Family pet.

SIZE
The shoulder height is 65 - 75cm (25½ - 29½in) for dogs and 60 - 70cm (23½ - 27½in) for bitches.

COAT
The coat is smooth and to be found in wolf grey, forest brown, cream, and white.
The most usual colors are wolf grey and forest brown.

CARE REQUIRED
The coat is easily looked after. The type of comb available for German Shepherds is ideal for this dog's grooming. Comb regularly and keep the inside of the ears clean.

CHARACTER
This intelligent, careful, and alert dog has a good scenting nose, and is lovable and affectionate.

Saarloos Wolfhound

Head of a forest brown Saarloos Wolfhound

This breed is patient with children. It barks rarely and the bitches come into season only once a year.

TRAINING
Early mixing with other dogs, animals and people is necessary – before the tenth week – if this breed is to grow up as a well-balanced dog. Let it be acquainted with all manner of situations in a positive way. This dog learns commands easily but this is not a breed from which to expect absolute obedience.

SOCIAL BEHAVIOR
These are really sociable dogs and they present no problem with other dogs or with children if you have heeded the advice given in the previous paragraph.

If the early contacts have been well handled, the Saarloos Wolfhound will behave perfectly. They tend to be cautious about both strangers and new situations.

EXERCISE
The breed has a fairly average need for exercise. If an occasion arises in which you are forced to miss a walk one day, it will accept it without fuss.

SPECIAL REMARKS
Saarloos Wolfhounds are healthy dogs. For a dog of its size it can live to be quite old – thirteen or fourteen years old is not uncommon. The breed is little known outside its native country and is a comparatively recent arrival, having been bred by crossing German Shepherds with wolves.

The Czech Wolfhound is a different breed that came into existence in a similar way. Both dogs have similar characters, although it is considered that the Czech breed is tougher and more independent in character.

Schapendoes

COUNTRY OF ORIGIN
The Netherlands.

SPECIAL SKILLS
Sheepdog and family pet.

SIZE
The shoulder height is 43 - 50cm (17 - 19½in) for dogs and 40 - 47cm (16 - 18in) for bitches. The weight is about 15kg (33lb).

COAT
The Schapendoes has a double coat: the outer layer is long, dry, and wavy, while the inner layer is thick and soft. All colors are permissible, but blue-grey to black is the most popular.

Schapendoes

CARE REQUIRED
Schapendoes are not dogs that are highly groomed but it is necessary to brush and comb them regularly to prevent tangles. Also clean in the ears but do not use cotton swabs. It is quite normal for the hair to cover the eyes. Do not hold it back with a hair band or bow. Check the eyes regularly for both dirt and loose hair.

CHARACTER
This happy, cunning dog is eager to learn, alert, brave, attentive, very loyal to the family, very playful and lively, and affectionate.

TRAINING
The Schapendoes will feel at home in a sporty family in which it can have a well-balanced upbringing. It will enjoy obedience classes, and greatly value subsequent agility classes and competition.

SOCIAL BEHAVIOR
It is this breed's nature to get on well with its own kind, other pets, and with children. These dogs bark if they detect trouble.

EXERCISE
Just as with countless other breeds, the Schapendoes needs exercise to rid it of its abundant energy.

It is advisable to let it run and play off the leash for at least an hour a day. Provided it gets sufficient exercise, it is extremely peaceful indoors.

Most Schapendoes love to play, swim, and retrieve.

Schapendoes

Schipperke

Schipperke

COUNTRY OF ORIGIN
Belgium.

SPECIAL SKILLS
Vermin destroyer and family pet.

SIZE
The shoulder-height is 25 - 30cm (9¾- 11¾in). In Belgium and France they are classified in two groups by weight: those of 5 - 8kg (11 - 17½lb), and others of 3 - 5kg (6½ - 11lb). In other countries the weight for the breed standard is usually 5 - 8kg (11 - 17½lb).

COAT
A tough coat with a soft under layer. Around the neck and by the hindquarters the hair is longer than elsewhere. The normal color is black; some countries permit other colors including blond.

CARE REQUIRED
This breed needs little grooming. An occasional brushing will keep this dog in excellent condition.

CHARACTER
These are attentive, self-confident, cunning and high spirited dogs that are lively, determined, constant, tireless, alert, and loyal to the family.

TRAINING
This breed is very alert and will bark at the first sign of trouble. If you live surrounded by other homes, teach your dog that a couple of barks are sufficient to arouse the family. This breed is usually easy to train as it is intelligent and eager to learn.

SOCIAL BEHAVIOR
This breed will defend its territory – whether that is an apartment or a large area of land – against both two-legged and four-legged intruders. If someone new visits, they will adopt a watchful position.

The pet cat will be happily accepted. Usually they are quite good with children.

EXERCISE
The Schipperke is a bundle of dynamite. To be happy, it needs to be able to play and run about a great deal.
In addition to daily walks, let it run in the yard or park off its leash.

Short-haired Border Collie with blue marbling

Border Collie, short-haired

COUNTRY OF ORIGIN
Northern England and Scotland.

SPECIAL SKILLS
Sheepdog and family pet.

SIZE
The shoulder-height is 56 - 61cm (22 - 24in) for dogs and 51 - 56cm (20 - 22in) for bitches.

COAT
The coat is dense and short-haired. They can be sable with white, a blue-black, or tri-colored (mainly black with white and tan markings).

CARE REQUIRED
These dogs need regular grooming with a brush and comb and lose copious amounts of hair when they are shedding.

CHARACTER
These are happy, very intelligent dogs which are eager to work, cunning, sociable, protective, energetic, alert, loveable, watchful, sensitive, and affectionate.

They bond very closely with their family members. Like most dogs in this group, they have no desire to run away.

TRAINING
This dog is a fairly quick learner who is pleased to work for you.
The best results are achieved by changing your tone of voice. Never scream at this dog or punish it severely.

Short-haired Border Collie, sable and triple-colored

SOCIAL BEHAVIOR
This breed gets on well with its own kind, other pets, and children. Friends of the family are given a cheerful welcome.

EXERCISE
Adult dogs need plenty of exercise although they can adapt if you fail to take them for a long walk now and then.
Most of them enjoy retrieving and playing with a ball and they do well in obedience and agility classes and enjoy playing catch and with Frisbees.
Care needs to be taken with young dogs during the growing stage so that their energy is directed into growing healthy bones, joints, and muscles.

Long-haired Border Collie

Border Collie, long-haired

COUNTRY OF ORIGIN
Northern England and Scotland.

SPECIAL SKILLS
Sheepdog and family pet.

SIZE
The shoulder-height is 56 - 61cm (22 - 24in) for dogs and 51 - 56cm (20 - 22in) for bitches.

COAT
The long-haired coat is very close; for show dogs a definite collar "ruff" is a desired feature.
These dogs come in sable, blue-black, and tri-color – usually black with white and tan.

Long-haired Border Collie

prevent tangles. During times when the dog is shedding, daily brushing and combing is necessary.

CHARACTER

These happy, very intelligent dogs are eager to work, sociable, cunning, protective, energetic, attentive, loveable, watchful, sensitive, affectionate, and bond very closely with their families.

TRAINING

The Border Collie learns quickly and is best trained by using the tones of your voice to show pleasure or displeasure.

SOCIAL BEHAVIOR

Most Border Collies get on well with other pets, their own kind, and with children. Friends of the family will be greeted with enthusiasm.

EXERCISE

These dogs are very adaptable to changes in their exercise routine but this is not a dog for a city apartment and three walks around the block a day. Allow your dog to run and play off the leash. Most of these dogs love playing with a ball and other forms of retrieving. They can compete with other dogs at such activities as agility skills and obedience competitions. During the growing stage it is important to ensure that their energies are available for building healthy bones, joints and muscles.

CARE REQUIRED

These dogs should be groomed about once a week, receiving a thorough brushing. In the areas of the coat that are thickest, the brushing should be worked right through to the skin to

Long-haired Border Collies

Shetland Sheepdog

Blue-black Shetland Sheepdog

Blue-black Shetland Sheepdog

COUNTRY OF ORIGIN
Scotland.

SPECIAL SKILLS
Sheepdog or family pet.

SIZE
The shoulder-height is 37cm (14½in) for dogs and 35.5cm (14in) for bitches. Deviation of 2.5cm (1in) above and below these standards is permissible.

COAT
These dogs have a double coat: the outer layer consists of long wiry hair, the inner layer is soft, short, and close. Shetland Sheepdogs are bred in sable (light sand to mahogany), with and without black tips to the hairs, and also in tri-colors (black with tan and white markings), blue-black, and black-white. The most attractive look is considered by some to be the tri-color with white feet, white chest, collar ruff, blaze, and tip of the tail.

CARE REQUIRED
The care of the Shetland Sheepdog is not demanding although grooming with brush and comb are needed, especially during shedding. Tangles form, particularly behind the ears, the hindquarters, and beneath the shoulders. Make sure these areas are attended to during grooming.

CHARACTER
This extremely intelligent and cunning dog is loyal to its handler and family, affectionate, obedient, responsive, and happy. It has considerable stamina and is fairly robust.

Shetland Sheepdogs

TRAINING

This is not a difficult breed to train. The Shetland Sheepdog learns happily and enjoys being busy. For this reason it is an excellent idea to enrol in obedience training classes and to follow a course for agility competition. Your dog will get much enjoyment from these activities.

SOCIAL BEHAVIOR

These are extremely sociable dogs who usually get on extremely well with their own kind, cats, and small animals. Provided children don't pester the dog, it will get along well with them, too. They are cautions and watchful with strangers.

EXERCISE

While these dogs will readily adapt to the circumstances you will harm an intelligent dog who is anxious to work if you do not engage it in plenty of activity. These dogs enjoy learning and love to be out with their handler. They are high performers in various areas of dog sports.

SPECIAL REMARKS

This breed does have a tendency to get "too big". If you wish to show it, bear this in mind.

Tatra Mountain Sheepdog

COUNTRY OF ORIGIN

Poland.

SPECIAL SKILLS

Watchdog, herding dog, family pet.

Tatra Mountain Sheepdog

SIZE

The shoulder-height is 65 - 70cm (25½ - 27½in) for dogs and 60 - 65cm (23½ - 25½in) for bitches.

COAT

The hair is short on the head and on the front of the legs; elsewhere, it is thicker and longer. Both straight and curly hair are permitted by the breed standard. The color is always white without markings.

CARE REQUIRED

Except during the time when the dog is shedding little attention is needed to maintain the coat on this dog, which does not readily tangle.

During shedding this breed needs regular grooming with brush and comb to remove loose and dead hair.

CHARACTER

Quiet, well-balanced, sociable, brave, obedient, intelligent, loyal, watchful, and affectionate. These dogs, unlike some other breeds, are not independent.

TRAINING

The Tatra requires a handler who has an air of calm control. Training needs to be consistent and conducted in peace and harmony. Treating these dogs severely works counter-productively. The breed can be somewhat stubborn and refuse to obey commands to which they see no point.

SOCIAL BEHAVIOR

Tatra Mountain Sheepdogs generally get on with other pets, dogs, and children. They will take the side of your children if play with other children becomes rough. They are somewhat reserved towards strangers.

EXERCISE

This is an outdoor dog which really is not suitable for an apartment or even a suburban house with a small yard. The coat protects it from all kinds of weather. Regular long walks are much to its liking but it is not interested in playing ball games or such.

The Tatra Mountain Sheepdog can cope perfectly well in a kennel outside provided it gets sufficient daily exercise and attention.

Welsh Corgi (Cardigan)

Welsh Corgi (Cardigan)

COUNTRY OF ORIGIN
Wales.

SPECIAL SKILLS
Herding dog and family pet.

SIZE
The ideal shoulder-height is 30.5cm (12in). Cardigan dogs are permitted to weigh 15 - 18kg (33 - 39½lbs); bitches are somewhat lighter.

COAT
The short-haired coat is weather-resistant. Any color is permitted provided that white areas do not exceed 30 per cent. Widely found colors are brindle, black with white, beige and blue-black.

CARE REQUIRED
The Corgi will be satisfied with as little grooming as possible. Brush occasionally to remove dead hairs.

CHARACTER
This intelligent dog is eager to learn, hardy and brave, bonds with its handler and family, is fairly calm by nature, and has an especially good sense of humor.

TRAINING
The Corgi is usually a problem-free breed to bring up; it will gladly learn from you, and is quick to understand. This makes it successful in several of the sporting activities for dogs. Care is needed during the growing stage, which means no extensive walks before the dogs is fully grown, and do not let it go up and down stairs too often during this time as its physical development can be harmed.

SOCIAL BEHAVIOR
The Corgi can be rather reckless with other dogs. It is important to socialize them early with cats and other animals to prevent problems in the future. Usually they get on well with children.

EXERCISE
This breed likes to be outdoors. Take it regularly for long and varied walks. With such a dog there are a number of sporting activities to involve both of you such as playing catch and tossing Frisbees as well as working on agility skills trials.
Corgis have been used as avalanche search and rescue dogs.

Welsh Corgi (Cardigan), brindle

Welsh Corgi (Pembroke)

COUNTRY OF ORIGIN
Wales.

SPECIAL SKILLS
Herding dog and family pet.

SIZE
The shoulder-height is 25 - 30.5cm (9¾ - 12in). The dogs weigh 9 - 11kg (20 - 24lb).

COAT
The coat consists of hard straight hairs and is water-resistant. They can have coats of red, beige (or sable), and black-and-tan, with and without white markings on the chest, neck, and legs. Some white markings are permitted on the head and muzzle.

Welsh Corgi (Pembroke), with undocked tail

CARE REQUIRED
The Pembroke's coat requires very little grooming. Use a good brush from time to time in order to remove any dead hair.

CHARACTER
This dog is full of energy and bonds with its handler and family easily. It is alert, hardy, very self-assured, intelligent, eager to learn, and sometimes foolishly brave.

TRAINING
These are not difficult dogs to train and to bring up because of their high intelligence and quick learning ability.

SOCIAL BEHAVIOR
Pembrokes get on well with children provided the children do not tease them. The breed is alert but not over-suspicious of strangers. They can be rather dominant towards their own kind.

EXERCISE
Give Pembrokes the chance to burn off their energy; three times a day quickly around the block is not sufficient.
They usually have no tendency to wander, even if your property is not fenced, since they become attached to your house and yard. It is advisable to ensure varied "work" for them; this might include agility skills and lots of time playing catch, both of which are very suitable for this breed.

Welsh Corgi (Pembroke), study of the head

dominant, but it is also sober, alert, cannot be led astray by bribes, is honest, loyal, demanding of itself, very brave, and intelligent. These dogs have extremely fast reactions, unusual for such large dogs. They are somewhat independent and make their own decisions.

TRAINING
Training needs to be founded on mutual respect and it is essential to treat the dog fairly and with careful consistency.

SOCIAL BEHAVIOR
This dog gets on with children but they must not be allowed to tease it.

If it grows up among other dogs and household pets, or cattle, the South Russian Owtcharka will accept and protect these animals from people who would harm them.

They do not usually form very good relationships with cats – their ancestors were fleet-footed hunting dogs.

The South Russian Owtcharka eyes strange visitors suspiciously, and unwanted ones will get no chance to step onto your property.
Regular visitors will be recognized and adopted as family.

South Russian Owtcharka

COUNTRY OF ORIGIN
Ukraine.

SPECIAL SKILLS
Sheepdog and watchdog.

SIZE
The shoulder-height is a minimum of 65cm (25½in) for dogs and 62cm (24in) for bitches.

COAT
The South Russian Owtcharka has a weather-resistant coat which is long, coarse, and bristly, with a thick under-layer.

The colors are white or grey-cream (in various possible tints), or white with grey markings.

CARE REQUIRED
This breed requires relatively little grooming. A weekly brushing will keep the coat in good condition.

CHARACTER
This breed is full of character and rather

South Russian Owtcharka

EXERCISE
The South Russian Owtcharka will take care of its own needs for exercise if it lives on a well-fenced, large, property.
They tend to inspect the boundaries of their territory, which keeps them fit. These are not suitable dogs for a small plot in a busy neigh-

borhood or for an apartment. This breed is happy to be outside and is not troubled in any way by bad weather.

SPECIAL REMARKS
The South Russian Owtcharka is suitable for people with enough room and space, preferably in remote regions. It is a good watchdog without presenting itself too much. This breed bonds strongly to its territory and usually has problems in adapting itself to a new boss and new surroundings.

Cattle drivers

Australian Cattle Dog

COUNTRY OF ORIGIN
Australia.

SPECIAL SKILLS
Cattle driver and family pet.

SIZE
The shoulder-height is 46 - 51cm (18 - 20in) for dogs and 43 - 48cm (17 - 18¾in) for bitches.

COAT
The outer layer of the coat is weather-resistant, short and fairly rough; the under-layer is short and thick. Two colors are permitted: the first is blue, by which is meant plain blue, blue speckled with and without black, and blue with tan markings.
The other color is described as speckled red, which may include dark speckled red markings on the head.

CARE REQUIRED
The coat of the Australian Cattle Dog does not require much attention. An occasional grooming with brush or comb is sufficient.

CHARACTER
The Australian Cattle Dog is very intelligent and willing to work, well-balanced, barks little, is loyal to its handler, brave, hardy, alert, optimistic, and active.

TRAINING
The Australian Cattle Dog is a very intelligent dog which is eager to learn and ready to work. This means that training it is easy.

You will be unfair to it if you do not work with it. Agility skill trials are an ideal activity, but the dog will equally enjoy playing catch, chasing after Frisbees, or any other sports.

Provided you keep it intensively active this dog will prove a joy to you. On the other hand, a bored Australian Cattle Dog will be a major and serious problem.

SOCIAL BEHAVIOR
This breed's behavior towards its own kind, other pets, and children is a perfect example for other dogs. This model behavior can only be achieved, though, if the dog is adequately socialized when very young.

EXERCISE
This breed needs lots of exercise and plenty to occupy it to keep it in good physical and mental health, and in top condition.

If you are seeking a family dog that won't require much from you, forget this breed.

Australian Cattle Dog

Bouvier des Flandres

COUNTRY OF ORIGIN
Belgium.

SPECIAL SKILLS
Historically a cattle driver, nowadays guard dog, defence dog, and family pet.

SIZE
The shoulder height is 62 - 68cm (24½ - 26¾in) for dogs and 59 - 65cm (23¼ - 25½in) for bitches. The ideal shoulder height is 65cm (25½in) for dogs and 62cm (24½in) for bitches.

COAT

The rough-haired coat is dry-textured, without a sheen. The hair, which may not be too long, has light whorls but is not curly. Permitted colors are dun or grey, streaked or highlighted. Plain black is not favored for showing but is permissible. Blond Bouviers are not considered acceptable.

CARE REQUIRED

A Bouvier needs to be trimmed at least three times a year. Between trims remove any excess hair inside the ears and trim hair between the pads of the feet.

Do not let the hair grow too long close to the feet but trim it so that the Bouvier has nice round feet. A well groomed Bouvier sheds little hair in the home.

CHARACTER

The Bouvier des Flandres is very loyal and bonds well with both its handler and family. This alert, brave, hardy, equable, and intelligent dog enjoys working and is sensible.

TRAINING

The Bouvier requires well-balanced training which remains consistent in nature. It is important to make the dog aware, without being too hard with it, that you are and will remain the boss.

This is an intelligent breed which learns new commands relatively fast though not quite as quickly as, for instance, a German Shepherd. Once a Bouvier has learned something, it will remember it for the rest of its life.

SOCIAL BEHAVIOR

Bouviers are generally sociable animals and provided they have been well socialized with cats when young, they get on well with other pets and their own kind. Children and Bouviers generally form a good combination. They regard strangers with suspicion and are very protective of their families. Their loyalty is world-famous.

EXERCISE

This dog has an average demand for exercise. It will enjoy going with you for a long walk or running alongside you while you bicycle.

During the growing stage exercise needs to be carefully regulated so that growing bones, joints and muscles are not too strenuously stressed. The dog requires all its energy to build a strong frame.

Bouvier des Flandres

Bouvier des Flandres puppies

2. Pinscher, Schnauzer, Molossian, Mastiff, and Swiss Sennenhund breeds

Pinschers and Schnauzers

Affenpinscher

COUNTRY OF ORIGIN
Germany.

SPECIAL SKILLS
Vermin destroyer, watchdog, and family pet.

SIZE
The shoulder-height is 25 - 30cm (9¾ - 11¾in).

COAT
The Affenpinscher has coarse hair which grows in whorls. The coat is usually plain black, but russet brown and grey markings are accepted.

CARE REQUIRED
It may be necessary to pluck the Affenpinscher's coat. This is usually done by a dog trimming specialist but it is possible to learn how to do it yourself. The hair should never be clipped because this ruins the coat for many years. Hairs sometimes grow in the corners of the eyes, causing irritation; these should be dealt with promptly.

CHARACTER
Lively, cheerful, friendly, alert, dependent, and sharp-witted.

TRAINING
Affenpinschers learn commands fairly quickly. Ensure consistency in the training but make sure there is ample variety in the drills so your dog will not become bored.

SOCIAL BEHAVIOR
Affenpinschers get on well with children, and can also be fine with their own sort, and other household pets. If you have visitors who are not known to your dog, the Affenpinscher may refuse to let them in without a great deal of reassurance.

Affenpinscher

EXERCISE
This breed is happy if you take it for a quick trot around the corner three times a day. If you also play with it regularly, then its happiness is complete.

Doberman

COUNTRY OF ORIGIN
Germany.

SPECIAL SKILLS
Guard- and defence-dog, and family pet.

SIZE
The shoulder-height is 68 - 72cm (26¾ - 28½in) for dogs and 63 - 68cm (25 - 27in) for bitches. The weight is between 32 - 45kg (70½ - 99lb) for dogs.

Clipped brown Doberman

COAT

The color of the sleek smooth coat of short hairs is often black and tan, or brown and tan. Coats of blue and tan, or grey-yellow and tan are not recognized in every country.

CARE REQUIRED

A Doberman's coat does not require much attention. During shedding use a rubber glove with knobbled surface to remove dead and loose hairs. Keep the claws short and check the teeth from time to time for tartar.

CHARACTER

The Doberman is an active, cunning dog which bonds closely and is brave, intelligent, a good guard-dog, loyal, dependent, occasionally noisy and boisterous. It has tremendous stamina. Dobermans have a tendency to become extremely loyal to one particular person.

TRAINING

This strong, handsome dog requires very careful and consistent training. Strive to ensure everything is harmonious throughout the training. If you have little experience of training dogs, then you are seriously advised not to acquire one of this breed. If   Dobermans are wrongly brought up they can become quite neurotic making them fearful and/or snappy – while their natural character is straightforward and reliable. Always act clearly and fairly with a Doberman.

Never hit it and make absolutely sure it is not pestered. Dobermans are ideally suited to defence-dog training, but do not start too young and avoid too much pressure on the dog in the early stages – never force it! Wait for really serious activity until a   Doberman has matured somewhat.

SOCIAL BEHAVIOR

A properly socialized Doberman can get along fine with other dogs, other household pets, and children. Unwanted visitors are stopped in their tracks.

EXERCISE

A Doberman cannot be fobbed off with a daily trot around the neighborhood. It is built for speed and has tremendous stamina.

Take it swimming, or let it run alongside your bicycle, or run free in the woods.

This breed is ideal for a variety of sporting activities.

Dobermans are excellent working dogs.

German Pinscher

COUNTRY OF ORIGIN
Germany.

SPECIAL SKILLS
Vermin destroyer, watchdog, and family pet.

SIZE
The shoulder height is 45 - 50cm (17¾ - 19½in).

COAT
The German Pinscher's coat is smooth-haired and plain red, or black and tan.

CARE REQUIRED
The German Pinscher requires little grooming. An occasional brushing to remove dead hairs is all that is necessary.

CHARACTER
This happy, very intelligent, and cunning dog is vigilant, alert, friendly, playful, patient with children, and loyal to its own family. It has a sense of humor, is brave, not squeamish, sober, and has considerable stamina. German Pinschers only bark when necessary.

TRAINING
This breed learns quickly and makes a keen pupil. It is necessary to be firm to some extent, but in a loving and consistent way. German Pinschers are capable of doing well in various sporting activities.

SOCIAL BEHAVIOR
German Pinschers usually get on very well with children. Visitors will be announced with loud barking but then things usually calm down quickly. The dog will defend its territory, handler, and the family to the end against those intent upon harm. Normally they get on without problems with other household pets.

EXERCISE
German Pinschers have an average need for exercise. They enjoy running alongside you when you bicycle, but when you are too busy for that they'll be happy with going around the block provided you also take time to play with the dog in the yard.

German Pinschers

German Pinscher

Miniature Pinscher

COUNTRY OF ORIGIN
Germany.

SPECIAL SKILLS
Family pet.

SIZE
The shoulder height is 25 - 30 cm (9¾ - 11¾in).

COAT
The Miniature Pinscher has a very short coat. The color is basically brown but can vary

Black and tan Miniature Pinscher

through various shades of brown, including deer red to black and tan.

CARE REQUIRED
The Miniature Pinscher requires little grooming. When it is shedding, use a rubber brush to remove dead and loose hairs; follow this by wiping the coat with a damp cloth to encourage the hair to shine.

CHARACTER
This lively, alert, and vigilant dog likes to bark, is intelligent, sober, (overly) courageous, dependent, loyal to its handler, and learns quickly.

TRAINING
Many people seem to feel that just rudimentary training is sufficient with a small dog. This is a pity because the Miniature Pinscher can learn extremely well and wants very much to do so. It is certainly valuable for its socialization to take the dog to puppy courses where it can meet other people and dogs.

You will be dumbfounded by the speed at which the little Pinscher understands and obeys. Pay particular attention to house breaking since a puddle from such a small dog can easily be overlooked, so that the Miniature Pinscher gets the idea that you are happy to accept it fulfilling its natural needs indoors.

SOCIAL BEHAVIOR
The Miniature Pinscher can get along well with other household pets and children, provided they do not pester it. These dogs can be rather suspicious towards strangers, but their behavior depends entirely upon how they were brought up as young dogs.

EXERCISE
A Miniature Pinscher is perfectly happy living in a small apartment provided it gets at least three outings a day when it can run and play.

These dogs are not really happy to spend their entire life in a basket or as a lap-dog.

White Miniature Schnauzer

Black and silver Miniature Schnauzer

Miniature Schnauzer

COUNTRY OF ORIGIN
Germany.

SPECIAL SKILLS
Vermin destroyer, watchdog, and family pet.

SIZE
The shoulder height is 33–36cm (13–14in).

COAT
The coat is rough-haired and salt-and-pepper colored (with dark face), or black (with black and silver markings on the head, legs, and belly). There are also, more rarely, white examples.

CARE REQUIRED
The rough-haired coat of the Miniature Schnauzer needs to be plucked by hand or with a blunt trimmer at least twice a year. They must never, in any circumstances, be clipped because this spoils the coat for many years.

The excessive hair between the pads of the feet should, however, be clipped, and the embellishments should be combed regularly to prevent tangles. By embellishments is meant the beard, moustache, and long eyebrows. When necessary, remove excessive hair growth within the ears.

CHARACTER
This lively, attentive, intelligent dog can be willful and stubborn, and is vigilant, untiring, loyal to the family, and is not led astray by bribes.

TRAINING
The Miniature Schnauzer needs a confident handler despite its size, and also needs to be handled fairly and with consistency. Schnauzers are quick and bright pupils, although they frequently have their own ideas about your commands. Vary the drills with play and do not repeat them too frequently.

SOCIAL BEHAVIOR
In general the Miniature Schnauzer gets on well with other household pets and children. They are uncertain about strangers and will announce visitors with full throated barking.

EXERCISE
The Miniature Schnauzer has enormous amounts of energy. Country walks and romping in the yard please them. Take them out of doors as much as possible.

Dutch Smoushond

COUNTRY OF ORIGIN
The Netherlands.

SPECIAL SKILLS
Stable dog, rat-catcher, and family pet.

SIZE
The shoulder height is 37 - 42cm (14½ - 16½ in)
for dogs and 35 - 40cm (13¾ - 15¾in) for bitches.
Dogs weigh about 10kg (22lb).

COAT
The coat of the Dutch Smoushond is rugged,
coarse, and wiry. The color is straw yellow.

CARE REQUIRED
Depending upon the quality of the coat, the
Dutch Smoushond generally requires the hairs
to be plucked by hand about twice a year, leaving
the hair on the head alone so far as possible.
Between these grooming sessions, remove any
excess hair from inside the ears.

They can also be troubled by too much hair
between the pads of the feet, so ensure this is
regularly trimmed.

CHARACTER
These friendly, engaging, cunning, and intelligent dogs have considerable adaptability, are
dependent, sober, sensitive, companionable,
alert, and have a sense of humor.

TRAINING
The Dutch Smoushond is an intelligent dog
which is eager to do things for you which means
training them is therefore quite easy.

Dutch Smoushond

It is important, though, to ensure that you are consistent towards them because some can try to rule the roost themselves if they get an idea that their handler is rather easy-going.

SOCIAL BEHAVIOR
They get on well with children and happily accept the family cat. Most Dutch Smoushonds get on well with their own kind.

EXERCISE
This breed is untiring and enjoys long walks, and swimming.
Decide to enrol it for agility skills or ball playing courses because it is ideal for both and will enjoy the activity enormously. However, if a week occasionally passes without a good long walk, the Dutch Smoushond will accept it without difficulty.

Standard Schnauzer with salt-and-pepper coat

Standard Schnauzer

COUNTRY OF ORIGIN
Germany.

SPECIAL SKILLS
Vermin destroyer, watchdog, and family pet.

SIZE
The shoulder-height is 45 - 50cm
(17¾ - 19½in).

COAT
The rugged wire-haired coat is black or salt-and-pepper colored with a dark face.

CARE REQUIRED
The coat of this Schnauzer needs to be plucked about twice a year. Such plucking is necessary with most wire-haired breeds because it is the only way to keep both coat and skin in the best condition. When necessary, remove any excess hair within the ears and between the pads of the feet.

CHARACTER
This is an even-tempered and intelligent breed which is eager to learn, sober, dependable, very dependent on its own family. It is not easily led astray with bribes, is observant, and vigilant.

TRAINING
Schnauzers learn quickly and are eager pupils but they possess a fair amount of stubbornness. They respond best to fair and consistent handling, with the sound of your voice being normally sufficient.

SOCIAL BEHAVIOR
Standard Schnauzers naturally get on well with dogs, other animals, and are extremely tolerant of children.

They are mistrustful of people they do not know.

EXERCISE
This breed has an average need of exercise. Despite this, it likes to be busy doing things such as swimming, running beside a bicycle, agility skill competitions, playing ball, running in the yard or the woods.
These are all suitable activities for a dog of this character.

Standard Schnauzer, tolerant of children

Austrian Short-haired Pinscher

COUNTRY OF ORIGIN
Austria.

SPECIAL SKILLS
Vermin destroyer and family pet.

SIZE
The shoulder-height is 35 - 50cm
(13¾ - 19½in).

COAT
This breed's short-haired coat is usually russet-brown, yellow, or streaked brown, with or without white markings.

Austrian Short-haired Pinscher

CARE REQUIRED
Austrian Pinschers are easy to take care of – all that is needed to keep the coat in good condition is to brush it from time to time to remove any loose and dead hairs.

CHARACTER
This dog is constantly alert, lively, and very active, demanding of itself, intelligent, and an outstanding rat-catcher. It bonds extremely closely with its family.

TRAINING
Give the Austrian Pinscher a caring, fair, but somewhat firm training. These dogs learn quickly and perform well in competitions testing skills. With the right handler they can also do well in obedience trials.

SOCIAL BEHAVIOR
The Austrian Pinscher can sometimes try to dominate other dogs.

There are usually no problems with cats and other household pets, provided, of course, that the usual advice to socialize them when young is followed. They can be somewhat remote and cautious with strangers.

EXERCISE
The Austrian Pinscher is by origin a farm dog so that a home in the country where it can get all the exercise it needs on its own is the ideal place for it.

If this does not match your life style, then take it for long walks regularly.

Austrian Short-haired Pinscher

Giant Schnauzer

COUNTRY OF ORIGIN
Germany.

SPECIAL SKILLS
Watchdog, guard-dog, and family pet.

SIZE
The shoulder height is 60 - 70cm (23½ - 27½in).

COAT
The coat is rough. The most usual color is salt-and-pepper; a dark face is desirable with any color.

CARE REQUIRED

About twice a year the hair needs to be plucked. Check regularly that there is not too much hair in the ears and snip it if necessary. Excessive hair growth between the feet pads must also be dealt with. To prevent tangles, comb the long decorative hair embellishments (beard, moustache, and eyebrows) that are a feature of its head.

CHARACTER

This is an alert, vigilant, hardy, and sober dog that does not wander, is very loyal to its handler and family, intelligent and eager to learn, thoughtful, and good-natured. It has considerable stamina, and is not led astray by bribes. Giant Schnauzers bond closely with the family of which they form part.

TRAINING

This breed, which is full of character, requires a sound upbringing. If the training is consistent, fair, and full of variety, it will enjoy it. Provided you bear in mind that a Schnauzer has its own ideas and will not follow every command slavishly, it can do well in various sporting activities – especially defence dog trials.

SOCIAL BEHAVIOR

The Giant Schnauzer causes few problems with dogs and other pets. As with other dogs, he must be correctly socialized when young. These dogs are naturally loving with children.

They are not interested in strangers and tend towards shyness, although to what extent depends largely upon their upbringing and socializing process.

EXERCISE

This is a breed that requires quite a lot of exercise. Make sure that it gets plenty of outdoor exercise.

Black Giant Schnauzer, study of the head

Black Giant Schnauzer

Russian Bear Schnauzer, study of the head

Russian Bear Schnauzer

COUNTRY OF ORIGIN
Former Soviet Union.

SPECIAL SKILLS
Watchdog, guard-dog, and family pet.

SIZE
The shoulder-height is 66 - 72cm (26 - 28½in) for dogs and 64 - 70cm (25½- 27½in) for bitches.

COAT
This breed of dog has a thick under-layer with a rough upper coat.
Colors are plain black, or black with some grey mixed in.

CARE REQUIRED
The coat requires plucking about two to three times each year. This is necessary to maintain a good tough coat. Between these occasions the excess hair in the ears and between the pads of the feet should be trimmed.
Comb the beard and moustache regularly to prevent tangles.

CHARACTER
This dog is vigilant and protective and, unlike some dogs, does not bark to excess. It is quiet in the house, intelligent, cunning, obedient, loyal to its handler and family, and sober.
Russian Schnauzers like to show their own initiative.

TRAINING
This interesting breed likes to work and quickly grasps what is required.
The training has to be clear and consistent in nature to succeed. The dogs react very well to voice commands and physical punishment is rarely necessary.

Russian Bear Schnauzer

SOCIAL BEHAVIOR
The Russian Bear Schnauzer is very friendly with children and can get along fine with cats and other household pets. Family friends will be enthusiastically greeted but strangers will be stopped in their tracks. The breed is naturally reserved with strangers but after its handler says the strangers are "all right", the dog will accept them.

EXERCISE
Russian Bear Schnauzers like to be kept busy but they do not misbehave if you do not have time to take them for a long walk. The breed is suitable for a wide variety of dog sports and particularly for defence dog trials.

SPECIAL REMARKS
A Russian Bear Schnauzer is an ideal family pet but is not a dog for beginners. Dogs which are imported from their country of origin or surrounding countries may often have sharper and stronger characteristics than those bred in Western Europe or North America.

Mastiffs

Argentinian Mastiff, or Dogo Argentinof

COUNTRY OF ORIGIN
Argentina.

SPECIAL SKILLS
Hunting dog.

SIZE
The shoulder-height is 60 - 65cm (23½ - 25½in).

COAT
The Argentinian Mastiff has a short coat which is always white, sometimes with pigment flecks in the skin. A small black patch between the ears is permissible.
There is also an extremely rare version with a long-haired coat.

CARE REQUIRED
The coat of the Argentinian Mastiff is very easy to keep in condition.
Remove dead and loose hairs during shedding with a rubber brush.
Keep the claws short and, as is necessary with all dogs, make sure the ear passages are kept clean.

Unclipped Argentinian Mastiff

CHARACTER

This brave, even-tempered dog is loyal to its handler and family, barks little, is demanding of itself, has considerable stamina, and a strongly developed hunting instinct. The dogs in particular may tend to try to dominate other dogs.

TRAINING

This dog is definitely not a breed for beginners. It requires a well-balanced, loving, but very consistent upbringing. Try to reward it when things go well and when they go wrong punish the dog solely with your voice. A combination of isolation in a kennel with a tough training regime is cruel and can lead to unpredictable behavior from this dog.

SOCIAL BEHAVIOR

These dogs usually get on well with children although some of them can be rather boisterous. It is possible to socialize them to tolerate cats and other pets but it is not advisable to expect an Argentinian Mastiff to share a house with them. Remember that this is a hunting dog which will regard a cat or sheep as prey.

They are not an ideal choice as watchdogs because of their hunting instincts although they are certainly likely to frighten away most wrong-doers.

EXERCISE

For this dog to be happy it should be taken regularly for long walks. A walk around the block three times a day is definitely not enough. In a large enough fenced yard it will burn-off its energy itself. Because of its strong hunting instincts and dominant behavior towards other dogs, an Argentinian Mastiff must be firmly controlled when walked on a leash.

SPECIAL REMARKS

This breed is banned in some countries. They are not suitable for beginners. Many of these dogs are deaf. Purchase puppies only from a trustworthy recognized breeder.

Dogue de Bordeaux

Dogue de Bordeaux

COUNTRY OF ORIGIN

France.

SPECIAL SKILLS

Watchdog and family dog.

SIZE

The shoulder-height is 60 - 70cm (23½ - 27½in) for dogs and their minimum weight is 50kg (110lb). The shoulder-height is 58 - 66cm (22¾ - 26in) for bitches and their minimum weight is 45kg (99lb).

COAT

The coat consists of soft short hair of mahogany red or red-brown, with a red or black face. White markings are considered unacceptable.

CARE REQUIRED

Brush the coat regularly when the dog is shedding with a rubber brush to remove dead and loose hairs. If necessary, clean the folds in the face.

In common with other large dogs, the Dogue de Bordeaux grows quickly and needs all its energy to build a healthy body. Do not allow a young dog to tire itself and ensure it gets ample food of sufficient nourishment.

CHARACTER
This is an equable, calm dog which rarely barks and is friendly, attentive, curious, very brave, and physically demanding of itself. It bonds closely with its handler and family. The Bordeaux will protect the family and guard the house and grounds.

TRAINING
Give the Bordeaux a consistent training in a fair and calm manner. This dog becomes very attached to and wants to please its handler.

Make a fuss of the dog and let it see you are pleased when it behaves well, and speak encouragingly to it.

SOCIAL BEHAVIOR
When the Bordeaux has had lots of positive experiences in its youth, enabling it to develop as a happy dog, its behavior with other pets will probably be fine.
These dogs are usually kind and protective with children. Visitors are initially eyed mistrustfully but once the dog's handler says the visitors are "all right", they are accepted by the dog. This breed can be rather dominant towards other dogs.

Dogues de Bordeaux are sociable animals.

EXERCISE
This breed has average exercise demands. Two walks (on the leash) each day together with running and playing off the leash a few times each week are sufficient for it.

SPECIAL REMARKS
This strong dog bonds figuratively and almost literally to the family. It will consider separation as a punishment. Do not choose this breed if you have to be away from the house for long periods.

Boxer

COUNTRY OF ORIGIN
Germany.

SPECIAL SKILLS
Working dog and family pet.

SIZE
The shoulder height is 53–63cm (21–25in).

COAT
"The Boxer has a short smooth coat, either brindle or yellow, possibly with white markings and a dark face. The white should not cover more than a third of the dog."

CARE REQUIRED
The coat can be kept in condition by grooming occasionally with a rubber brush. Pay special attention to this when the dog is shedding.

CHARACTER
This happy, friendly, spontaneous, and intelligent dog is eager to learn and curious. Learning quickly, it is also vigilant, boisterous, uncomplicated, straightforward, lively and constantly on the move, bonding very closely with the family.

TRAINING
Teach the Boxer not to be so boisterous and

Boxer

especially not to jump up at people. Since it learns quickly and has substantial intelligence, the Boxer is ideal for various sporting activities from defence trials to skill trials.

SOCIAL BEHAVIOR
Boxers are known for the way they get on so well with children. A well brought-up and properly socialized Boxer will also get on with his own kind and other household pets.

The Boxer's nature is to protect you, your family, and your home. Known visitors will be welcomed boisterously.

EXERCISE
Try to give a Boxer plenty of exercise. When it has grown up, you can carefully let it run beside a bicycle.

They love playing and romping with their own kind but a Boxer will happily leave its basket to play ball with you.

Bullmastiff

Bullmastiff

COUNTRY OF ORIGIN
England.

SPECIAL SKILLS
Watchdog and family pet.

SIZE

The shoulder height is 63.5 - 68.5cm (25 - 27in) for dogs and 61 - 66cm (24 - 26in) for bitches.

COAT

The coat is short and the colors, which may be streaked, are tan or red-brown, always with darker muzzle and ears. A little white on the chest is permitted.

CARE REQUIRED

Grooming a Bullmastiff is not difficult. Occasionally remove dead and loose hairs with a rubber brush or massage glove.

TRAINING

This breed reacts best to a fair, stable, and consistent approach carried out in a harmonious manner.

The Bullmastiff is very sensitive to the tone of your voice. It is not a difficult dog but does require a handler who can assert his authority. The Bullmastiff should never be banished to a kennel.

SOCIAL BEHAVIOR

Bullmastiffs are very tolerant towards children but can be rather dominant towards their own kind. Provided they are properly socialized when young, they can learn to get along with

Bullmastiff, study of the head

other household pets. Friends of the family will be accepted, especially if the handler indicates approval, but unwanted visitors will be stopped.

EXERCISE

The Bullmastiff has an average demand for exercise.

A couple of outings every day with several opportunities to run and play (on a leash) give it sufficient freedom of movement.

Estrela Mountain Dog

Estrela Mountain Dog

COUNTRY OF ORIGIN

Portugal.

SPECIAL SKILLS

Guarding the herd and the household, and family pet.

SIZE

The shoulder height is 65 - 72cm (25½ - 28½in) for dogs and 62 - 68cm (24½ - 26¾in) for bitches. Dogs weigh 30 - 50kg (66 - 110lb).

COAT

There are two types of coat for this breed: long-haired and with short hair. Both types of coat should be abundant, with an under-layer of fine, short hairs. Reddish-brown, wolf-grey, and yellow, plain or with white markings, are all permitted.

CHARACTER

This breed is vigilant (sometimes rather noisily alert), sober, equable, intelligent, and eager to learn, but it can also be stubborn and independent.

It is affectionate and bonds very closely with the family and with people it knows which can make it difficult for it to accept a new handler or owner in later life.

TRAINING

The Estrela Mountain Dog learns quite quickly; some examples of the breed have excelled at obedience trials. These dogs are intelligent and agile enough to perform well in skills trials but both the dog and the handler should enjoy the activity.

At competition level the Estrela will be overtaken by faster breeds.

Stubbornness and making up their own mind are characteristics of the Estrela but they will only appear if the dog finds the drills boring or feels it is pressured.

Do not over-tire the dog and adapt the extent and nature of exercise during the growing stage when it needs all its energy to build healthy bones, muscles and joints.

SOCIAL BEHAVIOR

Those who are known to the family and all the people and animals of the household will be seen as its responsibility to look after.

Strangers will be extremely suspiciously regarded.

EXERCISE

The Estrela Mountain Dog is happiest with plenty of space, indoors as well as out. They really enjoy going for walks with you, but if that is not always possible they will accept the situation without fuss.

Blue Great Dane with clipped ears

Unclipped Black Great Dane

Great Dane

COUNTRY OF ORIGIN
Germany.

SPECIAL SKILLS
Previously hunting dog for large game, now watchdog, and family pet.

SIZE

The shoulder-height is a minimum of 80cm (31½in) for dogs and 72cm (28½in) for bitches. There is no maximum standard and generally people like the dogs to be well over the minimum height. These dogs weigh 50kg (110lb) and upwards, depending upon the size and sex.

COAT

These dogs have short smooth coats which have three accepted colors: yellow (which can be streaked) with a black face; black, perhaps with a little white, or white with black spots (known as harlequin and the only variety permitted to have blue eyes and partially flesh colored muzzles); and blue.

Two other colors are accepted in some countries. These are the Mantle which has a black coat covering almost all the dog with white showing on just the chest, neck, blaze, belly, legs, and tip of the tail; and another variety where this mantle is broken with white. Both are considered as black in some countries. The different colors are not interbred.

CARE REQUIRED

The Great Dane's coat requires very little attention. During shedding it is best to remove dead and loose hairs with a rubber brush. The Great Dane must always be allowed to lie somewhere soft to avoid pressure marks. Fast-growing breeds like the Great Dane require care during the growing stage. The first essential is the right nutrition. The other point to watch is to limit exercise, avoiding pressuring and over-tiring the dog which can cause serious problems for the developing bones, joints, and muscles. These dogs do not belong in a kennel and like to be comfortable.

CHARACTER

These are affectionate, calm, and intelligent dogs that are sensible, sensitive, very loyal to the handler and family, not easily led astray by bribes, and are curious. Despite the fact that they do not bark much, these dogs make excellent watchdogs.

It is said that a burglar may get into a house watched over by a Great Dane but can never get out. Like other Mastiff types, the Great Dane is not very susceptible to pain and so it is possible that an illness or injury may be overlooked for some time.

TRAINING

The Great Dane grows in a very short period into a very large dog. You must therefore teach it as a very young dog that it must not pull on the leash. Train it with understanding and with great consistency.

These dogs are very sensitive to the intonation of the voice and your friendly request will quite often be sufficient to get them to do what you require.

SOCIAL BEHAVIOR

Generally Great Danes get on perfectly well with their own kind, other household pets, and children. Most of them are rather unsure with strangers but friends of the family will be warmly greeted.

EXERCISE

These strong and elegant dogs require a great deal of exercise.

They will enjoy being able to run free and romping, off the leash, in open country or woodland. They can also be exercised running alongside a bicycle provided they stay strictly by you.

Great Danes that get sufficient outdoor exercise will be very peaceful indoors.

English Bulldog

English Bulldog

COUNTRY OF ORIGIN

England.

SPECIAL SKILLS

Family pet.

SIZE

The English Bulldog weighs 22–25kg (48½–55lb) and stands 31–36cm (12–14in).

COAT

The coat is short and is found in beige, red-brown brindle (with or without a black face), white (with lots of dark pigment on the muzzle and eye) and piebald. Black, liver, and black and tan are not acceptable colors.

CARE REQUIRED

When the Bulldog sheds, it is easy to remove dead and loose hairs with a rubber brush. When necessary clean the folds in the face with a special lotion made for this purpose. The English Bulldog prefers to lie in a draught-free, soft, dry place, and a kennel can be suitable if it meets those requirements.

CHARACTER

The Bulldog is animated, spontaneous, uncomplicated, and equable with a sense of humor, gentle-natured, sensitive but demanding

English Bulldog puppy and adult

of itself. This dog can be fearless if necessary, intelligent in a thoughtful way, and peaceful in the house. These dogs are very affectionate and prefer to be close to the family.

TRAINING

Bulldogs are usually easy to train. They are very sensitive to your voice or voices and will often respond to a friendly but determined request. Consistency is most important in training these dogs and be sure they understand what you want.

SOCIAL BEHAVIOR

Mixing with other dogs and household pets is usually problem-free. They make ideal friends for children and are very tolerant. Most also have a well-developed sense of humor. Some English Bulldogs are extremely wary of strangers, while others are friends with everybody.

EXERCISE

This is not a breed requiring long walks. The English Bulldog will be quite happy with three short outings a day and for the rest of the time they will be pleased to stay in the house or yard, provided the family is close by, which makes them ideal for less active people. Bulldog puppies have a tendency to keep on running and playing when they are exhausted.

Make sure that they get sufficient rest and limit their exercise so that their energy can be used to build healthy bones, joints, and muscles.

They are not able to withstand heat, so make sure that they have somewhere cool to lie on hot days.

Fila Brasileiro

Fila Brasileiro, or Brazilian Molosser

COUNTRY OF ORIGIN
Brazil.

SPECIAL SKILLS
Watchdog and tracking dog.

SIZE
The shoulder-height is 65 - 75cm (25½ - 29½in) for dogs and 60 -70cm (23½ -27½in) for bitches.

COAT
The short-haired coat of the Fila Brasileiro is known in many different colors of which only white, mouse-grey, and spotted or piebald coats are not accepted. The most usual coat is brindle.

CARE REQUIRED
This is a breed which requires relatively little care. Let the dog lie somewhere soft to prevent callouses forming on the leg joints.

CHARACTER
The Fila Brasileiro can be very affectionate and always works with its handler, which it obeys totally. These dogs are suspicious of strangers and this can manifest itself as aggression or evasion, depending upon the person in question. Regular visitors are usually accepted. The breed has an exceptionally well developed sense of smell so that the dogs are very aware of whatever approaches.
They can act quite independently, depending upon the situation. They have very strong territorial instincts.

TRAINING
The owner of a Fila Brasileiro needs to be confident and have a well-balanced nature in order to train this breed successfully. Some people find the dog's character to be difficult and unfathomable. Training needs to be calmly carried out in a harmonious manner and with understanding for the dog's character. An occasional correction is acceptable but this breed is very sensitive to the intonation of your voice.
The potential owner must be aware that they react very quickly. For the right handler they are obedient.

Head of a Fila Brasileiro

SOCIAL BEHAVIOR

The Fila Brasileiro presents no problems for the children of its family but this is not true of their playmates.
It will also accept other household animals which it has met while young. New pets joining the family are usually not accepted.

EXERCISE

It is best to keep this breed in a large, securely fenced yard where it can take care of its own exercise needs.
From time to time take it to new places to provide a change of scene for it.

SPECIAL REMARKS

The Fila Brasileiro or Brazilian Molosser is banned in some countries. It is definitely not a breed for beginners, nor one to be kept in an urban environment.

Black and tan Hovawart

Hovawart

COUNTRY OF ORIGIN

Germany.

SPECIAL SKILLS

Watchdog and family pet.

SIZE

The shoulder-height is 63 - 70cm (24¾ - 27½in) for dogs and 58 - 65cm (23 - 26in) for bitches.

COAT

The Hovawart has a long-haired, wavy coat which lies flat.
The colors are plain black, black with a marking, and blond.

CARE REQUIRED

The coat does not require a great deal of attention. The use occasionally of a brush and comb (particularly in places where tangles might form) is sufficient.

CHARACTER

Good-natured, equable, demanding of itself, loyal to the family but with the tendency to become strictly devoted to one person in the family. This dog is affectionate, vigilant and protective, attentive, and a good watchdog. The Hovawart has a good scenting nose and remains playful until old age.

TRAINING

The Hovawart learns quickly what you expect of it. The best results are achieved with extremely consistent, loving, and well-balanced training. Hovawarts are ideally suited to be tracking-, avalanche-, watch-, and defence-dogs.

SOCIAL BEHAVIOR

These dogs generally behave well towards other household animals provided the dog has met these animals when it was young.
They are generally very patient with children but somewhat reserved towards strangers.

The Hovawart will protect your property against intruders with great zeal. When its handler indicates that visitors are "all right", it accepts them immediately.

EXERCISE

The Hovawart adapts itself to the circumstances. Take the dog for regular long walks and let it enjoy running and playing off the leash.

A great advantage of this breed is that it has a highly developed sense of territory and will not readily desert your property.

Blond Hovawart

Anatolian Shepherd Dog, or Karabash

COUNTRY OF ORIGIN
Turkey.

SPECIAL SKILLS
Sheepdog and protector for cattle herds.

SIZE
The shoulder-height is 74 - 81cm (29¼ - 31¾in) for dogs and 71 - 79cm (28 - 31¼in) for bitches. The dogs weigh 41 - 64kg (90 - 141lb).

COAT
The outer protective coat is smooth with a sheen and mainly short, but longer around the collar and tail. Any color is permitted, but the most acceptable colors are plain cream to fawn with a black face and ears.

CARE REQUIRED
The Anatolian Shepherd Dog requires little grooming. During the time when the dog is shedding use a comb with a double row of metal teeth to remove the dead and loose hairs of the under-layer of the coat.

CHARACTER
This equable dog is brave and demanding of itself, unsure of strangers, can be stubborn and dominant, is reasonably independent, and very vigilant.

TRAINING
The Anatolian Shepherd is not a dog for beginners. It needs a handler who naturally radiates leadership.
The best results are achieved with a determined, consistent, and loving approach. It is very important to begin training quite early because fully grown dogs are too strong and too big to be corrected.

SOCIAL BEHAVIOR
These dogs generally get on well with other animals provided they have been introduced to them when young.
They are rather reserved towards strangers but there are seldom problems with children from their own family.

They can be rather dominant towards other dogs. It's important to introduce the dog early in its life to its own kind, other animals, and people.

EXERCISE
Anatolian Shepherds require a lot of exercise. When they can run free in their own yard with a fence surrounding it, they can decide upon their own exercise needs. This breed is not suited to an apartment.

Anatolian Shepherd Dog, study of the head

Caucasian Owtcharka, or Caucasian Sheepdog

COUNTRY OF ORIGIN
Former Soviet Union.

SPECIAL SKILLS
Watchdog.

SIZE
The shoulder-height is a minimum of 65cm (25½in) for dogs and 62cm (24½in) for bitches.

COAT
The Caucasian Owtcharka has three different kinds of coat: long-haired with a collar and longer-haired hindquarters; short-haired; and medium-length hair without the collar and the long hairs on the hindquarters.
The main colors are different shades of grey with light to rust markings; yellow, white, dun, and rust-brown; they can be multi-colored and patterned.

CARE REQUIRED
The long-haired kinds require grooming from time to time with brush and comb, especially where tangles might occur. The coat of the short-haired variety needs less grooming.

CHARACTER
The Caucasian Owtcharka's original role was to protect livestock from four-legged and two-legged predators.
It is a very brave, vigilant, and strong, hardy dog. It distrusts people it does not know as it has a powerful urge to defend.

TRAINING
If you are thinking of owning a Caucasian Owtcharka you should be strong in character and physique. This dog has a strong sense of right and wrong and you must never treat it severely or punish it unfairly.

The right handler can develop a Caucasian Owtcharka which is obedient and very loyal through mutual respect. Such a dog will protect the family and home with its life.

Caucasian Owtcharka, study of the head

SOCIAL BEHAVIOR
Everything and everyone who belongs to the family – and that includes children, cats, chickens, or whatever – will be regarded by this dog as part of its family and respected and pro-tected.

Do not leave it alone with your children because if play should become rough when they play with other children, the Caucasian Owtcharka will defend your children, perhaps excessively. It has no time for strangers but will greet family friends warmly. It can be rather dominant towards other dogs.

EXERCISE
This breed of dog is best suited to a family with lots of space surrounding the home where it can attend to its own exercise needs. Because its thick coat protects it so well, it can happily cope with living outside.

Landseer (European Continental type)

COUNTRY OF ORIGIN
Canada/Europe.

SPECIAL SKILLS
Family pet.

SIZE
The shoulder height is 72 - 80cm (28½ - 31½in) for dogs and 67 - 72cm (26¼ - 28½in) for bitches. Small variations above and below these standards are permited.

COAT
The under-layer of the coat is soft, the outer coat is long, thick, and without curls. The color is white with black patches, and a black head with white blaze is much preferred. For showing, it is preferable not to have black spots on the coat.

CARE REQUIRED
Regular brushing and combing is sufficient, specifically paying attention to the places where tangles are likely to occur, such as between the hind and front legs.

Keep the ear passages clean and snip away excessive hair between the pads of the feet. The Landseer, in common with other big dogs, grows fairly quickly and needs high quality nutrition. Exercise should be adapted during this growing phase to prevent overworking a growing body.

CHARACTER
The Landseer is an amiable, soft-natured, straightforward, affectionate, docile, sociable, self-aware, and equable dog. It is friendly towards people and animals and enjoys sports.

It is a keen swimmer. It will protect the members of the family and the house and yard if necessary. The Landseer rarely barks.

TRAINING
Normally this breed is not difficult to train. Teach the young dog to walk to heel and not to pull on the leash, because when these dogs are fully grown they are much too strong to control by physical force.

SOCIAL BEHAVIOR
The Landseer is a fine family dog, which will live in harmony with other dogs and household pets.

Children often receive special attention from them (in a positive sense). Friendly visitors will be treated in a friendly manner.

EXERCISE
Do not take the Landseer on extremely long walks until it is fully grown. These dogs love to swim and this is an ideal form of exercise for them.

SPECIAL REMARKS
The Landseer is well protected against poor weather and it is not therefore necessary for it to live indoors.

Landseers

Leonberger

Leonberger

COUNTRY OF ORIGIN
Germany.

SPECIAL SKILLS
Family pet.

SIZE
The shoulder height is 72 - 80cm (28½ - 31½in) for dogs and 65 - 75cm (25½ - 29½in) for bitches. The ideal height is 76cm (30in) for dogs and 70cm (27½in) for bitches.

COAT
The Leonberger has a soft to firm coat of medium-length hair with a thick under-layer. The most usual colors range from golden-yellow to red-brown, with a dark face. The tips of the hairs should be black. The lack of a black face is accepted but not preferred.

CARE REQUIRED
Brush and comb the coat regularly to remove all the dead hair. In addition keep the ear passages clean. Because this breed grows so rapidly, it is very important that it receives a proper well-balanced diet.

Bear in mind that the bones, muscles, and joints of the young dog must not be too heavily taxed with long walks or by letting it run up and down stairs too often.

CHARACTER
This is a peaceful, self-confident, and equable dog which is straightforward, loyal, intelligent, and a quick learner. It will alert you to visitors.

TRAINING
This breed responds best to a well-balanced training program in a harmonious manner. It learns quickly and will rapidly grasp what is expected of it.

SOCIAL BEHAVIOR
Leonbergers get on well with other dogs and other household pets, and mixing with children presents no problems. However, it makes little difference to it whether visitors are friendly or not. Once it has alerted you the Leonberger considers its job done.

EXERCISE
The Leonberger requires extensive exercise. Take it with you regularly for long walks during which it can have an opportunity to run and play off the leash.

Leonbergers

Mastiffs

Mastiff

COUNTRY OF ORIGIN
England.

SPECIAL SKILLS
These dogs were originally hunting dogs for large game and watchdogs. Now they are watchdogs and family pets.

SIZE
The shoulder height is a minimum of 76cm (30in) for dogs and 70cm (27½in) for bitches.

COAT
The Mastiff's coat is short-haired and can be apricot, silver, yellow, or streaked. Whatever the color of the coat, the face should be black.

CARE REQUIRED
When the dog is shedding the loose and dead hairs can best be removed by using a rubber brush. Give the Mastiff a soft place to lie down to avoid ugly pressure marks.
Economies must not made with the young growing dog's diet. Good nutrition is essential for optimum growth. Like other mastiff types, the Mastiff has a high pain threshold and since it is very demanding of itself, injuries and illnesses can be overlooked.

CHARACTER
The Mastiff is a calm, self-confident, watchful, and patient dog who is gentle natured towards his family, intelligent, and dignified. It rarely barks but it is in its nature to defend its territory and family.

TRAINING
Training a Mastiff must be enjoyable, conducted calmly and in a harmonious manner.

Mastiff

Consistency, lots of love, and plenty of understanding work wonders.

SOCIAL BEHAVIOR
Provided it is correctly socialized, the Mastiff presents no problems mixing with other dogs and household pets.

Normally its behavior with children is good-tempered and friendly. When strangers visit it is likely to refuse to let them in unless they are accepted by its handler.

EXERCISE
Do not let a young Mastiff run about and play to excess. Control exercise during puppyhood and youth because this rapidly growing animal needs all its energy for development.

If the dog is too strongly pressured or becomes over-tired, it can have a bad effect upon the development of bones, joints, and muscles.

An adult Mastiff has an average need for exercise. In general these dogs do not really enjoy playing with a ball and similar activities.

Young Spanish Mastiff

Spanish Mastiff

COUNTRY OF ORIGIN
Spain.

SPECIAL SKILLS
Guard-dog for livestock.

SIZE
The shoulder-height is a minimum of 78cm

(30¾in) for dogs with a preferred height of 80cm (31½in). The shoulder-height is a minimum of 74cm (29¼in) for bitches with a preferred height of 76cm (30in).

COAT
The Spanish Mastiff has straight hair with a dense under-layer. The center of the back and the tail have longer hair.

The colors can be plain yellow, red, black, wolf-grey, and red-brown, or broken colors or spotted. White should not be too dominant.

CARE REQUIRED
Groom the Spanish Mastiff regularly with a brush, especially when it is shedding, and examine the ear passages for dirt.

CHARACTER
This breed is very gentle with its family, but it is very mistrustful of strangers. It is also self-confident and independent, intelligent, and very alert, and it will protect you and your family against unwelcome visitors to its full ability.

TRAINING
It is important to train the Spanish Mastiff with an equable, consistent, and loving approach. A tough or unjust approach to training will bring undesirable characteristics to the surface. Its handler needs to be a well-balanced, calm person who naturally exudes leadership.

Spanish Mastiff, study of the head

SOCIAL BEHAVIOR
Its own family is always the most important for a Spanish Mastiff. This dog takes its responsibilities as a watchdog very seriously and will allow no person or other animal onto the property where it lives.

This is a role it assumes naturally without training or commands. When its handler indicates that visitors are welcome, however, it will accept them without difficulty.
It is always friendly towards other animals regardless of whether they are cats or large or small livestock. It is usually extremely patient with children.

EXERCISE
These dogs are in their element if your home is surrounded by plenty of land.
Take them occasionally for an outing to the woods or open countryside for a change of scene.
This dog's thick coat protects it from cold and wet so that it can live happily outdoors.

Unclipped Neopolitan Mastiff

Neopolitan Mastiff

COUNTRY OF ORIGIN
Italy.

SPECIAL SKILLS
Watchdog and family pet.

SIZE
The shoulder-height is 65 - 75cm (25½ - 29½in) for dogs and 60 - 68cm (23½ - 26¾in) for bitches.

COAT
The coat is short and usually blue-grey; these

dogs can also be grey, black, brown, or fox red. All colors may be broken. A little white on the chest or feet is permitted.

CARE REQUIRED
When this dog is shedding the dead and loose hairs are best removed with a rubber brush.
The breed likes a draught-free and dry place to sleep which must be soft to prevent pressure marks.

CHARACTER
This is a dominant, watchful, equable, and peaceful dog which is brave, intelligent, not aggressive, affectionate, and demanding of itself. It rarely gives trouble by excessive barking.

TRAINING
This large Mastiff requires a well-balanced training. Be sure you are consistent in approach and do not keep repeating commands it has failed to obey.
These are not dogs for beginners but it is an exaggeration to describe them as difficult in their association with others. A calm handler with natural leadership will achieve the best results with this breed. It is in their nature to protect you and your possessions – it does not need to be reminded.

SOCIAL BEHAVIOR
The dogs can sometimes try to dominate other dogs, but with regard to children they are generally always loving, provided the children do not tease them. If the dog has had positive experiences with cats and other household pets when young, there should be no problems in this direction.

EXERCISE
Do not let the young Neopolitan Mastiff run and play too much. Limit its exercise because it must on no account be over-tired.
Avoid rough games in the growing stage and ensure that all its energy is available to make healthy bones and muscles. When full-grown the Neopolitan Mastiff has an average demand for exercise.

Newfoundland

Newfoundland

Newfoundland

COUNTRY OF ORIGIN
Canada.

SPECIAL SKILLS
Originally a fisherman's dog, now a family pet.

SIZE
The shoulder-height is about 71cm (28in) for dogs and about 66cm (26in) for bitches. Their weight is 50 - 69kg (110 - 152lb).

COAT
The Newfoundlander has a water resistant, double, medium-length, greasy and dense coat.

Permitted colors are brown or black, with some white on the chest, toes and tip of the tail. Black and white Newfoundlanders exist, but are seldom seen.

CARE REQUIRED
Brush and comb this breed regularly with special attention to the hindquarters and other areas where tangles quickly form.
Trim any excessive hair growth between the pads of the feet.

CHARACTER
Good humored, sociable, gentle, straight-forward, affectionate, and tractable, this breed is friendly with people and animals, loves to swim, is not particularly vigilant yet protects its family if it should become necessary. The Newfoundland rarely barks, is self-assured, and has an equable nature.

TRAINING
Training must be conducted in a calm and balanced manner. These dogs are very sensitive to the tone of your voice.

SOCIAL BEHAVIOR
The Newfoundland is a through and through household companion. Any dog, other animal, child, or visitor who has no evil intentions will receive a friendly welcome.

EXERCISE
Avoid all exhausting day-long hikes until the dog is fully grown. Newfoundlands usually love to swim and this is an ideal form of exercise for them. The thick coat protects them against cold and rain so that they can happily be kept out of doors.

Pyrenean Mountain Dog

Pyrenean Mountain Dog

COUNTRY OF ORIGIN
France.

SPECIAL SKILLS
Sheepdog (to protect flocks and herds of cattle), and family pet.

SIZE
The shoulder-height is 70 - 80cm (27½ -31½in)

for dogs and 65 - 72cm (25½ - 28½in) for bitches. The weight is 45 - 60kg (99 - 132lb).

COAT
The coat is abundant and tightly packed with fairly long hair that is even longer around the neck and tail. Pyrenean Mountain Dogs are plain white with markings on the head, ears, and root of the tail.
These markings can be grey, badger, pale yellow, or wolf-grey. Some markings on the body are permissible.

CARE REQUIRED
This breed requires thorough grooming to keep the coat in good condition.
The dog must be brushed or combed thoroughly once or twice a day in order to remove loose hairs. This is even more important during shedding.

CHARACTER
This is an equable, attentive, vigilant, brave and intelligent dog that is reasonably independent and hardy, and can sometimes be stubborn. The Pyrenean Mountain Dog rarely barks to excess.

TRAINING
If you decide to get this breed of dog, remember that it is essential to make it aware of everything it must and must not do when still very young – when fully grown the dogs are both too strong and too independent to be ·trained properly. Pyrenean Mountain Dogs require an equable handler who can be consistent and loving.

SOCIAL BEHAVIOR
The Pyrenean Mountain Dog can act aggressively towards dogs that might be a match for him but will leave smaller dogs alone. Normally this dog mixes well with children, but strangers are mistrusted, and it will protect you, your family, and your home against unwanted visitors.
There are no problems with regard to cats and other household animals.

EXERCISE
The Pyrenean Mountain Dog requires extensive exercise. Take it for long walks regularly and give it the opportunity during the walk to run and play off the leash.

This dog is always happiest with families that have plenty of space – indoors and out – but it will adapt to smaller homes provided it gets sufficient exercise. In common with all rapidly growing breeds this dog must not be exhausted during the growing stage.

Rottweilers

Rottweiler

COUNTRY OF ORIGIN
Germany.

SPECIAL SKILLS
Watchdog, guard-dog, and family pet.

SIZE
The shoulder-height is 61 - 68cm (24 - 26¾in) for dogs and 56 - 63cm (22 - 24¾in) for bitches.

COAT
The breed has a not very long, thick and coarse outer layer of hair with a thick under layer. The coat is always black with brown markings. Long-haired examples occur occasionally but are not considered desirable. A white chest marking is also not desirable.

CARE REQUIRED
The Rottweiler is relatively easy to care for. Use a rubber glove to remove loose hairs during shedding as you'll find it works better than a normal brush. If you wish to make the coat shine, there are special lotions which can be used. Keep the claws short and the ear passages clean.

CHARACTER
The Rottweiler is intelligent, obedient, unconditionally loyal to its handler and family, and is vigilant, protective, brave, strong, imposing. It can be jealous.

A Rottweiler will defend its family and property to the end. Most of them have a tendency to become loyal to one person.

TRAINING

Rottweilers can be rather dominant in nature and therefore require an equable, calm handler who is confident and always fair. Teach the puppy what it may and what it may not do and hold consistently to this. The breed is extremely sensitive to your voice so use it for praise as well as blame.

A varied training program gives the best results with this dog. Generally it is necessary to be more forceful with the dogs than the bitches, which have a slightly gentler nature. Rottweilers are ideally suited for security work and defence dog training and sports, although the Mechelen Belgian Shepherd can be trained more quickly for this type of work.

SOCIAL BEHAVIOR

When a Rottweiler has been consistently brought up and trained, it will be loyal to its family and a good playmate for the children. Cats and other household animals will be accepted unquestioningly, provided the dog has had positive experiences with them when young. Some Rottweilers can try to dominate other dogs and want to assert themselves.

Friends and relatives of the family are normally enthusiastically welcomed, whereas strangers can get no nearer than the sidewalk. The Rottweiler is an outstanding watchdog.

EXERCISE

Make sure that a Rottweiler gets plenty of exercise because it needs it.

Running in the woods and in open country makes it very happy and it has no desire to wander far from you.

Swimming or running beside a bicycle are perfect activities for this dog and it also adores retrieving a ball.

Rottweiler

Young Shar Pei

Shar Pei

COUNTRY OF ORIGIN
China.

SPECIAL SKILLS
Family pet.

SIZE
The shoulder-height is 48 - 58cm (18¾ - 22¾in) and the weight is about 18kg (39½lb).

COAT
The coat is very hard and is intended to be very short and bristly (the horsecoat variety). There is also a variety with longer hair (the brushcoat) but these are not considered the best. Permitted colors are black, brown, red, and fawn. A cream coat is also known but is not considered the best. Lighter tints of the main colors are permitted but never white or multi-colored. Shar Pei dogs have a blue tongue and blue pigment.

CARE REQUIRED
The Shar Pei has folds of skin over his entire body, especially when young. Check these folds regularly and clean if necessary. Some of these dogs have a tail which lies very close to the body and this too needs to be inspected and cleaned to prevent infections. Put drops in the eyes when necessary and groom the coat with a soft brush.

CHARACTER
This breed is loyal to its handler, playful, active, dominant, and brave. It is an intelligent dog that doesn't always follow orders slavishly, and it is reasonably vigilant.

TRAINING

Training of this dog needs to be extremely consistent. If you are too uncertain, too inconstant, too soft, or too lenient in the dog's eyes, it will take over as boss. The Shar Pei needs a confident handler.

SOCIAL BEHAVIOR

The Shar Pei bonds with the people who form its family but they are not unfriendly towards strangers.
Normally they are fine with children and cats present no problems if they have met them when young.
Mixing with other dogs can sometimes present problems. This dog is by nature always ready for a fight.

EXERCISE

Shar Peis have a considerable need for exercise. Provided they get enough outdoor exercise, however, they will be very peaceful indoors.

Shar Pei

St. Bernard

COUNTRY OF ORIGIN
Switzerland.

SPECIAL SKILLS
A long established search-and-rescue dog, now principally a family pet.

SIZE
The shoulder-height is a minimum of 70cm (27½in) for dogs and 65cm (25½in) for bitches. The weight depends upon the height and build of the dog but should be at least 60kg (132lb).

COAT
There are both short-haired and long-haired St. Bernards. The color is red with white or white with red, or white with streaked patches. The St. Bernard must have white legs, a white chest, and white tip to his tail, a white blaze, and a white neck patch or collar.

Short-haired St. Bernard, study of the head

Short-haired St. Bernard

CARE REQUIRED

Groom your St. Bernard with a brush or comb every day to remove loose hairs. Keep the ears clean and check the eyes of any dogs that have drooping eye-lids regularly.

CHARACTER

Good-humored, friendly, and equable, the St. Bernard is excellent with children, loyal to its handler, careful, and not given to barking. It will defend you and your possessions if necessary although this is not its primary role.

TRAINING

Young dogs must be taught early not to pull on the leash because this is hard to teach them when they are older.

In common with all mastiff types, the St. Bernard requires considerable understanding in its training from you.
Make sure also that they are not too pushed when they are young – they need all their strength for growing.

SOCIAL BEHAVIOR

St. Bernards get along fine with children, and other dogs and household animals usually present no problems.

EXERCISE

An average level of exercise is sufficient for the St. Bernard. Walks around the block three times a day with occasional longer walks when it can run free, off the leash, are all it needs.

Long-haired St. Bernard in traditional rescue harness

Tibetan Mastiff

Tibetan Mastiff

COUNTRY OF ORIGIN
Tibet.

SPECIAL SKILLS
Watchdog and family pet.

SIZE
The shoulder-height is a minimum of 66cm (26in) for dogs and 61cm (24in) for bitches.

COAT
This breed has a long, thick coat with a heavy under layer of hair. The Tibetan Mastiff's coat can be plain black, black and tan, golden brown or grey, with and without tan markings.

CARE REQUIRED
The breed requires regular grooming with a brush. In the winter the Tibetan Mastiff has an abundance of hair forming a very thick coat, but at the beginning of the summer much of this hair will fall out. During this period an owner must spend at least half an hour daily pulling out the loose hair with a brush and comb. The Tibetan Mastiff comes to adulthood somewhat later than other breeds.

CHARACTER
Equable, calm and thoughtful, the Tibetan Mastiff is dignified, very loyal to its own family, and reserved towards strangers.
It can be stubborn and also dominant as well as self-confident. It comes naturally to this Mastiff to guard its family and their property.

TRAINING
This special dog has to be raised to adulthood in a carefully well-balanced manner. Strong words and a readiness to hit the dog will only cause it to ignore its handler even more. The objective in training this dog is to achieve a bond of mutual respect, which can only be accomplished by showing respect.

SOCIAL BEHAVIOR
The Tibetan Mastiff is by and large loving with children but distrusts strangers. If it has come to know a variety of animals when young it will accept new ones when it is older. This dog usually also gets along well with other dogs.

EXERCISE
The dogs of this breed have an average demand for exercise and will enjoy going with you to the woods and open countryside but they are not particularly enthusiastic about playing games with a ball and the like. Take care that the bones, muscles, and joints of the young dog are not overtaxed during the growing stage by not over-doing the physical side of its life.

Head of a Tibetan Mastiff

Tosa Inu, or Japanese Tosa

COUNTRY OF ORIGIN
Japan.

SPECIAL SKILLS
Watchdog and family pet.

SIZE
The shoulder-height is a minimum of 61cm (24in) for dogs and 55cm (21½in) for bitches. As no maximum shoulder height is prescribed these heights are substantially exceeded.

COAT
The short-haired coat of the Tosa Inu is found in a number of colors including red-brown, black, yellow, streaked, and black and tan. Multi-colored is also permissible.

CARE REQUIRED
The Tosa Inu is fairly easy to look after. The coat can be kept in good condition by an occasional brushing to remove dead and loose hairs. Unlike many dogs, these dogs do not drool.

CHARACTER
The Tosa Inu is quiet and self-aware, patient, brave, and a very good watchdog. It is exceptionally intelligent and barks only when necessary although it has a strong protective urge. These dogs are very affectionate towards their family members but more reserved with strangers.

TRAINING
The Tosa Inu requires an equable and consistent but friendly approach to its training.

It is very sensitive to your voice. This is not a breed for beginners.

SOCIAL BEHAVIOR
The Tosa Inu places its family first and foremost. These dogs are usually fine with children but treat strangers cautiously. Known visitors are usually happily greeted.

Keep your dog away from other dogs which want to fight because your Tosa Inu will always win.

EXERCISE
In a well fenced and large enough area of land, this dog can happily look after its own exercise demands.

Take it with you to the beach, woods, or open countryside occasionally for a change of scene. In theory, it only requires an average level of exercise but it enjoys the opportunity for more.

SPECIAL REMARKS
The Tosa Inu or Japanese Tosa is banned as a dangerous breed in some countries.
Although other countries may permit these dogs, they are completely unsuitable for beginners.

They should never be placed in kennels because they like to spend the day close to their handler.

Tosa Inu

93

Swiss cattle-drivers

Appenzell Mountain Dog

Appenzell Mountain Dog or Appenzeller Sennenhund

COUNTRY OF ORIGIN
Switzerland.

SPECIAL SKILLS
Previously cattle-protector and driver, tracking, and watchdog. Nowadays mainly a watchdog and family pet.

SIZE
The ideal shoulder-height is 52 - 56cm (20½ - 22in) for dogs and 50 - 54cm
(19½ - 21¼in) for bitches. A variation of 2cm (¾in) taller is permitted for both sexes.

COAT
The coat is straight-haired with a thick under-coat. The basic color is black or brown with symmetrical rust and white markings.

CARE REQUIRED
The coat of the Appenzell Mountain Dog requires little attention. Remove loose and dead hairs from time to time with a rubber brush.

CHARACTER
The Appenzeller is a tough, sober, brave, intelligent, and lively dog which makes a good watchdog with a natural enthusiasm. These dogs do, however, like to bark so they are not suitable for areas with near neighbors.

TRAINING
The Appenzell Mountain Dog responds best to an equable manner of training that is consistent in approach. Try to ensure that it makes acquaintance as positively as possible with all kinds of situations, people and other animals. This dog learns quite quickly, in part because it is so bright but also because it really wants to have something to do. This dog does not belong in a kennel. It likes to be out of doors, but only when with its handler. Agility skill trials and games of catch and so forth are suitable sports for this breed.

SOCIAL BEHAVIOR
The Appenzell Mountain Dog usually gets along with other dogs and mixes well with livestock and household animals if it has become used to them when young. They are rather unsure of strangers but greet family friends effusively. A healthy and well brought up Appenzeller Sennenhund is fine with children. It is loyal to the whole family but tends to bond closely with one person.

EXERCISE
A dog such as this does not belong in a busy urban environment or in the suburbs. It likes to be outdoors and is closely bonded with its territory.

The dog's herding instincts keep it from running off. If the dog lives on a farm, it will get sufficient exercise on its own. In all other circumstances it must be taken on really long walks and if you can find work for it the dog will be completely happy.

Head of an Appenzell Mountain Dog

Bernese Mountain Dog, or Berner Sennenhund

COUNTRY OF ORIGIN
Switzerland.

SPECIAL SKILLS
Previously a cattle-driver, tracking dog, and watchdog among other uses, now a watchdog and family pet.

SIZE
The shoulder-height is 64 - 70cm (25½- 27½in) for dogs and 58 - 66cm (22¾ - 26in) for bitches.

COAT
The coat is medium-length and straight to slightly curly and has a thick under coat. The color is always chiefly black with rust and white markings.

CARE REQUIRED
In those places where the hair readily tangles (hindquarters, neck, the leg sockets, and behind the ears), it must be regularly groomed with brush and comb. When necessary, trim any excessive hair growth between the pads of the feet.

CHARACTER
The Bernese Mountain Dog is an equable,

vigilant, and friendly dog which is not easily bribed and is very loyal to its handler and family. It is also attentive, calm, and intelligent. It seldom barks unnecessarily.

TRAINING
The Bernese Mountain Dog requires an equable, consistent, and very loving approach to being brought up. This dog is a quick learner and an eager pupil and is very responsive to your voice. Never let a growing dog run up and down stairs and avoid them being overtaxed physically as the young animal needs all its energy to build strong bones and joints and to put on weight.

SOCIAL BEHAVIOR
Bernese Mountain Dogs are normally wonderful with children and will also protect them. If they have met cats and other household animals as young dogs, they will always behave properly in their presence. They are good watchdogs and they will never jump up and down and pace your yard fence barking. Unknown visitors will be announced with full-throated barking and then carefully watched. They will stand ready to defend you if required to. Some of these dogs try to dominate their own kind.

EXERCISE
This dog must be taken out regularly because it is very fond of exercise. When possible let it run and play off the leash. Make sure that a young

dog gets sufficient rest and sleep. Do not take it on long and tiring walks during the growing stage. These dogs do not run away because they have strong territorial instincts.

SPECIAL REMARKS
This is an extremely popular breed in some countries. It is probably, therefore, wise to obtain a puppy with the help of the recognized society for the breed.

Bernese Mountain Dog

Entelbuch Mountain Dog, or Entelbucher Sennenhund

COUNTRY OF ORIGIN
Switzerland.

SPECIAL SKILLS
Formerly a cattle-driver and estate dog among other duties, nowadays a watchdog and family pet.

SIZE
The shoulder-height is 44 - 50cm (17¼ - 19½in) for dogs and 42 - 48cm (16½ - 18¾in) for bitches. Examples of the breed 2cm (½in) higher than these standards are accepted.

COAT
The coat is straight-haired with a thick under coat. The color is predominantly black with white and rust-colored markings.

CARE REQUIRED
When the dog is shedding use a special comb with a double row of metal teeth to groom the underlayer of the coat. At other times little attention is required to the coat.

CHARACTER
This is a lively, temperamental, equable, and brave dog which is a good watchdog. It is also high-spirited, intelligent, and keen to learn.

TRAINING
The Entelbuch Mountain Dog responds best to an equable, caring handler who has a firm hand but is consistent at all times. Make sure that this dog, which learns very quickly, has plenty of positive experiences of other animals, people, and situations during its social training. This breed is not suitable for banishing to a kennel. The dog loves to be outdoors but only when it can be with its handler.

SOCIAL BEHAVIOR
The family comes as priority number one with this breed in common with all the Swiss Sennenhunds. The Entelbuch Mountain Dog will warn you when there is trouble. They tend to be rather uncertain with strangers and will certainly announce their presence. They are usually good with children and they rarely cause problems with household animals and livestock.

EXERCISE
This Sennenhund needs lots of exercise and must be kept busy. Do not expect it to adapt to conditions that are not right for it. It will become moody and uncertain if you limit it to three short outings around the block. These dogs have a fairly strong territorial instinct so that they are not likely to run away. They enjoy playing sports such as catch and agility skills.

Entelbuch Mountain Dog

Greater Swiss Mountain Dog

Greater Swiss Mountain Dog

COUNTRY OF ORIGIN
Switzerland.

SPECIAL SKILLS
Formerly a cattle driver, today a watchdog and family pet.

SIZE
The shoulder-height is 65 - 72cm (25½ - 28½in) for dogs and 60 - 68cm (23½ - 27in) for bitches.

COAT
The coat is straight-haired with a thick under coat.
The color is always black with rust and white markings.

CARE REQUIRED
The Greater Swiss Mountain Dog requires little grooming. An occasional session with a rubber brush to remove dead and loose hairs is adequate.

CHARACTER
This breed is intelligent, friendly, keen to work, watchful, reliable, and protective. Its is also equable, sociable, and obedient. The dogs only bark when necessary.

TRAINING
Even though this breed bonds closely with the family of which they form a part, they are not a suitable breed for everyone. The Greater Swiss Mountain Dog has a very strong character and needs a handler who is equally strong. It must get the chance to grow up in a well-balanced environment and have a clear understanding of what is permitted and what is not. It needs to be able to build a close bond with his family.

Make sure that you are always consistent with it. A severe approach will only ruin the dog's nature. Watch and control it carefully during the growing stage so that all its energy can be used for building healthy bones and muscles. For the same reason be generous with its food.

SOCIAL BEHAVIOR
This breed gets on well with dogs and other household animals. Under your care it will make a marvelous friend for your children too, but do not forget that it will protect your children against their friends if it thinks they are being pestered by them. They make excellent watchdogs which will protect you and your family together with all your possessions against wrongdoers. They are not suited to living in a kennel.

EXERCISE
This breed is a diligent worker which means, if you consider its intelligence, that it can make a multi-faceted and reliable working dog for you. In Switzerland it is used as a tracking dog. This dog has the potential to shine at obedience training and in various other areas of dog sporting activities. When it happens that a week passes in which you are too busy to get out with your dog, it will accept it easily and not mis-behave.

SPECIAL REMARKS
This beautiful, imposing dog requires plenty of living space. It will not be happy in an apartment or small house without a yard.

Greater Swiss Mountain Dog, study of the head

3. Terriers

Long-legged Terriers

Airedale Terrier

Airedale Terrier

Airedale Terrier

COUNTRY OF ORIGIN
England.

SPECIAL SKILLS
Originally used for hunting otters and other animals, now mainly a family pet.

SIZE
The shoulder height is 58 - 61cm (22¾ - 24in) for dogs and 56 - 58cm (22 - 22¾in) for bitches.

COAT
The hard wire-haired coat is smooth. The most common color is tan with a grey-black saddle.

CARE REQUIRED
The Airedale Terrier requires little grooming under normal circumstances. The hair should be plucked about twice per year, but for dogs that are to be shown much more intensive grooming is needed. When necessary, trim excess hair between the pads of the feet.

CHARACTER
The Airedale is tough on itself, loyal to its own people, but it can be stubborn. It tends to be playful, watchful, active, intelligent, and resolute. An Airedale does not often bark.

TRAINING
The Airedale Terrier is intelligent enough to perceive quickly what is required of it. Try to give some variety to its training, because if it is asked to do the same thing over and over it is likely to refuse.
Make the exercises a challenge. With the right handler, Airedale Terriers can do well in various dog sports including defence dog trials.

SOCIAL BEHAVIOR
In general, Airedale Terriers get on well with cats and other household animals, and they are very patient with children. They sometimes try to dominate other dogs, but this depends upon their training and the individual dog.

Staffordshire Bull Terrier

EXERCISE
The Airedale Terrier has an average demand for exercise and will be happy with three walks around the neighborhood a day on the leash plus playing in the yard.

Most of them love to play with a ball, swim, or retrieve objects, and once fully grown will happily run alongside a bicycle.

Bedlington Terrier

COUNTRY OF ORIGIN
England.

SPECIAL SKILLS
In the past the Bedlington Terrier was used to destroy vermin and for hunting hares and foxes, among other smaller animals. Today they are chiefly family pets.

SIZE
The shoulder-height is approximately 41cm (16¼in) with a permissible 2.5cm (1in) higher and lower latitude .

COAT
The Bedlington Terrier used to be called a wolf in sheep's clothing.
Its coat grows in curly short whirls, which stand out from the body.

They can be plain blue, blue with brown, liver, or sandy-colored. The most common color is blue. Puppies are born black or brown.

CARE REQUIRED
This dog needs to visit a professional at least once a year for its coat to be kept in order and also requires regular grooming with brush and comb. It does not shed. Keep the inside of the ears free of hair by removing the hairs yourself or get a professional to do it for you.

Bedlingtons should not be washed too often or the coat will become lank, which is not considered appropriate for the breed. Dogs which are to be shown require higher levels of grooming.

CHARACTER
The Bedlington Terrier is brave and tenacious, intelligent, peaceful indoors and equable.

It is loving with children, playful, barks little, is loyal, cheerful and has a mind of its own.

Blue Bedlington Terrier

Head of a liver-coloured Bedlington Terrier

These dogs tend to bond closely with one member of the family.

TRAINING
Bedlingtons are intelligent and they grasp things quickly, although they can be a bit stubborn. They react well to your voice, but the occasional sterner corrective measure may be required.

SOCIAL BEHAVIOR
This breed usually gets on well with children. They need to learn to like cats and other household animals when they are young. Usually they can get on with other dogs but keep them away from those that want to dominate, as once challenged they are terrifying fighters!

EXERCISE
The Bedlington Terrier can run fast and jump high and it loves doing both. Letting it run beside your bicycle is an ideal way for it to burn off energy.

SPECIAL REMARKS
This breed can cope perfectly well with life in an apartment or suburb provided it gets sufficient outdoor exercise.

Border Terrier

COUNTRY OF ORIGIN
England.

SPECIAL SKILLS
Hunting dog and family pet.

SIZE
The shoulder-height is approximately 35cm (13½in).
For dogs the weight is permitted to be 5.9 - 7.1kg (13 - 15½lb); the weight for bitches is between 5.1 - 6.4kg (11¼ - 14lb).

COAT
The hard coat is thick with a dense under coat. The recognized colors are red, wheat, and grey with grey markings.

CARE REQUIRED
Groom these dogs thoroughly at least once a week. Depending upon the condition of the coat, the Border Terrier's coat may need plucking occasionally but it must never be trimmed. Plucking by hand removes old and excess hair.

CHARACTER
The Border Terrier is a tenacious, brave, equable,

Border Terrier

It has been said of the Border Terrier that it can keep a horse under control which may or may not be true. It is true that these dogs love to run and play outdoors. A Border Terrier restricted to three short outings per day and spending the rest of its time indoors will adapt to this life but at the expense of some of its natural zest for life. Border Terriers are suitable for sports such as catch and playing with Frisbees. They also enjoy tests of agility.

Fox Terrier (Smooth)/ Fox Terrier (Wire)

stubborn, lively dog which is sportive and untiring. This breed can take a blow and is not sensitive to pain. It is loyal to its handler, patient with children, and adaptable.

TRAINING
Training is relatively easy because the Border Terrier learns so quickly.

SOCIAL BEHAVIOR
This dog gets on well with children. If you want it also to get on with other dogs, cats, and other household animals, then it is essential to introduce them when it is young.

COUNTRY OF ORIGIN
England.

SPECIAL SKILLS
Formerly a vermin destroyer and hunting dog for foxes and badgers. Today the Fox Terrier is a family pet.

SIZE
The Fox Terrier weighs 7 - 8kg (15½ - 17½lb). The shoulder-height may not exceed 39cm (15¼in) for dogs. Bitches may be slightly smaller.

Fox Terrier (Wire)

Fox Terrier (Smooth)

COAT

There are two types of Fox Terrier: the smooth and the wire-haired. The Smooth has a dense coat of sleek short hairs which may not be thin anywhere on the body. The Wire has a rough coat that is thick and hard and should be neither curly nor soft.

The Wire is required to have hair embellishments around the muzzle and eyes, and longer hair around the feet. The main color for both is white with markings of tan and/or black considered desirable.

CARE REQUIRED

The coat of the Wire generally requires plucking with the fingers several times each year. In addition to this the dog should be groomed several times a week with brush and comb. For showing, even greater levels of grooming will be required. The Smooth can be adequately taken care of with a weekly brushing. Use a rubber brush during shedding to remove dead and loose hairs.

CHARACTER

The Fox Terrier is a very intelligent and cunning, hardy, lively, and cheerful dog which is watchful, alert, brave, resolute, and self-confident.

TRAINING

Fox Terriers learn quite quickly. They can be rather stubborn but that is true of all Terriers. Make certain you remain consistent in your training.

SOCIAL BEHAVIOR

This breed usually gets on well with children. Some Fox Terriers can try to dominate other dogs. Teach the dog when young how to get on with cats and other household animals so that it

will not chase them later. Fox Terriers are ever alert and will go to the attack if there is danger, but they are not unfriendly towards strangers.

EXERCISE

These dogs are bursting with energy and like to be constantly active. Your Fox Terrier is certain to enjoy activities like agility skills and games of catch. If you enjoy sports, then one of the two types of Fox Terrier is the dog for you.

Young Fox Terrier (Smooth)

Glen of Imaal Terrier

COUNTRY OF ORIGIN
Ireland.

SPECIAL SKILLS
This Terrier was once used for such things as hunting badgers and destroying vermin. Today it is mainly a family pet.

SIZE
The shoulder-height may be no greater than 35.5cm (14in). In spite of its short height this is a robust dog.

COAT
The Glen of Imaal Terrier has a medium-length, hard and coarse outer coat, and a soft dense underlayer.
The colors range from dark grey (considered blue) with highlights, through to brindle, to wheaten.

CARE REQUIRED

If your Glen of Imaal Terrier is a pet, hand-plucking its coat about twice a year will be sufficient grooming; the coats of show dogs require more attention. Clip excess hair between the pads of its feet and also remove it from the ear passages.

CHARACTER

These dogs are calm, affectionate, brave, and very demanding of themselves. They are loyal and intelligent but late developers. They can be stubborn, are playful, lively, and boisterous. They are usually calm indoors and they rarely bark without reason.

TRAINING

The training of this breed need not be difficult. They are keen to learn, but they can try to dominate and be stubborn. The handler should be consistent at all times and have some play in every training routine.

SOCIAL BEHAVIOR

Glen of Imaal Terriers get on well with children. Some of the dogs of this breed can try to dominate other dogs, but provided they have had positive experiences with cats and other household animals when growing, they can happily mix with them.
Visitors that are known to the family will be cheerfully greeted, but unwelcome ones will be chased away. These dogs will bark if they detect danger.

EXERCISE

This breed will adapt its exercise needs to the family situation.

Irish Terrier

COUNTRY OF ORIGIN
Ireland.

SPECIAL SKILLS
Hunting dog, watchdog, and family pet.

SIZE
The shoulder-height is 46 - 50cm (18 - 19½in) and the weight should be about 14kg (31lb).

COAT
The outer-coat is very hard, while the under-layer is softer and finer.
The accepted colors are golden-yellow, wheat, and light red. Small white markings on the chest are permissible.

CARE REQUIRED
The Irish Terrier's grooming depends upon the condition of its coat and whether you wish to show the dog, but hand-plucking of the hairs will be necessary at least twice a year. Trim excessive hair between the pads of the feet and keep the ears clean.

CHARACTER
The Irish Terrier is a dog of character which is loyal, protective, vigilant, and playful. It has a sense of humor, is intelligent, tends to be over-courageous, sensitive, active, and bonds very strongly with its family.

TRAINING
This breed requires a confident handler who can train it in a very consistent and tactful way.

Irish Terrier

Head of an Irish Terrier

When this dog is in a good mood it can learn anything, but try to ensure that there is plenty of variety in the training routine.

SOCIAL BEHAVIOR
This dog may want to fight other dogs. Teach it when young not to chase cats. It is naturally friendly with people and adores children and is very tolerant of them. The bitches are generally calmer than the dogs.

The Irish Terrier becomes very dependent upon its family and regards it as a punishment to be left alone for a long time. It will defend its territory and that of its family against wrong-doers but is not as mistrustful of strangers as many other dogs.

EXERCISE
The Irish Terrier requires a lot of exercise so take it out regularly. These dogs enjoy playing with a ball in the yard or romping in open countryside. They also love riding in cars and want to go everywhere their family goes.

Soft-coated Wheaten Terrier

Soft-coated Wheaten Terrier

COUNTRY OF ORIGIN
Ireland.

SPECIAL SKILLS
Hunting dog and family pet.

SIZE
The shoulder-height is 46 - 48cm (18 - 18¾in) and the weight in the region of 15kg (33lb).

Soft-coated Wheaten Terrier with puppy

COAT
The coat of the Soft-coated Wheaten Terrier is very soft and silken with a light wave or curl. The color is a range of tints from light wheat to reddish gold. The attractive and distinctive adult coat can take as long as two years to grow. The coat of the Soft-coated Wheaten Terrier must not be wool-like.

CARE REQUIRED
This breed is normally trimmed to a set style, leaving the hair around the face, feet, neck, chest, and belly longer than elsewhere.
The dogs do not shed in spring and autumn but loose hairs should be combed out of the coat from time to time. Well-groomed dogs will shed very little hair in the house.

CHARACTER
This breed is cheerful and extroverted, active and playful, intelligent and eager to learn. They bond extremely closely with their family. The dogs are also slightly independent, self-confident. They seldom bark unnecessarily.

TRAINING
The Soft-coated Wheaten Terrier needs to be taught when it is young what it may and may not do. Because these dogs are very intelligent, they will generally grasp quickly what is required of them.

They have a straightforward nature and need to be handled in a straightforward manner.

SOCIAL BEHAVIOR
Soft-coated Wheaten Terriers are usually very loving with children and get on reasonably well

with other dogs. Provided they are socialized when young, they will also get along well with cats.

EXERCISE

Wheatens are active dogs which can be very calm indoors provided they get sufficient opportunities outdoors to burn off their energy. They are ideally suited to a number of sporting activities such as agility skills, catch, and chasing Frisbees. Make sure their training has plenty of variety and is a challenge for them because they will quickly lose their enthusiasm if the exercises are too easy.

Kerry Blue Terrier

Kerry Blue Terrier

COUNTRY OF ORIGIN
Ireland.

SPECIAL SKILLS
Watchdog and family pet.

SIZE
The shoulder-height is 45 - 48cm (17¾ - 18¾in). The weight is between 14 - 18kg (31 - 39½lb).

COAT
The Kerry Blue has a soft, thick and abundantly curly coat without an under coat. The color is light to dark blue. Puppies are born black and it can take up to a year and a half before the coat changes color to blue.

CARE REQUIRED
The Kerry Blue Terrier needs to be trimmed with scissors and a trimmer. In addition to this, they will need grooming occasionally with brush and comb. Dogs for showing will require higher levels of grooming. An advantage of the Kerry Blue is that does not shed.

CHARACTER
These dogs are intelligent and have a very good memory. They are lively and boisterous, self-confident, vigilant and brave. They bond very closely with their handler. They can be stubborn, are hardy, have a mind of their own, and tend to be always ready for a fight with other dogs. They rarely bark unnecessarily.

TRAINING
Because this dog is active, self-confident, and stubborn, it needs a handler who is very confident. These dogs are not, therefore, suitable for beginners. The dog may want to attack other dogs in the street and obviously this must not be tolerated – even though it is a natural character trait of the breed. The Kerry Blue has an aptitude for sports such as catch and agility training but make sure the dog enjoys the challenge. If lessons or drills are too monotonous for the Kerry Blue, its stubbornness will show.

Kerry Blue Terriers

SOCIAL BEHAVIOR

This Terrier is loving with children and very attached to its handler and family. Introduce it to cats and other household animals when very young so that it will get along with them when it is older.

Some of them very much enjoy the company of other dogs, while others prefer to go through life as an "only dog." This seems to depend not so much on early social training as the personality of the individual dog.

EXERCISE

The Kerry Blue is a sporty dog which likes to accompany its handler on long walks, but it will accept the occasional week without such a good outing.

SPECIAL REMARKS

The Kerry Blue Terrier is something special. Its coat is meant to look unkempt. If you want a dog which is not everybody's friend and which is also fairly unusual the Kerry Blue can be a good choice for you. Make sure you can be consistent and will value a dog which has its own distinct personality.

Lakeland Terrier

Lakeland Terrier

COUNTRY OF ORIGIN

England.

SPECIAL SKILLS

Hunting dog (for foxes and other small prey), and family pet.

SIZE

The shoulder-height may not exceed 37cm (14½in).The weight is about 7kg (15½lb).

COAT

The coat is thick and hard, and sheds water. It can be black and tan, blue and tan, red-grey, red, wheat, liver, blue, or black.

CARE REQUIRED

The Lakeland Terrier should have its coat plucked two or three times each year by pulling the old hair out by hand. Remove loose hairs also from the ear passages and trim excess hair between the pads of the feet. The coats of show dogs will require more intensive grooming.

CHARACTER

This a sporty, intelligent, and affectionate dog which is a good watchdog, self-confident and loving with children, and also lively and cheerful.

TRAINING

This dog learns quite easily. Make sure that the training is full of variety and offers the dog a challenge. You'll find the dog quickly learns what you want from it.

SOCIAL BEHAVIOR

Lakelands get on well with children but also with other dogs – which is unusual among Terriers. They can be unsure around strangers but this does not usually become extreme. Teach them when they are young to get on with cats and other household animals, so that they will not chase them later.

Lakeland Terrier

EXERCISE

A Lakeland Terrier can be kept in an apartment but it must get adequate exercise. These dogs need to run and play off the leash at regular intervals. They are certainly suitable for sports activities such as catch and agility skills.

Head of a Manchester Terrier

Manchester Terrier

COUNTRY OF ORIGIN
England.

SPECIAL SKILLS
Rat-catcher and family pet.

SIZE
The ideal height is 40 - 41cm (15¾ - 16¼in) for dogs and 38cm (15in) for bitches.

COAT
The coat is short, sleek, and shiny. The most usual color is black and tan.

CARE REQUIRED
The Manchester Terrier does not require much grooming.
When the dog is shedding the dead and loose hairs can be simply removed with a rubber brush. Rub the dog afterwards with a chamois to make the coat shiny.
Keep the ear passages clean and the claws short.

CHARACTER
This is a high-spirited, very intelligent, and cunning dog which is eager to learn, lively and sporty, alert and vigilant.
Normally this dog barks only when there is danger, and bonds very closely with its handler.

TRAINING

The Manchester Terrier likes to please its handler and learns quite quickly. These dogs can be outstanding in activities like agility skills and catch and also do well in obedience trials.

SOCIAL BEHAVIOR

Some of these dogs can try to dominate other dogs but they get on well with children. It is advisable to get them used to cats and other household animals quite early. Manchester Terriers make exceptional watchdogs because in spite of their size they do not hesitate to go into action when necessary. They are also first-rate rat- and mole-catchers.

EXERCISE

The Manchester Terrier demands plenty of exercise. In addition to the normal daily walks, let it run and play off the leash regularly. These dogs can run very fast and keep the speed up for a long time. This dog greatly enjoys exercising by running alongside a bicycle, provided the amount of exercise is built up gradually.

Manchester Terrier

Parson Jack Russell Terrier

COUNTRY OF ORIGIN
England.

SPECIAL SKILLS
Hunting dog and family pet.

SIZE
The ideal shoulder-height is 35cm (13¾in) for dogs and 33cm (13in) for bitches.

Smooth-haired Parson Jack Russell

COAT
There are smooth-haired and rough-haired Parson Jack Russell Terriers. Both types of coat should be wiry, dense, and thick. They are usually predominantly white with tan, lemon, black, or with markings in three colors – preferably restricted to the head and root of the tail.

CARE REQUIRED
The Parson Jack Russell Terrier is easy to care for. During shedding you should remove loose hairs every day with a rubber brush. The rough type requires its coat to be plucked occasionally.

CHARACTER
This is a very active, intelligent, and cunning dog that is vigilant, bold and enterprising, hard upon itself, brave (sometimes almost foolhardy). This dog usually has plenty of self-confidence – verging on a wish to dominate – and is quite independent.

Rough-haired Parson Jack Russell

TRAINING
These dogs can learn very quickly but try to have their own way in everything. Do not let yourself be won over by their mischievous charm; they know perfectly well what they are doing. Remain consistent at all times!

SOCIAL BEHAVIOR
Usually this breed produces uncomplicated and socially acceptable dogs. They get on well with other household pets and love to play with children. When their social training has been good, they can also get on with the household cat but they frequently cannot resist the urge to chase a cat which runs away from them – they are still hunting dogs! Some dogs with a more dominant nature can be foolhardy in the presence of larger dogs. Visiting strangers will always be announced.

EXERCISE
These dogs have enormous reserves of energy and you must do your best to find ways to burn this off.

They need much more exercise than three walks around the block a day. The Parson Jack Russell Terrier needs to run about and frolic every day. They love to dig. They will feel absolutely at home on a farm where they can also be useful in dealing with vermin. They are ideally suited for activities such as agility skills and playing catch.

Welsh Terrier

COUNTRY OF ORIGIN
Wales.

SPECIAL SKILLS
Hunting dog and family pet.

SIZE
The weight is about 9kg (20lb) and the shoulder-height should not exceed 39cm (15¼in).

COAT
The coat is wire-haired, hard, and very thick. These dogs are usually red-brown with black.

CARE REQUIRED
The Welsh Terrier needs to have its coat plucked two, three, or more times a year depending upon the condition of the coat. It also requires grooming with brush and comb a number of times each week. Those dogs that are to be shown will require even greater levels of

attention to their grooming. The longer hairs at the feet, on the belly, and around the face, give the Welsh Terrier its typical appearance.

CHARACTER
The Welsh Terrier is a vigilant, active, cheerful and uncomplicated dog, which is affectionate and intelligent.

Although it can sometimes try to dominate other dogs, it is brave, and obedient. It bonds very closely with its handler and family but is usually more cautious with strangers.

TRAINING
The Welsh Terrier is bright enough to understand quickly what you want of it but is also cunning enough to try to divert you from your intentions.

Give these dogs constant variety in their training and remain consistent towards them.

SOCIAL BEHAVIOR
The Welsh Terrier can be rather reserved with people it doesn't know. It is usually patient with children and can withstand a bit of rough play.

Make sure it becomes confident with cats and other animals of the house when it is young to prevent the dog from chasing them when it is older.

EXERCISE
The Welsh Terrier is untiring; it is always ready to play with a ball and to run and gambol off the leash in the open countryside. On the other hand, if you occasionally find it impossible to spend this kind of time with your dog it will accept it without making a fuss.

Short-legged Terriers

Australian Terrier

COUNTRY OF ORIGIN
Australia.

SPECIAL SKILLS
Hunting dog and family pet.

SIZE
The shoulder-height is about 25cm (9¾in) and the weight is in the region of 5.5 - 6.5kg (12 - 14½lb).

Welsh Terrier

Head of an Australian Terrier

COAT
The hair is straight, hard, and of medium length. The breed has a blue back and deep shades of tan on legs and muzzle. The locks of hair over the eyes may be blue or silver, but sandy or red is also accepted.

CARE REQUIRED
The Australian Terrier's coat requires plucking about every three months. Groom with brush and comb between these times once a week and check to be sure that no hair is growing inside the ear passages. Because the breed standard is for a hard coat, don't wash this Terrier too often, which will make the hair lank. An Australian Terrier in good condition sheds very little hair.

CHARACTER
The Australian Terrier is vigilant and alert, brave, lively, self-confident, and very adaptable, intelligent, playful, independent, and a bit stubborn. These dogs are excellent vermin destroyers and like to bark.

Australian Terrier

TRAINING
The training of the Australian Terrier needs to be strict because this self-confident dog prefers to follow its own ideas. They learn quite quickly.

SOCIAL BEHAVIOR
Provided children do not tease it, this breed gets along fine with them.
Strangers, on the other hand, may find these dogs unfriendly although they are really not excessively suspicious.

Teach the dogs when young to live with cats so that they can live together without major conflict.

EXERCISE
The adaptability to a variety of living conditions of the Australian Terrier is phenomenal but it is most happy when able to romp and play.

Cairn Terriers

Cairn Terrier

COUNTRY OF ORIGIN
Scotland.

SPECIAL SKILLS
Vermin destroyer, hunting dog, and family pet.

SIZE
The shoulder-height is 28 - 31cm (11 - 12¼ in) tall, but this must be in proportion to the weight, which can vary from 6 - 7.5kg (13¼ - 16½ lb).

COAT
The Cairn Terrier – like the West Highland Terrier – has a double-layered coat of which the topcoat is hard and abundant and the undercoat is soft and short. The hair must not curl. Permitted colors are grey, wheat, cream-red, or almost black. Darker markings on the ears and muzzle are highly regarded. Cairns may not be white or totally black.

CARE REQUIRED
The Cairn's coat needs regular grooming with a brush and comb.
About twice per year – depending upon the condition of the hair – the dead hairs need to be plucked out by hand. This can be done by a dog grooming shop but it is good to learn how to do it yourself. From time to time remove excess hair from the ear passages.
A Cairn Terrier should have a somewhat rough appearance and is therefore not excessively groomed for showing.

For showing, any excessive hair around the feet, ears, and tail is removed.

CHARACTER
This is an intelligent, brave, cheerful, lively, playful and extroverted dog which is hard upon itself, uncomplicated, affectionate, eager to learn, alert and vigilant.

TRAINING
Teach this dog early to get on with cats and other household pets so that it will not chase them when it is older. Puppies can take a game of pulling on a rope quite seriously. You must decide when the game is to end by giving it the command "drop it". The antics of puppies are often both cute and funny but remember that the tricks the dog might pull as a puppy will be less amusing when it is grown up. The Cairn needs loving but also strict and consistent training.

SOCIAL BEHAVIOR
The Cairn Terrier makes a first-class friend for children; it can tolerate rough play and has a well-developed sense of humor. These dogs can also get on reasonably well with other dogs, although some dogs of this breed will fight for their rights as they see them. They go into action when they detect danger.

EXERCISE
This breed is bursting with energy and must get ample opportunity to run and play. It is an ideal dog for a sporty family. It likes to be taken for a walk in the woods or in open countryside where it can run free, but make sure before you do so that the dog will return to you when you call – the hunting instinct is so strong in these dogs that they can run away if you aren't careful.

Cairn Terrier

Cesky Terrier or Bohemian Terrier

Cesky Terrier or Bohemian Terrier

COUNTRY OF ORIGIN
Czech Republic or Slovakia.

SPECIAL SKILLS
Hunting dog and family pet.

SIZE
The shoulder-height is 27 -35cm (10½ - 13¾in) and the weight is 6 - 9kg (13¼ - 20lb).

COAT
The coat consists of thick shiny hair. The most usual color is blue-grey in different shade variations; light coffee brown is rarer. Both colors are permitted, with and without white markings. The Cesky does not shed.

CARE REQUIRED
The Cesky should be trimmed regularly, leaving the hair long on the stomach and legs and around the face (moustache, beard, and eyebrows).

If the dog is a pet, it will need to be trimmed about four times a year; dogs for showing require more frequent grooming. The longer hair needs to be brushed or combed twice a week or more, depending on the condition of the coat, to prevent tangles. Clip the excess hair between the pads of the feet and remove loose hairs in the ear passages.

CHARACTER
The Cesky is a good-humored dog which is affectionate, very adaptable, stalwart and hardy, sporty but calm. It is intelligent and sociable.

TRAINING
The training of this breed is not very demanding. It is important to let the puppy meet with various

people and different animals in positive circumstances and to experience a variety of situations to enable it to grow up to be a happy adult.

SOCIAL BEHAVIOR
This sociable dog gets on well with its own kind and with other household animals. It is always loving with children but can be somewhat cautious with strangers.

EXERCISE
The Cesky Terrier has an average demand for exercise.
This dog likes to frolic and play but it also enjoys walks through a wood or across open countryside.

SPECIAL REMARKS
Cesky Terriers are always born black. The coat lightens later – in some cases not until the dog is over two years old.

Dandie Dinmont Terrier

COUNTRY OF ORIGIN
Scotland.

SPECIAL SKILLS
Hunting dog and family pet.

Dandie Dinmont Terrier

SIZE

The shoulder height is approximately 23cm (9in) and the weight 7 - 11kg (15½ - 24lb).

COAT

This Terrier has a double-layered coat: the undercoat is soft, the topcoat is hard. Dandie Dinmonts' colors are pepper (almost black to a light silver-grey) and mustard (reddish brown to pale beige).

CARE REQUIRED

These dog needs to be brushed regularly and should have professional grooming to have the dead hair plucked out once or twice each year. Dogs that are to be shown will require additional grooming.

CHARACTER

This is a high-spirited yet calm dog which will be devoted to its handler and family. It combines the characteristics of intelligence, vigilance, and tenaciousness with sensitivity.

TRAINING

The training of this dog is not difficult, but allowance must be made for the fact that it can be stubborn.

SOCIAL BEHAVIOR

This is a very sociable breed of dog that usually leaves other dogs alone and acts perfectly with cats and other household animals, provided it has met them when young. These dogs are normally very loving with children and visitors should also cause no problem.

EXERCISE

The Dandie Dinmont Terrier has an average demand for exercise and will adapt to the family circumstances.

Norwich Terrier

Dandie Dinmont Terriers

Norfolk and Norwich Terriers

COUNTRY OF ORIGIN
England.

SPECIAL SKILLS
Much used previously as a true terrier (a dog which hunts animals underground), today mainly a family pet.

SIZE
The shoulder-height of both breeds is about 25cm (9¾in) and both weigh about 4kg (8¾lb).

Norwich Terriers

COAT
These Terriers have hard wire-haired coats. The hair on the head and ears is shorter than at the neck, belly, and shoulders.
The dogs can be a variety of shades of red, but also straw-yellow, black with rust-brown, and grey. A small amount of white is permissible although not preferred.

CARE REQUIRED.
Brush and comb the coat regularly and pluck out the old hair about twice a year, depending on the condition of the coat.
This is a job that you can do yourself or leave to a professional.
Excess hair between the pads of the feet must also be trimmed.

CHARACTER
These are cheerful, lively, and intelligent dogs which are friendly, brave and bold, cunning, enterprising, straightforward, and playful. They are sometimes willful.

TRAINING
Both Norwich and Norfolk Terriers learn quite quickly. Make sure you are consistent with them

Norfolk Terrier

because these Terriers tend to have minds of their own and want to show it.

SOCIAL BEHAVIOR
For a Terrier, these are fairly easy dogs in their relationship with other dogs. Children too are seldom a problem. Visitors will be initially announced by loud barking but then all will be calm.

EXERCISE
These dogs adapt to the circumstances, but Terriers are natural diggers and they must be allowed to dig if they are to be happy.

SPECIAL REMARKS
The difference between a Norwich and a Norfolk Terrier is that the former have erect ears while the latter have drooping ears.

Scottish Terrier

COUNTRY OF ORIGIN
Scotland.

SPECIAL SKILLS
Hunting dog, for foxes and rabbits and other small prey, and family pet.

SIZE
The shoulder-height is 25 - 28cm (9¾ - 11in) and the weight 8.5 - 10.5kg (18¾- 23lb).

COAT
The coat is hard and wire-haired. The Scottish Terrier or Scottie, as it is commonly known, is bred as plain black, broken black with high-lights, and wheat.

Sealyham Terrier

COUNTRY OF ORIGIN
Wales.

SPECIAL SKILLS
Hunting dog and companion.

SIZE
The ideal shoulder-height is 31cm (12¾in). Dogs weigh about 9kg (20lb) and bitches are slighter lighter.

COAT
The long, hard, wire-haired outer-layer of the coat covers a weather-resistant under-layer. The colors are entirely white, or white with lemon, brown, blue, or badger markings on the head and/or ears.

CARE REQUIRED
Comb the coat thoroughly on a regular basis and take the dog twice each year to a professional for a trim. Not every professional knows the special requirements for clipping Sealyham Terriers so check to be sure the one you go to has had experience.

Sealyham Terrier

CARE REQUIRED
The coat needs to be hand-plucked by a professional about twice per year; the chest, legs, and head are usually clipped. Between the plucking sessions the hair should be regularly brushed and combed. Remove any food remnants from the beard and moustache regularly. Show dogs require more intensive grooming.

CHARACTER
The Scottie is straightforward and sober, becomes very attached to its family, is vigilant, noble, sporty, and sometimes has a mind of its own. Keep it mind that it loves to dig.

TRAINING
For the right handler who is consistent this aristocrat of a dog is easy to train. Remember, though, that for all its loyalty to you, this is an independent dog. Training needs to be founded on mutual respect.

SOCIAL BEHAVIOR
The natural inclination of a Scottie is to get on well with other household animals and its own kind. Provided children do not treat this dog as a toy and don't pester it, they will get along together. Much depends upon the puppy's social training.

EXERCISE
The Scottie will adapt its exercise demands to the circumstances where it finds itself living.

CHARACTER

This is an equable dog which is brave and often tough on itself. It tends to be very active outdoors but calm indoors. The dog has a loud bark but uses it only when it senses danger. It remains playful into old age, and can have a mind of its own. Sealyham Terriers are very loyal.

TRAINING

The Sealyham Terrier is generally an intelligent dog which learns easily, but it can try to undermine your authority from time to time. If it does, correct it, of course, but make sure you are always consistent with the dog.

SOCIAL BEHAVIOR

The Sealyham gets on reasonably well with other dogs. If you want it to get along with cats and other animals it will have to meet them when it is young. Provided it has had positive contact with children when a puppy, it will get along with them when grown up. With visitors it can be friendly or cautious – much depends upon its early social training.

EXERCISE

This breed has average demands for exercise and usually adapts to the circumstances. However, a Sealyham Terrier loves to get out of its basket for a good long walk in the woods.

They usually love to root around in the ground – bear this in mind if you have a neatly laid out yard. Most Sealyhams like to ride with you in the car.

Skye Terrier

COUNTRY OF ORIGIN
Scotland.

SPECIAL SKILLS
Historically used to hunt the fox, badger, and otter. Today they are principally family pets.

SIZE
The shoulder-height is a mere 25 - 26cm (9¾ - 10¼in) for dogs, while the length between the

Skye Terriers

nose and the tip of the tail can be more than 100cm (39½in). The bitches are slightly smaller.

COAT

The Skye Terrier has a double-layered coat. The topcoat is long, hard and straight, without curls, while the undercoat is short, thick, and woolly. These dogs can be black or grey, but brown and blond with dark markings on the ears, muzzle, and tail, are also permitted.

CARE REQUIRED

The Skye Terrier requires little grooming. A good brushing once a week is sufficient to keep it in good condition. The hair should fall into a parting from the centre of the back. Remove loose hairs and dirt from the ear passages. Trim excess hair between the pads of the feet.

Skye Terrier

CHARACTER

This is an affectionate dog which is calm, noble, makes a good watchdog, and is full of character. The Skye Terrier is a little reserved with strangers and very loyal to its own family. Some of them have the tendency to become loyal to only one person in a family.

TRAINING

The training needs to be done with mutual respect, with you being fair and consistent, while giving the dog room for its own initiative.

SOCIAL BEHAVIOR

Most of the dogs from this breed get on with their own kind and with other household animals, although this can depend on their early social training. They also get along fine with children but they do not like being teased. Some dogs try to dominate other dogs.

EXERCISE

Give the Skye Terrier lots of exercise. This dog will love to go with you for long walks (on the leash) in woodland or open countryside.

If you do not feel like a walk one day, or even frequently, the dog will adapt without misbehaving.

SPECIAL REMARKS

Skye Terriers can live to be quite old – fourteen or fifteen is not unusual. There is a variety with drooping ears, but these are very rare.

West Highland White Terrier

COUNTRY OF ORIGIN
Scotland.

SPECIAL SKILLS
Family pet.

SIZE
The shoulder-height is about 28cm (11in) and the weight about 7.5kg (16½lb).

COAT
The West Highland Terrier or Westie, as it is commonly called, has a double-layered coat: the topcoat is rough and hard, without curls, whilst the undercoat is soft and short.

This breed is always white with darker eyes and darker pigmentation on the pads of the feet, nails, jowls, and nose.

West Highland White Terrier

CARE REQUIRED

The Westie is required to have a hard coat so it should not be washed too frequently or the coat will become lank. When the dog gets dirty playing outdoors, it's best to let the hair dry and then brush the dirt out. Its coat should be plucked by hand two or three times each year. The coats of dogs which are to be shown will require more grooming.

CHARACTER

This is a lively, playful, intrepid, vigilant, and alert dog which is cheerful, and loyal to its handler. It is an extrovert, cunning and ingenious but also stubborn, resolute, and independent. The Westie is extremely self-confident and not easily impressed.

TRAINING

Despite the straightforward and cheerful character of this dog it must not be a allowed it to get away with whatever it likes.

It may occasionally need to be corrected. Westies can sometimes be naughty over and over, so stay consistent and firm.

SOCIAL BEHAVIOR

Westies generally get on well with their own kind and make excellent playmates for children because they can withstand rough play. Teach them when young to tolerate cats or they will chase them when they are older.

Some of this breed can try to dominate other dogs, but this depends greatly upon their early social training.

EXERCISE

Westies love playing with balls, running around, and having fun.
They need lots of exercise. They enjoy digging and some of them like to wander off so make sure your yard is well fenced.

Terriers of the Bulldog type

American Staffordshire Bull Terrier

COUNTRY OF ORIGIN
United States of America.

SPECIAL SKILLS
Watchdog and family pet.

SIZE
The preferred shoulder-height is 45.7 - 48.4cm (18 - 19in) for dogs and 43.2 - 45.7 (17 - 18in) for bitches. The correct relationship between height and weight is more important than these specific heights.

COAT
The coat of this dog is short and shiny. Any color is permitted, although black and tan, liver, plain white, or more than 80 per cent white are less favored than broken red and beige with highlights, either with and without white patches.

American Staffordshire Bull Terrier

CARE REQUIRED
Remove the dead and loose hairs from time to time with a rubber brush.

CHARACTER
This is a brave dog which is loyal to its family, tenacious, and tough on itself. It makes a good

American Staffordshire Bull Terrier

watchdog, is boisterous with tremendous stamina, and tends to dominate other dogs.

TRAINING
The American Staffordshire is not suitable for anyone with little experience of dogs. These dogs must be taught when they are young not to pull on the leash because they are amazingly strong when fully grown. This breed can learn a great deal if well trained with a consistent approach. They have often succeeded very well in obedience trials.

SOCIAL BEHAVIOR
These dogs can make good family dogs provided the family is always consistent and can cope with a boisterous dog. Enthusiasts for these dogs claim that they are loving with children.

This dog will protect house and home and accept cats and other household animals provided it has become acquainted with them when young. Some examples of the breed can be rather eager to fight with other dogs.

EXERCISE
If you own an American Staffordshire Bull Terrier make sure it gets plenty of exercise.
These dogs like running alongside a bicycle and playing ball games; they also enjoy retrieving things.

Bull Terrier

COUNTRY OF ORIGIN
England.

SPECIAL SKILLS
Family pet.

SIZE
There is no standard size for this dog; the most important point is for the build to create an impression of a substantial dog.

Bull Terrier

COAT
The short-haired coat can be plain white, white with markings on the head, and or coloring broken with highlights. Red, broken black, fawn, and black and tan with a little white are all accepted. With non-white animals, one color must predominate.

CARE REQUIRED
A minimum of grooming is required for a Bull

Terrier. Brushing the coat with a rubber brush to remove dead and loose hairs is considered adequate to keep it in good condition. In addition, you should regularly clean the ears. These dogs need a soft place to lie down.

CHARACTER
Bull Terriers can be hard on themselves (they seem to have almost no sensitivity to pain), and are affectionate but often stubborn and with a mind of their own, lively and boisterous, loving with children, spontaneous, and cheerful. Some Bull Terriers are rather keen to fight other dogs.

TRAINING
Take your puppy to a good obedience training course. When fully grown, this dog is very strong for its size and it is very difficult to train when it is an adult. The Bull Terrier is intelligent and learns relatively quickly, but it is also stubborn, with a mind of its own. The handler needs plenty of patience but must also be consistent towards the dog, possess understanding and be able to express affection.

SOCIAL BEHAVIOR
This breed usually gets on well with children and, provided they have social training when young, will not present difficulties with cats or other household animals later. Some Bull Terriers may try to dominate other dogs but this depends on the basic nature of the individual dog and the manner in which its social and other

Bull Terrier

Staffordshire Bull Terrier

COUNTRY OF ORIGIN
England.

SPECIAL SKILLS
Family pet.

SIZE
The shoulder-height should be 35 - 41cm (13¾ - 16¼in) and the weight 11-17kg (24 - 37½lb).

COAT
The coat is short and smooth. Staffordshires can be black, red, soft brown, white, or blue with any mixture that does not include white. Black and tan and liver are not considered desirable.

CARE REQUIRED
The Staffordshire Bull Terrier requires little grooming. Remove the loose and dead hairs occasionally with a rubber brush to keep the coat in optimum condition.

CHARACTER
This breed is loving with children, obedient, brave, affectionate, and has a sense of humor. It is intelligent, and tenacious, possesses tremendous stamina, and can be boisterous.

training was carried out. If you already own dog, don't buy a Bull Terrier as a second dog. It may take years before it happens, but sooner or later there will be a major battle between the two dogs.

EXERCISE
When they get enough exercise, Bull Terriers are calm indoors. These dogs enjoy running alongside your bicycle but don't try this until they are fully-grown, and even then not for too long at one session. These dogs also like going for long walks and running and playing off the leash.

Staffordshire Bull Terrier

Staffordshire Bull Terrier

TRAINING
The Staffordshire learns fairly quickly but can be stubborn. Teach this dog early that it must let go when you tell it to stop when you have had enough with rope-pulling games. Remain consistent throughout its training but always treat it as an equal. Introduce the young dog to other household animals.

SOCIAL BEHAVIOR
These dogs normally get on well with children and they can take rough play without a fuss. If these dogs have been properly introduced to cats and other household animals when young, there should not be any problems with such animals.

Most Staffordshires (and particularly the males) do not like the company of other dogs when they are adult – and they will make this quite obvious.

EXERCISE
When these dogs get sufficient exercise, they are very peaceful in the house. Most of them love to romp, play with a ball, and retrieve things.

SPECIAL REMARKS
The Staffordshire Bull Terrier has many of the characteristics of a larger dog and is therefore a suitable choice for people who would like that type of dog but do not have sufficient space.

Dwarf and Toy Terriers

Silky Terrier

COUNTRY OF ORIGIN
Australia.

SPECIAL SKILLS
Rat-catcher and family pet.

SIZE
The shoulder-height is about 23cm (9in) for dogs; bitches are generally a little smaller.

Silky Terrier

Coat

The coat is long, smooth, shiny, and silky, without an under-layer. The most common color is light to dark blue-grey (in various shades) with brown, although steel-blue is the most sought-after color. Silky Terriers are all born black.

Head of a Silky Terrier

Care required

In order to keep the coat in top condition, it is necessary to groom it daily with brush and comb, spending about fifteen minutes on the job. An occasional bath is acceptable. Check the teeth for tartar. The Silky seldom sheds.

Character

This is a lively, cheerful dog which is eager to learn, full of energy, intelligent, affectionate, loyal, docile, and in spite of its small size, vigilant and protective. The Silky Terrier likes to be close to its handler.

Training

The training of the Silky Terrier is very straight-forward because these dogs learn quite quickly.

Social behavior

Normally these dogs are very loving with children. Let them get used to cats when they are young as, otherwise, they will chase them when they are older. Expect these dogs to bark when visitors arrive.

Exercise

They adapt their exercise requirements to the family circumstances.

Yorkshire Terrier

Yorkshire Terrier

Country of origin

England.

Special skills

Historically a rat-catcher but nowadays usually a family pet.

Weight

The weight is about 2 - 3kg (4½ - 6½lb).

Coat

This breed has very long, silk-like hair, colored

golden-brown with steel-grey. As puppies the grey hairs are black.

CARE REQUIRED
The Yorkshire Terrier needs intensive daily grooming with brush and comb. If you do not have the time or the inclination to do this, you should have the coat trimmed by a professional. The hair is normally kept out of the eyes with a rubber band or a ribbon tied in a bow. Show dogs' coats are usually protected to keep their condition by being rolled up on curling papers. Check the ears regularly and remove loose hairs from the ear passages.

CHARACTER
This is a lively, intelligent, sometime too-brave dog, which is loving, vigilant, and becomes attached to its family. Yorkshire Terriers are very alert and bark whenever they sense danger.

TRAINING
The Yorkshire Terrier is a fairly quick-learning pupil. Provided you are consistent in your approach and ensure the lessons are positive, enjoyable and varied, it will soon learn to obey.

SOCIAL BEHAVIOR
Provided children do not treat them as a toy and do not invade their territory, these dogs will not cause any problems with them. Some of this breed can be rather foolhardy in their courage towards other dogs but usually get along very well with cats and other household animals.

Strangers will always be announced by loud barking.

EXERCISE
This breed adapts its exercise needs to the family circumstances and the dogs can readily be kept in an apartment.

SPECIAL REMARKS
The beautiful long hair of this breed is much admired at dog shows but to keep such a coat in good condition requires considerable work.

Most Yorkshire Terriers which are kept as pets go through life with shorter clipped coats. Although purists may find this upsetting, it is better for the dog than an unkempt coat with tangles which hurt and bother the dog.

Yorkshire Terrier

4. Dachshunds

Dachshund (Smooth-haired)

COUNTRY OF ORIGIN
Germany.

SPECIAL SKILLS
Family pet but also a hunting dog for above and below ground. These dogs are fanatical hunters of badgers, rabbits, deer, wild boar, and foxes.

SIZE
Dachshunds are divided into three size groups. The largest are the Standard, with a chest girth upwards from 35cm (13¾in).
The Standard should have a maximum weight of 9kg (20lb). The Miniature Dachshund has a chest girth of 30 - 35cm (11¾ - 13¾in), and the smallest sort, the Kaninchen or "little rabbit" is recognized by a chest girth smaller than 30cm (11¾in).

COAT
The coat consists of short smooth-hairs and is most frequently reddish-brown or black and tan. Some dogs, however, are chocolate brown and there are dogs with almost tiger-like markings.

CARE REQUIRED
The coat of the Smooth-haired Dachshund needs little attention.
Remove dead and loose hairs with a rubber brush from time to time. Keep the ear passages clean and the claws short. Most Dachshunds are dainty feeders. Be careful not to give them too much to eat because a fat Dachshund is an unhealthy one.

CHARACTER
The Dachshund is brave, dominant, has a mind of its own, is cunning, vigilant, resourceful, lively, tenacious, and curious. It has a sense of humor.

The Smooth-haired almost literally attaches itself to its own people, except when the hunting instinct rears its head.
A Dachshund needs to be introduced when it is young to many different situations for it to develop properly as an adult.

Red Long-haired Standard Dachshund

TRAINING
The Smooth-haired likes to dominate other dogs and has a mind of its own so it has to be consistently trained. With the right approach and much patience it is possible to teach this dog quite a lot but it will never slavishly follow your commands.

Dachshunds can sulk terribly if they feel they have been unfairly punished and they are very determined when they want something. Puppy training courses can be very good for young Dachshunds.

SOCIAL BEHAVIOR
The family comes first with Dachshunds and they have little time for strangers which they will show by a rather reserved manner to people they don't know. If they are introduced early to children so that they have positive experiences with them, the Smooth will not cause any problems.

They usually get on reasonably well with other dogs, although some of them can be over-courageous in their approach to larger dogs. Because of their passion for hunting, these dogs are definitely not suitable playmates for other small household animals. Introduce to cats when young to prevent later problems when it's older.

Red Smooth-haired Standard Dachshund

EXERCISE
Give this breed plenty of exercise to keep it fit. Don't allow it to run free as there is a strong possibility that its hunting instincts will cause it to run off.

If you wish to hunt with your Dachshund, contact the breed association. Dachshunds are strong healthy dogs which can live quite long but try to keep their backs from becoming injured through excessive strain from constantly running up and down stairs.

SPECIAL REMARKS
The Smooth-haired Dachshund is the original strain of this family of dogs. The Wire-haired and Long-haired Dachshunds were attained by crossing the Smooth with other breeds.

Dachshund (Long-haired)

COUNTRY OF ORIGIN
Germany.

Black and tan Standard Long-haired Dachshund

SPECIAL SKILLS
Family pet but also a hunting dog – above and below ground (for badgers, rabbits, deer, wild boar, and foxes).

SIZE
See Smooth-haired Dachshund.

COAT
The Long-haired Dachshund is most often seen with a plain deep chestnut coat, in reddish-brown, and black and tan.

CARE REQUIRED
This Dachshund is happy with an occasional grooming, giving those places where tangles can form special attention. If necessary clip excess hair growth between the pads of the feet. Keep the claws short.

CHARACTER
This Dachshund is brave, has a mind of its own, and is vigilant and intelligent. It has a good sense of humor, and is lively, sociable, and playful. The Long-haired variety has a gentler

nature than its Smooth-haired cousin. It has been suggested that this is due to the crossing with Spaniels and Irish Setters which is how the long hair was created.

TRAINING
Long-haired Dachshunds are easier to train than Smooth ones but because they, too, have minds of their own the training needs to be patient and you will constantly need to feel your way with this dog.

SOCIAL BEHAVIOR
The family is number one with this Dachshund too, though they are friendlier towards strangers than the Smooth-haired. They get on well with children provided their first youthful experiences with them were positive ones.

They usually get along with other dogs but the contact with other animals can be a problem – they are, after all, hunting dogs. Cats will be tolerated provided they have learned to live with them early but do not expect any affection in the relationship.

EXERCISE
The Long-haired Dachshund needs substantial exercise so take it for regular long walks.

Dachshund (Wire-haired)

COUNTRY OF ORIGIN
Germany.

SPECIAL SKILLS
Family pet but also a hunting dog – above and below ground (for badgers, rabbits, deer, wild boar, and foxes).

SIZE
See the Smooth-haired Dachshund.

COAT
The coat consists of wire-hairs which lie flat and should be as hard as possible, with a dense under-layer.
The hair on the head and ears should be very short and there should be a definite beard and moustache.

The color is an indeterminate mix of natural colors often found in wild animals – black and tan occurs less frequently.
Occasionally dogs with a red or chocolate coat may be encountered.

CARE REQUIRED
The Wire-haired Dachshund needs to have its coat plucked about twice per year, depending on the condition of the coat. The hair on the top of the head should be kept short. Trim excess hair which may grow between the pads of the feet.

CHARACTER
This is a brave, dominant dog with a sense of humor and a mind of its own. It is cunning, vigilant, resourceful, lively, tenacious, and curious. It is essential to introduce the Wire-haired Dachshund to all manner of situations early in its life to encourage its development.

TRAINING
See Smooth-haired Dachshund.

SOCIAL BEHAVIOR
See Smooth-haired Dachshund.

EXERCISE
See Smooth-haired Dachshund.

Wire-haired Standard Dachshund

Wire- and Smooth-haired Miniature Dachshunds

5. Spitz and other primitive breeds

Arctic breeds and sled dogs

Alaskan Malamute

Alaskan Malamute

COUNTRY OF ORIGIN
North America (Alaska).

SPECIAL SKILLS
Sled dog and family pet.

SIZE
The shoulder-height is about 64cm (25¼in) for dogs and about 58cm (22¾in) for bitches.

COAT
The Alaskan Malamute has a thick, coarse outer-coat with a greasy and woolly under-coat. The normal colors are wolf-grey, or black with white – always with white on the stomach and a white face or top of the head. Other colors are permitted but white is the only plain solid which is accepted.

CARE REQUIRED
This breed's coat does not need much in the way of grooming. When it is shedding use a coarse comb with a double row of teeth to remove loose and dead hairs.

CHARACTER
This is an affectionate dog which is intelligent, friendly, loyal, and noble, but can have a mind of its own. It will never slavishly follow your whims. The Alaskan Malamute learns quite quickly and has tremendous stamina.

TRAINING
Despite its friendly nature, this dog needs a firm hand in its training.

The Malamute calls for a handler with plenty of confidence who understands the character of this dog. With such a handler these dogs can learn a great deal even including agility skills, although they will be outperformed in competition by one of the sheepdogs.

Japanese Spitz

SOCIAL BEHAVIOR
Alaskan Malamutes generally get on well with children. They are friendly with everyone which makes them, of course, unsuitable as watchdogs.

They can occasionally try to dominate other dogs of the same sex, but that's exceptional. If they have been introduced to cats when young there is no problem with them.

EXERCISE
Exercise is probably the most important element in an Alaskan Malamute's life. This breed needs copious amounts of exercise and if at least an hour each day of hard exercise with this dog is impossible get another type of dogs.

In some places there are sled dog organizations which arrange competitions these dogs can enter with a wheeled cart in place of a sled where there is no snow.

Malamutes are happy whether they are indoors or outdoors but they do not like to be alone. Keep this dog on the leash whenever it is taken out because it may try to run away.

Alaskan Malamute

Head of an Alaskan Malamute

Greenland Dog

Greenland Dog

COUNTRY OF ORIGIN
Scandinavia.

SPECIAL SKILLS
Sled dog.

SIZE
The shoulder-height is a minimum of 60cm
(23½in) for dogs and 55cm (21½in) for bitches.
There is no maximum height.

COAT
The Greenland Dog has a double-layered coat:
the under-layer is soft and thick, the outer-layer
protects well against the weather.
All colors are accepted with the exception of
albino.

CARE REQUIRED
This breed does not need much attention to its
coat. During shedding, when the under-layer of
the coat is shed, the best way to remove loose
hairs is to use a comb with a double row of metal
teeth.

CHARACTER
This breed is independent, equable, dominant,
tough on itself, and with a mind of its own. The
Greenland Dog rarely barks but howls quite a
lot.
This is definitely not a family pet. These dogs
have an amazing amount of energy with tremendous stamina.

TRAINING
Training this dog is not particularly easy due to
its independent nature. This is a sled dog, not a
family pet.

It can cover enormous distances and will do so
given half a chance, staying away for days at a
time so that a good fence around your property
is essential if you decide to get this dog. These
dogs are happiest pulling a sled.

SOCIAL BEHAVIOR

This breed cannot stand being left on its own. If you decide this is the dog you want, get two. These dogs are perfectly happy in an outdoor kennel.

They do not usually get on well with either cats or other household animals.
Friends and strangers alike will be exuberantly greeted, probably with howling, which means they are not suitable as watchdogs in spite of their size.

EXERCISE

It should be obvious that the Greenland Dog needs a great deal of exercise. The best form of exercise is what they love most – pulling a sled or wheeled cart. If you know you won't be able to provide this dog with such exercise, choose another breed.

They are too strong to be exercised running alongside a bicycle. These are cold weather dogs so don't let them work when the temperature is over 60°F (15°C).

Samoyed

Samoyed

COUNTRY OF ORIGIN
Western Siberia.

SPECIAL SKILLS
Herding-dog, watchdog, sled dog, hunting dog, and family pet.

SIZE
The shoulder-height is 57cm (22½in) for dogs and 53cm (20¾in) for bitches. Variance of 3cm (1¼in) above and below these heights is permitted.

COAT
The protective topcoat is wiry and erect, while the undercoat is short and dense. The coat is white, cream, or white with light brown.

CARE REQUIRED
Do not brush the Samoyed too much because this can harm the under-layer of its coat. If the dog tends to shed too much use a comb with a

double row of metal teeth to remove the loose hairs from the undercoat.

CHARACTER
The Samoyed is a dog of contradictions. It is friendly and cheerful, intelligent and reasonably obedient, but it will never follow orders slavishly and can be very stubborn. It is sensitive and gentle-natured but dominant and vigilant, affectionate but not too much so. The Samoyed loves to wander, has considerable stamina, and remains playful into old age. These dogs like to hear themselves barking so they can be very noisy.

TRAINING
Training the Samoyed is no easy task and needs to begin very early. Make sure there is plenty of variety in the drills. Constantly practising the same command can be a mistake as it will become stubborn and refuse to do what you want. Teach it when very young that it must come to you when you call and arrange for as many positive encounters with cats and other household animals as possible. Your authority should be clearly seen but always make sure it knows you are its friend. It will not respect screaming, shouting, or being hit.

SOCIAL BEHAVIOR
These dogs are gentle-natured and patient with children but can be try to boss other dogs. Remember that the Samoyed is a hunting dog which enjoys chasing something if it gets the chance.
Train it early to get along with cats and other pets. The dog is reasonably vigilant.

EXERCISE
The Samoyed needs lots of exercise. Once it is fully grown, take it on really long walks or get it to run alongside a bicycle to keep it in good condition.

Because these dogs like to wander, make sure your yard is properly enclosed with a fence.

Siberian Husky

COUNTRY OF ORIGIN
Alaska.

SPECIAL SKILLS
Sled dog.

Siberian Husky

SIZE

The shoulder-height is 53 - 60cm (20¾ - 23½in) for dogs and 51 - 56cm (20 - 22in) for bitches.

COAT

The Husky has a double-layered, medium-length coat. Every color and combination are accepted and even partially blue eyes are permissible.

CARE REQUIRED

An occasional brushing and combing, particularly when the dog is shedding, is adequate for this breed.

The coat is usually more handsome when the Husky is kept in an outdoor kennel as this causes it to grow more.

CHARACTER

This breed is independent with a mind of its own, is very intelligent, full of energy, cheerful, loves to wander, and is very fond of its handler and family. Because these dogs want to make friends with everyone, they are not ideal watchdogs.

TRAINING

Most Huskies do not fill the role of family pet very well, although perhaps a very sporty family might manage. Remember that the Husky is a sled dog in heart and soul.

To teach the Husky anything will require a careful approach and great consistency. The handler should also have considerable patience and an understanding of the character of Arctic dogs.

A Husky will only obey a command in which it sees a point. If you are considering acquiring a Husky, it is sensible to contact a specialist on Arctic dogs and/or the breed society before doing so.

SOCIAL BEHAVIOR

Siberian Huskies generally get along with their own kind but the contact with other household animals needs careful handling and training. Cats and other small animals are not suitable companions for this dog.

Fortunately children are not a problem. This breed finds it hard to be left on its own so it is advisable to have more than one Husky.

EXERCISE

This dog needs lots of exercise and there can be no compromise in this. If you want to get involved in dog sledding then there is no better choice than the Husky. This breed is world-famous for its speed. If you cannot or do not wish to have your Husky pull a sled at least twice a week, then you must come up with an alternative exercise for it such as bicycling alongside it for at least an hour a day.

Lonely Huskies that are locked up with too little exercise will howl and become destructive. This is not the fault of the dog but of an owner who has made a wrong choice of dog. Take a Husky out on a leash. Fence your yard or it will run away.

Siberian Husky

SPECIAL REMARKS

Siberian Huskies will usually be happy to share an outdoor kennel with one or more other dogs. The thick coat protects these dogs against rain and cold.

These dogs need protection from the heat, so never work them in the summer.

Scandinavian Arctic dogs

Finnish Spitz

COUNTRY OF ORIGIN
Finland.

SPECIAL SKILLS
Hunting dog for birds, estate dog, and family pet.

SIZE
The shoulder-height is 53 - 60cm (20¾ - 23½in) for dogs and 51 - 56cm (20 - 22in) for bitches.

Finnish Spitz

COAT

The coat consists of thick, erect, medium-length hair with a thick under-layer of straight hair. The color may be red-brown or a yellowish red and small white markings are permissible. Puppies are born much darker and acquire their reddish coat later.

CARE REQUIRED

The Finnish Spitz has a self-cleaning coat as do most other Arctic dogs.
Regular grooming with brush and comb is, however, still necessary. The coat of this breed does not have the customary odor usually associated with dog hair.

CHARACTER

This breed is lively and curious, though not overwhelmingly so. It is a watchdog that only barks when necessary.

These dogs are delightful with children, home loving and sociable, and very loyal to their own family but do not follow their handler's orders slavishly.

TRAINING

The Finnish Spitz is a dog that requires much patience and understanding, together with a consistent manner.
If these elements go into its training it can be a very satisfactory pet.

Finnish Spitz

SOCIAL BEHAVIOR

Finnish Spitz usually do not cause problems in the intercourse with other dogs. They get along fine with children.
Visitors will always be announced. But that is all, it is no defender.

EXERCISE

This dog likes to be outdoors but will be lonely on its own in a kennel. With some companions of its own kind it will be quite happy. This is the perfect dog for the country but there are plenty of examples of this breed living successfully in towns.
Be sure the dog has plenty of exercise. If it has the exercise, it will be content to spend the evening at its handler's feet.

Elkhound with Elk

Elkhound or Jämthund

COUNTRY OF ORIGIN
Sweden.

SPECIAL SKILLS
Hunting dog for large game.

SIZE
The shoulder-height is 60 - 65cm (23½ - 25½in) for dogs and 55 - 60cm (21½ - 23½in) for bitches.

COAT
The Elkhound has a cream thick undercoat with thick, densely packed covering hair. The color of the outer-coat is dark or light grey and there should be cream patches on the nose, cheeks,

throat, stomach, front of the chest, legs, and underside of the tail.

CARE REQUIRED
The coat hardly needs any grooming. During shedding is best to use a comb with a double row of metal teeth to remove loose hairs from the under-layer of the coat. In common with other Arctic dogs, the hair of the Elkhound does not have the typical dog smell.

Elkhound

CHARACTER
This breed is equable, straightforward, intelligent and cunning, has a sense of humor, is sensitive to nuances in the voice, and is physically demanding of itself.

TRAINING
This dog needs a calm handler who exudes a natural authority.
A calm and consistent manner of approach to its training is essential.

SOCIAL BEHAVIOR
The Elkhound gets on with other dogs even though its bark can have a frightening effect upon them.

They are rather reserved with strangers but they don't make good watchdogs. These dogs get on well with children and also with any other animals in or around the home.

EXERCISE
The Elkhound is a hunting dog through and through and is still used for this purpose in its native country.

Its task is to track large wild animals independently and bring them down and it will search large areas to do this.
This dog is not suitable for life in an urban

environment. If it is allowed off the leash, the chance is its hunting instincts may well cause it to run away.

In wild countryside, the Elkhound will normally be constantly on the move. It verges on cruelty to animals to enclose such a dog and limit it to three short walks each day.

Head of an Elkhound

Karelian Bear Dog

COUNTRY OF ORIGIN
Finland.

SPECIAL SKILLS
Hunting dog for large wild game.

SIZE
The shoulder-height is 54 - 60cm (21¼ - 23½in) for dogs and 49 - 55cm (19¼ - 21½in) for bitches. The ideal height is 57 - 58cm (22½ - 22¾in) for dogs and 51 - 53cm (20 - 20¾in) for bitches.

COAT
The short-haired coat consists of straight and stiff hairs while the under-layer is soft and dense. The Karelian Bear Dog is white with black. Black speckles in the white are considered a fault.

CARE REQUIRED
The coat of these dogs requires little attention. Use a special metal comb when the dog is shedding for easy removal of loose hairs from the undercoat.

Karelian Bear Dog

CHARACTER
This dog is very loyal to its own family and makes a good household companion. It may try to dominate other dogs but it is also sensitive, independent, intelligent, cunning, tough on itself, and energetic. It has a good a sense of humor. These dogs can often be rather unfriendly towards other dogs.

TRAINING
This dog needs a handler with natural authority. The training should be very consistent, with both a firm hand and affection. This is not a breed for inexperienced dog owners.

SOCIAL BEHAVIOR
As far as other dogs are concerned, Karelian Bear Dogs tend to try to dominate and are perfectly willing to fight. They are affectionate

Head of a Karelian Bear Dog

towards people, however, which means they are unsuitable as watchdogs.

They'll announce both welcome and unwelcome visitors but that is all. Those visitors that the dogs know well will get an enthusiastic welcome while strangers may be treated coldly. The Karelian Bear Dog can live with other household animals if the training is properly handled.

EXERCISE
This breed can be kept in an outdoor kennel. The Karelian Bear Dog needs to be able to exercise for at least an hour per day.
If you can keep this dog well under control it will enjoy exercising by running alongside a bicycle.

If it gets too little exercise or becomes bored inside your house it may take this out on your furniture.

Make sure that your yard is well fenced because Karelian Bear Dogs have a tendency to go hunting.

SPECIAL REMARKS
In common with most Arctic dogs, the Karelian Bear Dog does not have the usual smell of dog hair. It also has a comparatively small appetite.

Lundehund

Lundehund

COUNTRY OF ORIGIN
Norway.

SPECIAL SKILLS
The Lundehund was originally used especially to catch Puffins and bring them to their handler.

Puffin nests were often found high up in rocky crevices on cliffs.

Size
The shoulder-height is 35 - 38cm (13¾ - 15in) for dogs and 32 - 35cm (12½ - 13¾in) for bitches. Dogs should weigh about 7kg (15½lb) and bitches 6kg (13¼lb).

Coat
The Lundehund has a short coat of reddish brown to drab red hairs which have slightly black tips. There is a soft undercoat.

Care required
The coat of this breed does not require much attention. When it is shedding remove the loose hairs with a strong comb.

These dogs need special care with their diet because they lack an enzyme that is necessary for the digestion of food. Seek specialist advice from your veterinarian.

Character
These dogs have a mind of their own and a sense of humor. They are cheerful, mischievous, intelligent and cunning, and like to be the boss. They rarely bark.

Training
When you are training this dog try to have as much variety as possible. Repeating the same exercise will bore the dog and undermine your authority. Make sure that you are always consistent with it.

Exercise
This breed does not require much exercise. Take it for a walk three times a day and give it some time to play in the yard.

Special remarks
Experts cannot agree whether or not this breed is really a part of the domesticated dog family of *Canis familiares*.

It is possible that it really is part of the primitive wild dog family *Canis ferus* because it possesses a number of features unknown in any other domesticated breed.

This dog can close its ears not just to orders it does not like but, more practically, when creeping through rocky crevices in order to prevent dirt getting in. This protects the dog's exceptional hearing ability. In addition to this, they have six toes and eight pads on each foot, compared with five toes and six pads on other dogs (see photograph p. 141).

Lundehunds are the only breed of dog to possess – like humans – collar bones so that they can spread the front legs out to the side. Finally, they can bend their head right back over themselves which is also useful for crawling through narrow rock crevices. No other breed shares this feature with them.

Norwegian Elkhounds

The feet of a Lundehund has six toes

Norwegian Elkhound

Norwegian Elkhound

COUNTRY OF ORIGIN
Norway.

SPECIAL SKILLS
Hunting dog for large wild game.

SIZE
The shoulder-height is ideally 52cm (20½in) for dogs and 49cm (19¼in) for bitches. Variance of 2cm (¾in) is permitted.

COAT
The Elkhound has a thick, woolly, cream undercoat and a hard, dense, and longer outer coat. This outer coat comes in various shades of grey, with black markings behind the ears and around the muzzle.
There are also black Elkhounds, which are recognized as a separate breed. The black Elkhounds are permitted to have white markings.

CARE REQUIRED
The coat of an Elkhound requires little grooming. An ideal way to remove loose hairs when the dog is shedding is to use a wooden comb with a double row of metal teeth. In common with other Arctic dogs, they do not have the usual smell of dog hair. The coat is both water- and dirt-resistant.

CHARACTER
The Elkhound is tough on itself, straightforward, equable, friendly, and gentle. However quiet it may be indoors, it will be a bundle of energy outside.

TRAINING
Like other Arctic dogs, the Norwegian Elkhound has a mind of its own and is fairly independent. It is important to be firm with this dog but show your affection as well and make sure you are fair.

You can upset the dog for a long time by punishing it unfairly – and it will let you know how it feels.

SOCIAL BEHAVIOR
The Norwegian Elkhound is somewhat reserved with strangers but will greet family friends it knows with enthusiasm.
These dogs can try to be bossy around their own kind but this tends to be the exception rather than the rule. These dogs usually get on well with each other and reasonably well with children too provided the children do not pester the dogs. They will let you know you have visitors but that is all.

Head of a Norwegian Elkhound

EXERCISE

For this dog to be happy it must have at least an hour a day of exercise.

Let it run alongside your bicycle or let it have a really good run in the woods but don't forget that if it gets the scent of wild game, it will run away from you and you'll find it's deaf to your calls.

Norbottenspets

Norbottenspets

COUNTRY OF ORIGIN
Sweden.

SPECIAL SKILLS
Hunting dog.

SIZE
The shoulder-height is about 45cm (17¾in) for dogs and 42cm (16½in) for bitches.

COAT
The very short coat is dense, protecting the soft undercoat. Every color is permitted but the ideal color is white with yellow or reddish brown patches.

CARE REQUIRED
Little grooming is needed for the coat of this breed. An occasional brushing, particularly when it is shedding, is sufficient to keep it in good condition.

CHARACTER
This is an alert dog which is independent, extremely active, friendly, likes to bark, is intelligent and cunning, and has a mind of its own. The Norbottenspets has considerable stamina and is very energetic. Be aware that it likes to wander.

TRAINING

The very individual nature of this dog means that its handler needs considerable patience, power of persuasion, and an insight into the character of the dog to be able to achieve the most basic levels of training. In other words, this is another dog that really isn't suitable for beginners.

SOCIAL BEHAVIOR

This dog gets on well with other dogs. Visits by strangers will be announced but that is all so don't expect this dog to act as a watchdog. These dogs will be friends with animals that were already present in the household when they joined it and there are no problems worth mentioning in their attitude to children although they don't, of course, like being pestered.

EXERCISE

The Norbottenspets is very energetic and requires considerable exercise. Despite its small size, it can happily run alongside a bicycle provided it builds up to this gradually. If you let this dog run freely off the leash it will pay no attention when you call – their hunting instincts are stronger than the bond with you. If you live surrounded by open countryside, this need not be a problem but if you live in a more built-up area be sure your yard is well fenced.
Norbottenspets are usually very strong dogs.

West Siberian Laika

West Siberian Laika

COUNTRY OF ORIGIN
Western Siberia.

SPECIAL SKILLS
Hunting dog, sled dog, and family pet.

SIZE
The shoulder-height is 55 - 62cm

(21½ - 24½in) for dogs and 51 - 58cm (20 - 22¾in) for bitches.

COAT

The coat consists of straight, rough top coat with masses of hair in the undercoat. Permitted colors are white, salt and pepper, grey, any shade of red, black and multi.

CARE REQUIRED

The coat of the West Siberian Laika does not need much attention.

When the dog sheds, a period which is usually short but with a very large amount of hair loss, the loose hairs are best removed using a comb with a double row of metal teeth.

CHARACTER

This is a friendly dog which is intelligent, eager to learn, uncomplicated, and calm.

TRAINING

The West Siberian Laika is not difficult to train. It learns commands quickly and likes to work. Both agility skills and obedience training will be easily absorbed.

SOCIAL BEHAVIOR

This very original and healthy breed usually gets on well with its own kind and is very patient and loving with children.

The West Siberian Laika is a true friend to humans. When strangers come to your home they'll let you know but they won't attack them.

EXERCISE

The West Siberian Laika has an average demand for exercise but try to give it more than three brief trots around the block a day.

Scandinavian Spitz guard- and watchdogs

Finnish Lapphund

COUNTRY OF ORIGIN
Finland.

SPECIAL SKILLS
Sheepdog, farm dog, and watchdog.

SIZE
The shoulder-height is 46 - 52cm (18 - 20½in) for dogs and 40 - 46cm (15¾ - 18in) for bitches.

COAT

The Finnish Lapphund has an abundant coat. The outer layer is long and coarse, the undercoat is soft, thick, and dense.

Every color is permitted provided the main color predominates.

Finnish Lapphund

Finnish Lapphund

CARE REQUIRED

The wire brush used for German Shepherds is ideal to remove the loose hairs from the thick undercoat of this breed when it is shedding.

CHARACTER

This is a friendly, intelligent and sociable dog which wants to work for its handler. It is very active, energetic, hard on itself, and affectionate.

TRAINING

The Finnish Lapphund is intelligent, and keen to learn and therefore makes an excellent pupil. It can compete on level terms with the best in dog sports such as catch and agility skills trials.

This dog is naturally very sociable. It gets on extremely well with children and in normal circumstances can take a great deal of rough housing from them. It also gets on well with other household animals and dogs.

The Finnish Lapphund is alert in the sense that it will warn you of visitors but it is too gentle-natured to defend your property.

EXERCISE

This breed needs fairly substantial exercise and running alongside a cycle is one of the possibilities, but it will also really enjoy long walks through the woods. Its sheepdog instincts will keep it close to you and prevent it from wandering off.

Iceland Dog

COUNTRY OF ORIGIN

Iceland.

Iceland Dog

Iceland Dog puppies

SPECIAL SKILLS

Sheepdog and family pet.

SIZE

The shoulder-height is 42 - 48cm (16½ - 18¾in) for dogs and 38 - 44cm (15 - 17¼in) for bitches. The dog weighs about 14kg (31lb).

COAT

The Iceland Dog has a double-layered coat of soft, sleek hairs. The predominant colors are white with pink markings and light brown with black tips to the hairs.

A few dogs turn up that are black with white markings.

CARE REQUIRED

The coat of the Iceland Dog does not require much attention. Comb out the loose hairs of the undercoat when it is shedding.

CHARACTER

This is a high-spirited and friendly dog which is sociable, equable, intelligent, and eager to learn. It is affectionate, attentive, and vigilant, hard on itself, and brave, but it can be stubborn. It likes to bark so keep that in mind if you have near neighbors.

TRAINING

The training of the Iceland Dog is not usually difficult. The breed learns quickly and is intelligent. Handle them always with utmost consistency and in a friendly manner, trying to bring as much variety as possible into the exercises. Bear in mind that the dog must see the purpose of the command. These dogs do quite well at both catch and agility skills trials.

SOCIAL BEHAVIOR

This delightful family dog needs quite a lot of exercise to keep it happy. Take it regularly for longer walks, giving it the chance to run and play off the leash.

These are dogs that like to be part of the family and regard being left on their own as severe punishment.

EXERCISE

This nice family dog needs quite a bit of exercise to feel happy. Take it on long walks regularly and let it run and play freely. This breed bonds strongly to the family. If they are left alone major parts of the day, this will be felt as a severe punishment.

Norwegian Buhund

COUNTRY OF ORIGIN

Norway.

SPECIAL SKILLS

Farm estate dog and sheep-herder. *Bu* in Norwegian means farm or homestead.

Norwegian Buhund

SIZE

The shoulder-height is 43 - 47cm (17 - 18½in) for dogs and 41 - 45cm (16¼ - 17¾in) for bitches. The weight is 14 - 18kg (31 - 39½lb) for dogs and 12 - 16kg (26½ - 35¼lb) for bitches.

COAT

The Buhund has a soft, woolly thick undercoat with an abundant thick topcoat. The color should be wheaten or biscuit, although black with a little white is also known.

CARE REQUIRED

It is not difficult to keep the coat in good condition. Loose hairs can be removed from the undercoat when the dog is shedding with a wooden comb that has a double row of metal teeth.

CHARACTER

This dog is vigilant, cheerful, active, and untiring, intelligent, attentive, and affectionate.

It also likes to bark but Norwegian Buhunds are normally quite calm indoors.

TRAINING

The Norwegian Buhund likes to be taught, is intelligent, and also learns very quickly. It requires a firm hand in its training which should be as varied in nature as possible to keep it interested.

These dogs like to be busy, enjoy retrieving, and with the right approach to training can shine in various dog sports.

SOCIAL BEHAVIOR

These dogs are generally very good with children and get on fine with other dogs and animals of the household.

This dog will warn you of any strange visitors but that is all – it is no watchdog.

EXERCISE

The Norwegian Buhund is an energetic dog with considerable stamina. One of its favorite pastimes is retrieving objects. Let it run free off the leash.

You needn't worry that it will run away as its shepherding instincts prevent it from roaming. It will run alongside a bicycle very nicely.

Norwegian Buhund

Vastgotaspets

COUNTRY OF ORIGIN

Sweden.

SPECIAL SKILLS

Livestock herder, watchdog, and family pet.

SIZE

The ideal shoulder-height is 33cm (13in) for dogs and 31cm (12¼in) for bitches.

COAT

The coat consists of smooth-lying yet coarse, wiry hairs with a soft woolly undercoat. The color is steel grey with darker outer hairs or slightly reddish yellow with lighter patches. Streaked, spotted, grey-brown, and yellow-brown are also permissible but not preferred. Small white markings are also acceptable but they must never cover more than a third of the total coat.

Vastgotaspets

CARE REQUIRED

Regular brushing and combing will keep the coat in good condition.

The ear passages should be kept clean and the claws kept short.

CHARACTER

This dog is vigilant, alert, active, eager to learn, intelligent, and both affectionate and very loyal.

TRAINING

This dog is easy to train because it understands quickly what is expected of it.

SOCIAL BEHAVIOR

The Vastgotaspets can get along well with children and it enjoys playing with them. It will always protect them from strangers who try to get close to them which is a characteristic of herding dogs.

These dogs generally get along with other dogs but tend to be rather reserved towards strangers.

EXERCISE

The Vastgotaspets is a working dog that needs plenty of exercise.
Given its size, it can be kept in an apartment but it is essential to give it ample opportunities to burn off its energy.

Nothing will make this dog happier than to train it for agility skills trials, or some similar activity which will provide it with a constant stream of new challenges.

Swedish Lapphund

COUNTRY OF ORIGIN
Sweden.

SPECIAL SKILLS
Sheepdog.

SIZE
The ideal shoulder height is 48cm (18¾in) for dogs and 43cm (17in) for bitches. A difference of 3cm (1⅓in) is permitted.

COAT
The Swedish Lapphund has a thick woolly topcoat, the hairs of which should be erect, and a dense curly undercoat of fine hairs.

Colors are brown, black, and a combination of the two. For the show ring, plain colors are preferred. White markings occur in some dogs but are considered a fault.

CARE REQUIRED
During shedding when the hairs begin to fall out of the thick undercoat deal with them by using one of the special combs designed for grooming German Shepherds.

CHARACTER
This is an intelligent, sociable, and friendly dog which is similar in nature to the Finnish Lapphund, meaning that it loves children, is very tolerant of them, and is keen to learn. It is affectionate, lively, and not squeamish about pain.

TRAINING
This dog learns quickly and easily, so that you can consider involving both of you in agility skills and obedience training or perhaps games of catch or chasing Frisbees.
Handled properly, this breed can compete at the highest levels.

SOCIAL BEHAVIOR
A Swedish Lapphund from good breeding lines gets on well with other dogs and is very tolerant of children. The dog will bark to let you know strangers are around but that is all because this dog is friendly with everyone.

EXERCISE
This breed has tremendous stamina and likes to be kept busy.
These dogs love to be taken for walks and will always stay close to you.

SPECIAL REMARKS
This breed looks very much like the Finnish Lapphund.

European Spitz

Pomeranian

COUNTRY OF ORIGIN
Germany.

SPECIAL SKILLS
Companion and pet.

SIZE
The shoulder-height of the smaller Pomeranians is 18 - 22cm (7 - 8½in) and 23 - 28cm (9 - 11in) for the larger ones.

COAT
These dogs have long, erect hairs and a thick undercoat.
Colors are plain white, orange, black, brown, or grey.

Small Pomeranian

CARE REQUIRED
The coat should be well combed with a coarse comb every three weeks and then lightly brushed.
If you use too fine a comb or groom the dog too frequently you run the risk of damaging the undercoat.

CHARACTER
This is a lively dog, which is boisterous, can be too brave, is intelligent, eager to learn, very loyal to its handler and family, vigilant, and energetic. It has a delightful nature and does not cling to its handler.

TRAINING
Teach this dog early that it may bark a couple of times when the doorbell rings or there are visitors but then to keep quiet. Be very consistent about this! Pomeranians are generally fairly easy to train because they are so intelligent and eager to learn.

SOCIAL BEHAVIOR
Too much attention from children can make these dogs rather nervous. They usually get along with other dogs and household animals without any problems.

Some of them seem to think they are much larger than they actually are and do not hesitate to attack much bigger dogs. You need to protect them from themselves.

EXERCISE

Both breeds are happy with short walks and like to play in the yard but they can walk a longer distance without becoming overtired.

Keeshond

COUNTRY OF ORIGIN
Germany.

SPECIAL SKILLS
Vermin destroyer, watchdog, and family pet.

SIZE
The ideal shoulder-height for Keeshonds is 46cm (18in) with deviations of 4cm (1½in) accepted.

A slightly larger related variety is known in The Netherlands, where most Keeshonds come from, as the *Wolfkeeshond*.
The ideal shoulder-height for this 'Wolf Spitz' is 50cm (19½in) with deviations of 5cm (2in) accepted.

Wolf-grey Keeshond

COAT
These dogs have a thick undercoat with longer covering hair. They are wolf-grey, plain black, brown, or white.

CARE REQUIRED
When these dogs are shedding the coat needs to be brushed and combed regularly to remove the dead hair.

At other times there should be a minimum of combing to avoid damaging the undercoat.

CHARACTER
These dogs are boisterous, loyal to their handler, vigilant, not easily led astray by bribes, intelligent, and eager to learn.

TRAINING
These dogs quickly figure out what is expected of them which means training them is fairly easy.

Keeshonds are often stars in dog sports such as agility skills trials.

SOCIAL BEHAVIOR
Keeshonds are naturally good with other dogs and children but they need to be introduced when young to cats.

Strangers will also be announced by barking.

EXERCISE
The Keeshond has an average need for exercise and will usually adapt to family circumstances.

Medium-sized Keeshond

Smaller Keeshond

COUNTRY OF ORIGIN
Germany.

SPECIAL SKILLS
Vermin destroyer and family pet.

SIZE
The ideal shoulder-height is 32cm (12½in) but heights of 29 - 36cm (11½ - 14¼in) are acceptable.

COAT
This dog has a thick undercoat with longer erect covering hair.

The Smaller Keeshond can be plain white, black, brown, orange, or wolf-grey.

CARE REQUIRED
When this dog is shedding groom it regularly with a coarse comb and with a brush to remove dead hairs. At other times this must not be done too often to avoid damaging the undercoat.

CHARACTER
This breed is boisterous, loyal to its handler and family, vigilant, not easily led astray by bribes, and intelligent. Some of these dogs like to bark to excess.

TRAINING
The Smaller Keeshond quickly grasps what is intended which makes training it fairly easy.

Teach your dog not to bark unnecessarily.

SOCIAL BEHAVIOR
These dogs get on well with their own kind and with children. Let them make the acquaintance of cats early in their lives. Strangers will always be announced by barking.

EXERCISE
This breed has an average need for exercise and will normally adapt to the family circumstances.

Primitive Asian Spitz breeds

Japanese Akita

COUNTRY OF ORIGIN
Japan.

SPECIAL SKILLS
Vermin destroyer and family pet.

SIZE
The ideal shoulder-height is 67cm (26¼in) for dogs and 61cm (24in) for bitches. Variations of 3cm (1¼in) will be accepted.

COAT
The dog has straight, coarse covering hair with a soft dense undercoat.

Permitted colors with the Japanese breed society are red, white, and streaked.

A dark face is regarded in Japan as a fault. In some countries spotted and speckled dogs with a black face are permitted at shows.

Smaller Keeshond

Japanese Akita

Japanese Akita

CARE REQUIRED
This breed is easy to care for. About twice a year they have a brief period of heavy shedding when a good comb with a double set of metal teeth should be used.

CHARACTER
These are calm, thoughtful, intelligent, and friendly dogs which are reasonably obedient, imperturbable, and have a strong hunting instinct. They are good watchdogs but won't bark too much. But they can also be independent and try to dominate. They will become friends with their family but never slaves.

TRAINING
With a confident handler who is consistent in his approach, the Japanese Akita can learn a great deal. They do best if the training drills are not constantly repeated.

They are not a suitable breed for beginners unless expert advice is followed very closely.

SOCIAL BEHAVIOR
Most Japanese Akitas have no time for other dogs and prefer not to have any other dog for company. They virtually all tend to be extremely dominant with other dogs, especially ones of their own sex. They need to become acquainted with cats and other animals early in their lives to prevent later problems. They usually get on reasonably well with children, provided the children do not invade the dog's own territory. They should never be considered a children's playmate. Strangers will get a rather reserved reception from this dog.

EXERCISE
Japanese Akitas have considerable stamina but if you miss a long walk one day, they will accept it without a fuss.

Never forget that they have strong hunting instincts so that if they are permitted to run free, there is a strong possibility they will run away.

SPECIAL REMARKS
The Akita is highly revered in Japan and is viewed almost as a national icon.

Chow Chow (Short-haired)

COUNTRY OF ORIGIN
China.

SPECIAL SKILLS
The Chow Chow had various roles in the past, including as a hunting dog and as a delicacy in Chinese cuisine. Today it is a vigilant family pet.

SIZE
The shoulder-height is 48 - 56cm (18¾ - 22in) for dogs and 46 - 51cm (18 - 20in) for bitches.

COAT
The coat is short (the name is said to mean short-haired). The most common colors are plain red, black, blue, and cream.
The Chow Chow has a blue tongue and blue pigmentation.

Short-haired Chow Chow

CARE REQUIRED

The care of the Short-haired Chow Chow is much less than that of the longer-haired variety. Nevertheless, it must still be groomed regularly with thorough brushing, especially when it is shedding.

CHARACTER

This is an attentive dog with a mind of its own. These dogs are calm and independent, reasonably active, like to dominate other dogs, vigilant, brave, quite demanding of themselves and full of character.

TRAINING

The Short-haired Chow Chow calls for a handler who is calm and fair and exudes natural authority. Some experts claim this shorter-haired variety of Chow is more active and learns faster than its longer- haired family member.

SOCIAL BEHAVIOR

Most Chow Chows like to dominate other dogs but, in contrast, they are quite good with children. If they get to know cats and other household animals when they are young they will get along with them when they are adults. They tend to be reserved with strangers.

EXERCISE

This breed does not require a great deal of exercise but likes to be outdoors.
Find this dog a cool place to lie in summer where it can hide in the shade because it doesn't like hot weather.

Chow Chow

Head of a Chow Chow

Chow Chow (Long-haired)

COUNTRY OF ORIGIN
China.

SPECIAL SKILLS
The Chow Chow had various roles in the past, including hunting dog and a delicacy in Chinese cuisine. Today it is a vigilant family pet.

SIZE
The shoulder-height is 48 - 56cm (18¾ - 22in) for dogs and 46 - 51cm (18 - 20in) for bitches.

COAT
The coat consists of long erect hairs and the colors that are most common are plain red, black, blue, and cream. Chow Chows have a blue tongue and blue pigmentation.

CARE REQUIRED
The Chow Chow needs regular thorough brushing, especially in those places where tangles may form.

Get your dog used to this when it is young so that grooming doesn't become a battle when it is fully grown and stronger.

CHARACTER
This breed has a mind of its own but is calm and independent, vigilant, brave, demanding of itself, and full of character. It may try to dominate other dogs.

TRAINING
The owner of this breed of dog should be a calm person who is naturally fair and firm. With such a handler, the Chow Chow can develop well.

Eurasian

Don't expect great obedience from them – they are born stubborn and with minds of their own.

The dogs can learn because they are certainly not stupid but they must see the point of your command. Be consistent at all times.

SOCIAL BEHAVIOR
The majority of Chow Chows like to dominate but are usually good with children. They should get to know cats and other household animals when they are young to avoid jealousy problems when they are older. The Chow Chow is cautious with strangers.

EXERCISE
This dog does not need a great deal of exercise but does like to be outdoors. Make sure it has a cool place where it can rest in the summer as it does not like heat.

Eurasian

COUNTRY OF ORIGIN
Germany.

SPECIAL SKILLS
Family pet.

SIZE
The shoulder-height is 52 - 60cm (20½ - 23½in) for dogs and 48 - 56cm (18¾ - 22in) for bitches. The ideal height is 56cm (22in) for dogs and 52cm (20½in) for bitches.

The optimum weight for dogs is 26kg (57lb) and 22kg (48½lb) for bitches.

COAT
The outer coat is of medium-length stiff hair with a ruffled appearance.

The undercoat is thick and woolly. Every combination of colors is permitted except white, white patches, or liver.

CARE REQUIRED
Avoid regular grooming of the Eurasian as this might loosen too much of the woolly under-layer.

When the dog is shedding a comb with a double row of metal teeth should be used to remove dead and loose hairs.

Eurasian

Japanese Spitz

COUNTRY OF ORIGIN
Japan.

SPECIAL SKILLS
Family pet.

SIZE
The shoulder-height is 30cm (11¾in) for dogs and slightly less for bitches.

COAT
The long-haired coat, which has a thick under-layer, is always white.

CARE REQUIRED
Do not groom the Japanese Spitz with brush and comb too often as that will damage the under-coat. When the dog is shedding use a comb with a double row of metal teeth to remove loose hairs from the under-layer.

CHARACTER
This is a high-spirited, intelligent, and playful dog which is vigilant and obedient.

TRAINING
The Japanese Spitz is not difficult to train although the handler must always be consistent.

These dogs learn quickly and really enjoy learning agility skills and playing games of catch with balls or Frisbees.

SOCIAL BEHAVIOR
This dog is usually good with children. The majority of these dogs tend to be rather reserved

CHARACTER
This is a calm, equable dog which is alert and friendly. Although it can have a mind of its own it will be fairly obedient. It is intelligent, and very loyal to its family. The Eurasian does not bark much.

TRAINING
This breed is not difficult to train although the handler needs to be consistent. Eurasians are house pets and should not be made to live in a kennel.

SOCIAL BEHAVIOR
This breed gets on well with children but is reserved towards strangers.

Unlike many other breeds, these dogs usually get along well with other dogs. Get them used to other animals when they are still young.

EXERCISE
This breed needs fairly substantial amounts of exercise, at least a good hour a day of walking.

These dogs also love to run around and play off the leash.

towards strangers but they usually get along well with other dogs and other household pets.

EXERCISE
To keep the dog healthy in body and soul, take it for at least three good walks every day and let it regularly run and play off the leash.

Japanese Spitz

Shiba Inus

Shiba Inu

COUNTRY OF ORIGIN
Japan.

SPECIAL SKILLS
Hunting dog and family pet.

SIZE
The shoulder-height standard is 39.5cm (15½in) for dogs and 36.5cm (14¼in) for bitches. Variations of 1.5cm (½in) are permitted.

COAT
The Shiba Inu has a short straight-haired coat with a soft undercoat.

Red, red highlighted with white, white, black, black and tan, and salt and pepper are the most common colors.

CARE REQUIRED
The coat of the Shiba Inu does not require much attention. Remove dead hairs from time to time to keep the coat in good condition, using a coarse comb with a double row of metal teeth.

Shiba Inu

CHARACTER
This is a lively, pleasant dog which barks little and bonds closely with its handler while remaining independent. It is also curious, cheerful, and vigilant. Shiba Inu are naturally fastidious so it is easy to house-break these dogs.

TRAINING
The training of this dog is not much of a problem, provided you make allowance for it having a mind of its own and being naturally

independent. Vary the exercises with play so that the dog will enjoy itself.

SOCIAL BEHAVIOR
The Shiba Inu normally gets along well with other dogs and animals. It may be a bit reserved with strangers but children do not usually cause any problems.

EXERCISE
This undemanding dog will adapt to your circumstances but should it ever be necessary it can walk for hours on end as it has tremendous endurance.

Primitive Spitz breeds

Basenji

COUNTRY OF ORIGIN
Africa.

SPECIAL SKILLS
Hunting dog and companion.

SIZE
The ideal shoulder-height is 43cm (17in) for dogs and 40cm (15¾in) for bitches.

Head of a Basenji

COAT
The coat is short-haired, dense and fine. Basenjis are usually red with white, but black with white, and black with tan and white are also permitted.

Not every country accepts those dogs having blends of colors with highlights.

CARE REQUIRED
Groom occasionally with a coarse rubber brush or with a rubber glove. These dogs naturally keep themselves very clean.

CHARACTER
This remarkable breed acts in many ways like a cat.
They clean themselves by licking their coat and do not bark instead making a sound that some say is like a yodel. They are independent dogs with minds of their own yet bond very closely with their handler and family and need to be in their company. The majority detest rain and hate the cold.

TRAINING
Basenjis are independent and headstrong dogs which are extremely difficult to train. A great deal is demanded of the trainer including considerable cunning to get this breed to listen and respond combined with the odd corrective measure.

Pharaoh Hound

COUNTRY OF ORIGIN
Malta.

SPECIAL SKILLS
Hunting dog (by sight, hearing, and scent), and family pet.

SIZE
The ideal shoulder-height is 56cm (22in) for dogs and 53cm (20¾in) for bitches.

COAT
These dogs have a short, shiny coat in colors ranging from light to dark reddish-brown. A white tip to the tail is a desirable feature, and white markings on the chest, feet, as well as a small white blaze are all permissible.

CARE REQUIRED
The Pharaoh Hound needs little grooming. It is

Keep in mind if you decide to keep a Basenji that it is unrealistic to try to make it into the ideal obedient dog. If you succeeded, you would destroy the dog's very special character.

SOCIAL BEHAVIOR
To a degree these dogs can be trusted with children, provided the children do not invade the dog's own domain, but they can never be considered real playmates for children. They are naturally reserved towards strangers and have a natural instinct to protect their handler.

Contact with other dogs is not usually a problem. Do not forget that the origin of the Basenji is as a hunting dog for wild game so get them to know cats and other animals when they are young and teach them that these animals are not to be hunted.

EXERCISE
This breed will adapt to the circumstances so that it can live in an apartment, provided it is taken out for regular walks.

SPECIAL REMARKS
The bitches of this breed normally come into season only once a year.

Pharaoh Hound

only necessary to remove dead and loose hairs with a rubber brush.

CHARACTER

This is a reasonably independent dog which is playful, brave, calm, not intrusive, affectionate, and loyal to its handler and family. It is also peaceful in the house, friendly, intelligent, and reasonably obedient.

The Pharaoh Hound has considerable stamina and deeply rooted hunting instincts.

TRAINING

Training should not be too difficult. The handler needs to understand the dog's character and to be consistent in approach.

SOCIAL BEHAVIOR

Dogs of this breed can be rather dominant towards other males. They tend to get on with children but treat strangers with reserve.

Cats and other animals will be regarded as prey by these dogs, although with the right approach and very early social training they can be taught to live with the household cat.

EXERCISE

The Pharaoh Hound needs lots of exercise. Try to set aside an hour each day to bicycle while the dog runs alongside you. These dogs can run away from you, however, if they spy or scent wild game because they never lose their instinct to hunt alone. To prevent this, you will need a sound high fence around your yard. They can jump very high to get out of a space.

SPECIAL REMARKS

The Pharaoh Hound is often considered to be a bit of a Greyhound because it hunts by sight, sound, and scent.

Primitive Spitz-type hunting breeds

Cirneco dell' Etna

COUNTRY OF ORIGIN
Sicily.

SPECIAL SKILLS
Hunting dog and family pet.

SIZE
Dogs 46-50cm (18 -19in), bitches 16 to 19in.

COAT

This Sicilian dog has a short-haired coat. All shades of red are permissible and one white marking is accepted, although this is fairly rare.

CARE REQUIRED

This breed's coat does not require much attention.
The shine on the coat can be kept in good condition by occasionally running a rubber glove over it. Check at frequent intervals that the ear passages are clean and keep the claws short.

CHARACTER

This is a friendly, affectionate, active dog which is intelligent and very loyal to its handler and the family and is also vigilant.

Most of these dogs like to bark and tend to demand plenty of attention.

TRAINING

The Cirneco dell' Etna is a relatively easy dog to train but the handler needs to be very consistent.

SOCIAL BEHAVIOR

This breed tends to be rather reserved with other dogs but generally gets on with its own breed. There will be no problems with your own cat but it will chase any strange cats.

These dogs are loving and patient with children. They will bark at strangers but that is all.

Head of a Cirneco dell' Etna

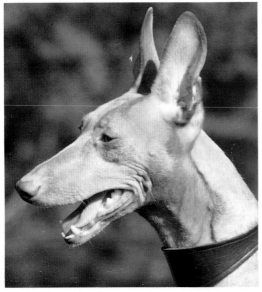

EXERCISE

Because this breed needs lots of exercise it is necessary to set aside an hour every day for this purpose.

Running alongside a bicycle or actual hunting if there is hunting in your area are ideal forms of exercise for them.

SPECIAL REMARKS

The Cirneco del' Etna is considered a bit of a Greyhound, because it hunts by sight and sound as well as by nose.

Don't let these dogs run free off the leash unless you are absolutely certain there is no wild game nearby or their hunting instincts will come into action and the dog will run away.

These dogs can jump extremely high so your yard needs a good high fence. They like to be near you and are definitely house dogs, unsuitable for kennel life.

Ibizan Hound

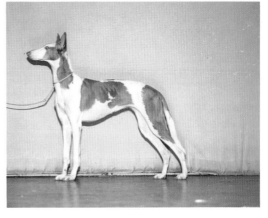

Ibizan Hound

COUNTRY OF ORIGIN

The Balearic Islands.

SPECIAL SKILLS

Hunting dog (by sight, sound, and scent), and family pet.

SIZE

The shoulder-height is 66 - 72cm (26 - 28½in) for dogs and 60 - 67cm (23½ - 26¼in) for bitches.

COAT

The Ibizan Hound comes in short-haired, long-haired, and rough-haired varieties. The most usual is the short-haired; the long-haired is very rare.

The rough-haired has a longer coat of rough hair that is softer textured than the other two varieties. Predominant colors are various shades of red, white, or a combination of them.

CARE REQUIRED

The short-haired version can be groomed occasionally with a rubber brush. The rough versions do not need hand-plucking and can also be groomed by an occasional brushing.

CHARACTER

This is a calm and affectionate dog which is very loyal to its family, and reasonably independent, vigilant, alert, intelligent, and keen to learn.

It is also fairly obedient, has tremendous stamina, is energetic, and brave. The Ibezan Hound has a strongly developed hunting instinct.

TRAINING

This breed likes to learn and does so quickly. Provided they have been properly trained, they can participate in many types of dog sports. These dogs are very sensitive to the voice of their handler and a friendly request will always achieve more than a gruff command.

SOCIAL BEHAVIOR

These dogs get on well with children but hold back watchfully with strangers. Once they decide the stranger means no harm, they will relax very quickly.

The dogs of this breed can be rather dominant towards other males. If they were introduced to your cat when they were young, there will be no problems.

EXERCISE

Despite the enormous ability to adapt of this breed – it can even be kept in an apartment – it still needs a great deal of exercise. These dogs enjoy running alongside your bicycle but don't do this until your dog is fully grown as it can harm a young puppy.

Keep in mind that these are basically hunting dogs and fence your yard with a fence of at least 2m (6ft 8in) as they can climb fences to escape if they want to go on the chase. These dogs will greatly enjoy retrieving for you.

SPECIAL REMARKS

Given their character, these dogs do not belong in a kennel.
They are considered half Greyhound because they hunt by sight, scent, and sound.

Thai Ridgeback Dog

Thai Ridgeback Dog

COUNTRY OF ORIGIN
Thailand.

SPECIAL SKILLS
Hunting dog and watchdog.

SIZE
The shoulder-height is 53 - 61cm (20¾ - 24in) for dogs and 48 - 56cm (18¾ - 22in) for bitches.

COAT
The coat is very short and soft, with a definite ridge of hair along the back (the pile of this hair grows in the opposite direction to the rest of the hair).
They can be blue, silver, chestnut, or black.

CARE REQUIRED
This Ridgeback requires little grooming. Brushing occasionally will keep the coat in good condition.

CHARACTER
This is a vigilant, intelligent dog which has a mind of its own, with considerable stamina, that is lively and active, but reserved in the company of strangers.

TRAINING
The training of the Thai Ridgeback calls for a gentle but very consistent approach.

SOCIAL BEHAVIOR
The company of other household animals does not cause any problems provided the dog grows up with them. These dogs are rather reserved towards strangers.

EXERCISE
This Thai breed needs quite a lot of exercise. Running alongside a bicycle or regular long walks are certainly necessary to keep the dog fit.

They have been known to complete various training courses successfully.

SPECIAL REMARKS
The Thai Ridgeback Dog is quite rare outside Thailand.

Thai Ridgeback Dog

6. Hounds

Hounds

Basset Artésien Normand

COUNTRY OF ORIGIN
France.

SPECIAL SKILLS
Hound and family pet.

SIZE
The shoulder-height is 30 - 36cm (11¼in) for both dogs and bitches.

COAT
The short-haired coat is dense. Only tri-colored examples or ones with a white and orange coat are permitted. White feet are preferred.

CARE REQUIRED
Run a rubber brush over the dog occasionally to remove loose hairs. Keep the ears clean using a recognized brand of ear cleaner for this purpose – never cotton swabs, which will push any dirt and wax further into the ear. Keep the claws short by filing them whenever necessary.

CHARACTER
This is a sociable, companionable, and friendly dog which is gentle, independent, and possesses a good scenting nose.

The Basset Artésian Normand has a deep bark which it lets be heard from time to time. This is usually not a problem if the dog is kept indoors.

TRAINING
This is a sociable, companionable, and friendly dog which is gentle, independent, and possesses a good scenting nose. The Basset Artésian Normand has a deep bark which it lets be heard from time to time. This is usually not a problem if the dog is kept indoors.

SOCIAL BEHAVIOR
In France these dogs live in packs so, obviously, they can get along happily with other dogs. If they get to know cats and other animals when they are young they will get along with them, too.

Petit Bleu de Gascogne

Basset Artésian Normand

Bassets Artésian Normand

Although these dogs will bark loudly when visitors arrive, they will still receive a warm welcome.

EXERCISE
Take this Basset regularly for longish walks but remember that this is a dog which will run away if it comes across the scent of wild animals when it is off the leash. If this happens, put a piece of your clothing or another item with your scent on it where the dog disappeared. The odds are that you will find it at this spot within a few hours or not later than the next morning.

Petit Bleu de Gascogne

Petit Bleu de Gascogne

COUNTRY OF ORIGIN
France.

SPECIAL SKILLS
Hound and family pet.

SIZE
The shoulder-height is 34 - 40cm
(13½ - 15¾in).

COAT
The short-haired and very dense coat has a white
ground speckled with black, and with black
patches, or a large black area with tan markings.

CARE REQUIRED
These dogs do not require much grooming.
Groom them occasionally with a rubber brush to
remove loose hairs.

The ears, however, must be carefully looked
after. Check regularly that they are clean and use
a special ear cleaner. Keep the claws short by
filing them.

Bassets Bleu de Gascogne

CHARACTER
These are friendly, sociable dogs with a sense of
humor that are gentle, independent, and have a
good scenting nose.

The Basset Bleu de Gascogne has a loud bark
which is music to people who like hunting. This
is rather less valued in a household pet, but
fortunately it does not usually become a real
problem. They welcome both welcome and
unwelcome visitors.

TRAINING
This dog is born with a mind of its own, but that
does not mean they cannot be trained.

If the dog's training is not pushed too quickly
and you take its character into account, this
French dog can become a fine companion in the
home.

SOCIAL BEHAVIOR
Since these dogs live in packs in France they can,
obviously, get along with other dogs. Children
and visitors will also present no problems. Let
them get used to cats and other animals when
young so that they will share their company
without difficulty when they are older.

EXERCISE
Take this dog for regular long walks but beware:
once they catch a hint of wild game, they will run
off after it and pay no attention to your calls.

Basset Fauve de Bretagne

COUNTRY OF ORIGIN
France.

SPECIAL SKILLS
Hound for hunting wild game, and a family
pet.

SIZE
The shoulder-height is 32 - 38cm (12½ - 15in)
with a variation of 2cm (¾in) taller or shorter
permitted.

COAT
The coat consists of short hard dense hairs.
Golden or darker shades of pink are most
common. Small white patches are considered a
fault.

CARE REQUIRED
Remove excess hair in the ear passage and keep
the claws short. Comb the hair regularly and

have it plucked professionally about twice a year (depending upon the condition of the coat) or pluck it yourself. The coat must never be trimmed.

CHARACTER
This is a cheerful dog with something of a mind of its own. It is intelligent, friendly, brave, and active with a good scenting nose.

TRAINING
The Basset Fauve de Bretagne is a hound through and through. To prevent it from using its skills during a walk in the woods and running away as a result, teach it at a young age that it must come to you on command.

SOCIAL BEHAVIOR
This dog gets along well with children and other dogs and animals.

In common with most other dogs, it needs to be introduced when young to cats and other household pets.

EXERCISE
The dogs of this breed have an average need for exercise. Let them romp and play regularly. In countries like France, they are kept in packs to hunt rabbits.

Basset Fauve de Bretagne

Basset Griffon Vendéen (Grand and Petit)

COUNTRY OF ORIGIN
France.

SPECIAL SKILLS
Hound (pack hound for hunting wild game) and family pet.

Small (Petit) Basset Griffon Vendéen

Small (Petit) Basset Griffon Vendéen puppy

SIZE
The shoulder-height of the smaller or Petit Basset Griffon is 34 - 38cm (13½ - 15in) and 38 - 42cm (15 - 16½in) for the larger or Grand Basset Griffon.

COAT
The rough-haired coat is hard, not very long, and has a somewhat unkempt look. These dogs are either single-colored, two-colored, or tri-colored.

The single color is grey-white or tawny; the two-colored are white with either grey, red, orange, or black patches; and the combination of three colors are either white-black-red, or white or tawny grey with a greyish white and red. Single-colored drab red is considered undesirable.

CARE REQUIRED
The coat requires regular grooming with brush and comb. Keep the ears, and especially the ear passages, clean. File claws that become too long and clip any hair that becomes too long between

the pads of the feet to prevent tangles. About once a year pluck the loose and dead hair out by hand.

If you wish to show the dog, the neck should be emphasized by removing more hair from this area.

The breed standard requires the Petit Bassett Griffin to have small ears and a tail which is accentuated by clipping excessive hair.

CHARACTER
These are high-spirited, lively, sociable, clever, loving, and sensitive dogs.
They have minds of their own but are quite straightforward.

TRAINING
As these dogs are quite independent there is no point in hoping to turn one of them into a perfectly obedient dog. With the right approach, however, and with patience it is possible to train these dogs to a certain extent.

SOCIAL BEHAVIOR
Dogs, pets, children, and visitors are all accepted without problem – this dog seems to like to have lots of people and animals around.

EXERCISE
Because these hounds need substantial amounts of exercise, it is necessary to take them for long walks regularly.

In France they hunt in packs. The larger Grand Bassett Griffon is used to hunt for hares and roe deer, while the smaller Petit is used for rabbit hunts. They usually adapt well to becoming family pets.

Grand Bassets Griffon Vendéen

Basset Hound

COUNTRY OF ORIGIN
England.

SPECIAL SKILLS
Hound and family pet.

SIZE
The shoulder-height is 33 - 38cm (13 - 15in). They are heavy dogs for their size.

COAT
Bassets have a dense smooth short-haired. The most usual color combination is brown, black, and white.

Other colors include red and white but almost any hound-coloring is permissible.

CARE REQUIRED
There is little to the grooming of a Basset Hound. Remove dead and loose hairs when the dog is shedding with a rubber glove. Keep the ears clean by attending to them about once a week, inside and out.

Keep the claws short and when necessary clean the folds of skin. Do not give Bassets too many snacks as they have a tendency to become fat which is bad for them. Dogs with drooping eye-lids should be given eye-drops, prescribed by the veterinarian, occasionally. These dogs grow very rapidly when young and you must be sure they have a good nutritious and ample diet during this period.

CHARACTER
The Basset Hound has a mind of its own but is lovable, sociable, calm, playful, and patient. It enjoys companionship, has a sense of humor and a real personality which can be influenced positively by its handler. They have a very good scenting nose.

TRAINING
These dogs tend to be quite independent so don't expect them to jump to your command. A consistent approach with much patience can work wonders, though.

Never wear out a young Basset by taking it on too long a walk. Young dogs need all their energy to develop a strong body.

SOCIAL BEHAVIOR
These dogs make superb playmates for children and fortunately get along fine with their own kind and with other animals. They are friendly towards strangers but if they sense danger they will bark loudly. They do not like to be left alone. If you know that it will be necessary to leave your dog alone quite often, get two Basset Hounds so they will have each other for company.

EXERCISE
This breed does not require much exercise and will be quite content with three trots around the block each day provided they can also play in the yard.
Make sure your yard is adequately fenced because these dogs love to explore.

Basset Hound bitch

Beagle

COUNTRY OF ORIGIN
England.

SPECIAL SKILLS
Hound and family pet.

SIZE
The shoulder-height is 33 - 41cm (13 - 16¼in) and the dog weighs about 15kg (33lb).

COAT
The coat is short and weather-protective. The three toned Beagle is the most usual – that is a white ground, a brown head and back, with a black saddle, but any recognized hound colorings are permissible. Liver-colored Beagles are not acceptable.

CARE REQUIRED
Brush the coat daily to remove dead and loose hairs.
In common with other breeds with hanging ears, the ears should be regularly checked to ensure they are clean.

CHARACTER
This is a lively, cheerful, sociable, brave, and intelligent dog with a mind of its own, that is resolute, and vigilant. They have the tendency to follow their nose.

TRAINING
The Beagle is both an independent hunting dog and also a highly suitable pet for your home.

Take your Beagle to an obedience class so it can learn what is expected of it.

SOCIAL BEHAVIOR
Beagles normally tend to get on well with other dogs and children but even strangers will get a friendly greeting. Get them used to cats and other household animals when they are young to avoid possible problems later.

EXERCISE
This breed needs quite a bit of exercise. A well-fenced yard will prevent your Beagle from running away.

Take it for long walks regularly but do not allow it to trot around freely off the leash until you are certain that you have the dog well under control or you run the risk of it disappearing in search of wild game.

SPECIAL REMARKS
For sporty people this is an ideal family pet but it is not suitable for life in an apartment. These dogs like to be outdoors and can happily live in an outdoor kennel with other dogs.

Bloodhound

COUNTRY OF ORIGIN
Belgium.

SPECIAL SKILLS
Hound or tracking dog, and family pet.

SIZE
The shoulder-height is 63 - 69cm (24¾ - 27¼in) for dogs and 58 - 63cm (22¾ - 24¾in) for bitches.

COAT
The Bloodhound has a short smooth coat. The most usual colors are black and red, liver and

red, and plain red. A small amount of white on the chest, feet, and tip of the tail is permissible.

CARE REQUIRED
There is little to the grooming of a Bloodhound. Brush them from time to time to remove loose and dead hairs.

More attention is necessary for the ears. Check them for dirt to prevent infections and wash them occasionally (for example after the dog's ears have dropped into its dinner).

The majority of dogs of this breed have drooping eye-lids. If necessary administer eye-drops containing vitamin A.

CHARACTER
The dogs of this breed are gentle and affectionate, boisterous when young, friendly, tenacious, and independent. They have a very loud bark but will bark no longer than necessary and they possess a very good scenting nose. Once their interest is aroused by something, it is very difficult to get their attention to anything else.

Bloodhound

Bloodhound

TRAINING
The new owner of a Bloodhound will need to have plenty of patience and to possess great tact for training to succeed. The most important consideration is to be consistent – these dogs know full well how successfully they can get around you with a pathetic look and make use of it to get their own way.

Do not expect too much by way of obedience from this dog – they are naturally gentle animals but they do have minds of their own and will often make their own decisions rather than following your orders. Do not overtire them with long walks until they are fully grown. The Bloodhound is a big dog that grows rapidly and needs all its energy for developing strong bones, joints and muscles.

SOCIAL BEHAVIOR
The Bloodhound usually gets on well with children. Make sure they do not pester the dog. These dogs are so good-natured that they will lie there and meekly let children clamber all over it which isn't fair to the dog. Both wanted and unwanted visitors will be greeted happily because this dog seems to love company. They can live in harmony with other dogs and household pets.

EXERCISE
This breed has a phenomenal level of stamina and can walk for hours on end. If you have one as a pet, you will have to do a fair bit of hiking quite regularly.
As is well-known, they are primarily tracking dogs which means when they encounter an interesting scent they will want to find its source. Make sure that your yard is well fenced. Consider hunting with this hound or having it trained as a search dog. They are resistant to cold and can be kept in a kennel provided they get sufficient exercise and attention.

Long-legged French Bassets

Short-legged hounds such as the Basset Bleu de Gascogne, the Basset Fauve de Bretagne, and the Bassets Griffon Vendéen make ideal household pets and are kept as such in many countries.

The long-legged French Bassets are, in contrast, almost always kept in kennels in packs for hunting. In this category are included breeds such as the Poitevin, Billy (Grand), Anglo

Petit Bleu de Gascogne

in their presence. Because they hunt together without orders from their owner, they have developed as very independent dogs which are brave and very sociable.
This group of dogs is rarely seen outside of France.

Because of their loud voices (which they like to use), these are less suitable dogs for keeping in a home as a pet than the short-legged Bassets or the French Pointing Bassets.

An exception to this is the Petit Bleu de Gascogne, which with the right training can make a reasonably good family pet.

Porcelaine

Anglo Français de Petite Vénerie

Porcelaine

Français de Petit Vénerie, Briquet Griffon Vendéen, long-legged Griffons, Petit and Grand Blue de Gascogne, and Porcelaine.

All these breeds hunt large wild game in packs, letting the hunters know where the quarry is by their loud cries. Such dogs have deeply rooted hunting instincts and a good nose.

It is obvious that these dogs, which live in packs, are able to get on with other dogs, but they are also friendly to children, if somewhat boisterous

Jura Hound

Swiss hunting dogs

This category includes dogs such as the Niederlaufhund and the Laufhund. There are eight types in all: the Berner, the Luzerner, Schweizer, and Jura Niederlaufhunds; and the same group of Laufhunds. The Jura is often called the Jura Hound.

Head of a Jura Hound

The difference between the two groups is their size. In every other respect, they are identical. The Niederlaufhunds have a shoulder-height of 33 - 41cm (13 - 16¼in) with an ideal height of 36 - 38cm (14¼ - ⅛in). The Laufhunds have a shoulder-height greater than 40cm (15¾in). In addition, they have different colors: the Berner is white with black, the Jura is either light brown or brown with a black saddle, the Luzerner is blue or mottled grey, and the Schweizer is white or yellowish-brown.

These Swiss hounds are specially bred as pack dogs for hunting wild game. When they find the trace of a wild animal, they give chase, baying as they go so that the hunters know where they are. Generally speaking such dogs make fine household pets provided you involve them in some activity, such as drag-hunting or other activity which fulfills their natural instincts. In Switzerland the Jura and Luzerner Hounds are often kept as single dogs for such activities. All of the dogs in these breeds like the company of other dogs and can be unhappy if they are without companions.

Deutsche Bracke

Deutsche Bracke or Steinbracke

COUNTRY OF ORIGIN
Germany.

SPECIAL SKILLS
Hunting and family pet.

SIZE
The shoulder-height is 40 - 53cm (15¾ - 20¾in).

COAT
The smooth-coat is hard to the touch. The colors usually range from red to yellow with a black

saddle, or a black mantle with a white blaze, collar, and chest and more white markings on the feet and tip of the tail. The undercoat is light-colored. A flesh-colored patch on the nose is considered important.

CARE REQUIRED
The Deutsche Bracke does not require much grooming. Run a rubber brush over the coat occasionally to remove dead and loose hairs. Check the ear passages regularly to ensure they are clean and remember that this breed is supposed to have fairly long claws.

CHARACTER
This is a friendly, sociable, affectionate, sensitive, shy, yet curious dog which has great reserves of stamina. It is reasonably obedient although independent-minded and vigilant.

These dogs have a good scenting nose and make excellent hunting dogs.

TRAINING
Training this breed is not too difficult. They grasp quickly what is required of them so don't go over and over the same material as it will annoy them. With patience, love, and under-standing, plus a consistent approach, the handler can achieve a lot.

Pair of Deutsche Brackes

SOCIAL BEHAVIOR
These are sociable dogs which will rarely cause any problems in the company of other dogs. They are also fine with children.

These dogs always will warn you of any strangers. Introduce them when young to cats and other household animals. They hold their ground with strangers.

EXERCISE
The breed is ideally suited for hunting hares, rabbits, and foxes. Most of them like to swim. If you do not intend to hunt with them, make sure you find some other means of fulfilling their exercise needs. In common with other hounds, they are likely to forget everything they learned in their training lessons in the interest of chasing an exciting scent, so do not let them run around off the leash.

Otterhounds

Otterhounds

COUNTRY OF ORIGIN
Great Britain.

SPECIAL SKILLS
Hound and family pet.

SIZE
The shoulder-height is about 67cm (26¼in) for dogs and 63cm (24¾in) for bitches.

COAT

The coat is rough and weather-resistant. All recognized hound colors are permitted, including plain grey, blue, red, wheaten, sandy, black and tan, and blue and tan.

CARE REQUIRED

The Otterhound must not be clipped because it is supposed to look natural; therefore, brush it as little as possible.

CHARACTER

These dogs are friendly, cheerful, boisterous, intelligent, independent, affectionate, equable, but have a mind of their own. They are calm dogs indoors if they have had sufficient exercise.

TRAINING

The Otterhound is not exactly the most obedient dog you could wish for but that does not prevent you from being able to succeed with basic training.

The best results are achieved with a soft but consistent hand.

Use the classic "iron fist in a velvet glove" approach when training these dogs. They have a good scenting nose and are ideally suited to drag-hunting or searching.

SOCIAL BEHAVIOR

The Otterhound is a friend to all – other dogs, the family pets, children, and people in general.

EXERCISE

They need plenty of exercise, but because they have a tendency to forget everything in the chase after an exciting scent, you should only allow them to run free off the leash where they can be controlled and it is safe. Make sure your yard is well fenced.

SPECIAL REMARKS

Otterhounds can be kept indoors or outside in a kennel.

Dalmatian

COUNTRY OF ORIGIN
Croatia.

SPECIAL SKILLS
Family pets. Dalmatians used to be bred as carriage dogs as they were highly decorative when running ahead of a coach. They also acted as watchdogs in the stables.

SIZE
The shoulder-height is 56 - 61cm (22 - 24in) for dogs and 54 - 59cm (21¼ - 23¼in) for bitches.

COAT
The coat is always short. The most attractive coat does not have the spots overlapping each other. The ideal size for the spots is a diameter of 2 - 3cm (¾ - 1¼in). There are white with black-spotted Dalmatians and those with liver-colored spots.

CARE REQUIRED
The Dalmatian sheds very little hair in your home. Remove loose hairs daily by grooming with a rubber glove during when the dog is shedding.

CHARACTER
This is a high-spirited dog with lots of stamina that is friendly, affectionate, intelligent, vigilant, curious, equable, and sociable.

TRAINING
This is not a difficult dog to train. Praise excessively when it does something well and it will quickly understand your intentions. These dogs can turn a deaf ear to commands they do not like. In such cases hold your ground and don't give in.

Dalmatian

SOCIAL BEHAVIOR
These are excellent playmates for children, although they can be too boisterous for smaller children. With other dogs and household pets, there is also generally no difficulty. With visitors, they either act very vigilantly or rather half-heartedly, depending on the character of the individual dog.

EXERCISE
The Dalmatian will adapt to your family circumstances but you do it an injustice if you limit this dog to three little outings per day. Running alongside a bicycle, swimming, playing, and running free through woods and in open countryside will all be good for this dog. Avoid over-exercising before the dog is fully grown.

SPECIAL REMARKS
It is extremely difficult to breed good show dogs. Dalmatians are born white and acquire their spots later. Some puppies are born deaf and it is really advisable to get your puppy from a really reliable breeder.

Dalmatian puppy

7. Pointers

Continental European Pointers

Bracco Italiano

COUNTRY OF ORIGIN
Italy.

SPECIAL SKILLS
Field sports dog and family pet.

SIZE
The shoulder-height is 58 - 67cm
(22¾ - 26¼in) for dogs and 55 - 62cm
(21½ - 24½in) for bitches.

COAT
The Bracco Italiano has a coat of short, dense, and shiny hair. Permitted colors are white; white with large or small patches of orange, amber, or chestnut; and white with light orange or chestnut-brown mottling.

CARE REQUIRED
The coat of this dog does not require much attention. When the dog is shedding you can remove dead and loose hairs by grooming with a rubber brush. Keep its ear passages clean.

CHARACTER
This is an equable and compliant dog which is intelligent, has a sense of humor, is thoughtful, gentle, calm in the house, affectionate, and sensitive.

These dogs are not fully mature mentally until they are two and a half to three years old. They are used as all-round field sports dogs for game birds.

TRAINING
They need to be trained with a consistent but gentle approach. They are very sensitive to and react strongly to the sound of your voice. Praise them if they do well. When trained in the right way, they pick things up quickly.
Too tough an approach has an adverse effect which will achieve nothing except to lose the dog's respect for you. Avoid over-taxing them physically during early growth and limit their going up and down stairs and steps as this can be harmful.

Drentse Patrijshond

Bracco Italiano

Bracco Italiano

SOCIAL BEHAVIOR
Bracco Italianos get along well with other dogs and do not usually cause any difficulties with other household animals. They become close friends with children.

They will always go into action at the hint of danger.

EXERCISE
It is important for this breed to get sufficient exercise. These dogs are best living with a family which has a large yard – they are definitely not dogs for apartment living. They love to swim and retrieve and once they are physically mature (at about ½ years), they can begin controlled exercise running alongside a bicycle. As hunting dogs, they are considered sound workers with an outstanding scenting ability.

Cesky Fousek

COUNTRY OF ORIGIN
Czech Republic and Slovakia.

SPECIAL SKILLS
Field sports dog and family pet.

SIZE
The shoulder-height is 60 - 66cm (23½ - 26in) for dogs and 58 - 62cm (22¾ - 24½in) for bitches.

COAT
The coat is rough and the most usual color is a brown (with or without patches), but plain brown with a white chest is also possible.

CARE REQUIRED
The condition of the coat determines how often the Cesky Fousek needs to have its hair hand-plucked: never, once a year, or more often. The beard, moustache, and eyebrows are left alone during this process.

Between plucking sessions, brush the coat occasionally and clip any excess hair between the pads of the feet. Check for any hair growth in the ear passages and remove it.

CHARACTER
This is a friendly, intelligent, and gentle-natured dog which is affectionate, tractable, obedient, and vigilant. Indoors they are calm; outdoors they are very active and tough on themselves. The Cesky Fousek is an all-round field sports dog but is a specialist pointer (they stand unmoving facing their prey as the wind carries the scent of wild game to them).

TRAINING
Because they are quick and eager pupils, the training of this breed is not particularly difficult.

Make sure, though, that there is plenty of variety because when they are made to do the same thing over and over they will protest.

SOCIAL BEHAVIOR
Cesky Fouseks get on fine with other dogs and other household animals, although their hunting instincts can cause problems with cats, for example.

They are fine with children provided they are not pestered by them.

EXERCISE
These through-and-through hunting dogs need lots of exercise to get rid of their energy. If you are unable to hunt with the dog or do not wish to do so, then it is essential to let them trot alongside a bicycle regularly and to let them run and play off the leash.
This will keep the dog mentally as well as physically fit.

Drentse Patrijshond

Drentse Patrijshond

COUNTRY OF ORIGIN
The Netherlands.

SPECIAL SKILLS
Field sports dog and family pet.

SIZE
The shoulder-height is 55 - 63cm
(21½ - 24¾in). Provided the dog is attractive and well-proportioned in its build, a variance of 1cm (½in) taller or shorter will be accepted.

COAT
The Drentse Patrijshond has a dense coat of medium-length hair. Colors are white with

brown or orange patches, which can include tan markings or mottling. A brown mantle is permissible but not preferred.

CARE REQUIRED
Brush these dogs once per week and, using a special "German Shepherd" comb, give particular attention to the parts of the coat with longer hairs. The ear passages need checking from time to time to ensure they are clean and excess hair between the pads of the feet should be trimmed.

CHARACTER
These are attentive, intelligent, curious, and vigilant dogs, which are affectionate, gentle, obedient, and equable. They do not take well to life in a kennel. They normally bark only when they sense danger.

TRAINING
Train these dogs with a consistent but gentle hand. The Drentse Patrijshond makes an easy pupil because it quickly grasps what is expected of it.

SOCIAL BEHAVIOR
This breed gets on extremely well with children and does not cause any problems with other dogs or household animals. They are vigilant but not badly behaved towards strangers.

EXERCISE
For their size, these dogs do not need a great deal of exercise. Let them swim or run beside a bicycle. They enjoy playing games in which they retrieve things and going for long walks.

If a week passes when you have less time for such activities, they will not misbehave, provided they feel part of the family.

Drentse Patrijshonds

Wire-haired German Pointer

German Pointer (Wire-haired)

COUNTRY OF ORIGIN
Germany.

SPECIAL SKILLS
Field sports dog and family pet.

SIZE
The shoulder-height is 60 - 67cm (23½ - 26¼in) for dogs and 56 - 62cm (22 - 24½in) for bitches.

COAT
The rough, wire-haired coat is close and dense, as is the undercoat. The colors are brown, brown with or without white, and white with a brown head and brown markings. A black is also permissible.

CARE REQUIRED
The hairs of the coat should be as hard as possible but must not look untidy. The hairs should be hand-plucked occasionally depending on the condition of the coat. Between such plucking sessions, brush thoroughly about once per week. This is a good chance to check the ear passages to make sure they are clean.

CHARACTER
This is an affectionate, active, and intelligent dog which is loyal to its own family, and is eager to learn, equable, vigilant. It has a good nose for a scent and can try to dominate other animals.

TRAINING
Wire-haired German Pointers learn quickly, though they need a handler who is consistent in approach.

In common with the short-haired variety, they like to be occupied and enjoy working for their handler. They are outstanding all-round field sports dogs. The Wire-haired is more likely to try to dominate than the Short-haired type.

SOCIAL BEHAVIOR
This breed usually gets along well with other dogs and household animals. They are normally patient with children.

They are friendly with those they know but, when necessary, they can perform watchdog functions.

EXERCISE
The Wire-haired German Pointer is best-suited to a sporty family. This is a dog that needs plenty of exercise and three walks around the block are completely inadequate. Most of these dogs love swimming and retrieving. When they get enough exercise they are calm indoors.

Short-haired German Pointer

German Pointer (Short-haired)

COUNTRY OF ORIGIN
Germany.

SPECIAL SKILLS
Field sports dog and family pet.

SIZE
The shoulder-height is 62 - 66cm (24½ - 26in) for dogs and 58 - 63cm (22¾ - 24¼in) for bitches.

COAT
The short-haired coat is recognized in brown (with and without white markings), dark brown, light brown, and white with brown markings on the head or with brown patches or spots.
There are also black coats with the same

combinations of markings as the brown varieties. Yellow markings are also permissible.

CARE REQUIRED
This breed does not need much attention to its coat – an occasional brushing will keep the hair in good condition. Check from time to time to ensure that the ears are clean.

CHARACTER
These dogs are tractable, intelligent and eager to learn. They are loyal and active, brave with a friendly, playful disposition. They also have a good scenting nose.

TRAINING
Because they are intelligent and eager to learn, Short-haired German Pointers are not difficult to train if their handler is consistent in approach. They like to be busy and enjoy working for their handler. They are outstanding all-round field sports dogs.

SOCIAL BEHAVIOR
German Pointers generally get on well with their own kind, other animals, and with children. Although they tend to be friendly with everyone, they can also play a role as a watchdog.

EXERCISE
The Short-haired German Pointer is best-suited to a sporty family. Remember that this is a hunting dog that likes to be kept busy and it cannot and will not adapt to an easy-going life.

Head of a Long-haired German Pointer

Most of these dogs enjoy swimming and retrieving. If you are unable to hunt with the dog, you will need to take it for regular long walks and give it the chance to run and play off the leash. When these dogs get enough exercise to keep them busy, they will be calm when indoors.

Long-haired German Pointer

German Pointer (Long-haired)

COUNTRY OF ORIGIN
Germany.

SPECIAL SKILLS
Field sports dog and family pet.

SIZE
The shoulder-height is 63 - 66cm (24¾- 26in) for dogs and 60 - 63cm (23½ - 24¾in) for bitches.

COAT
The long-haired coat can be plain brown, but also brown with a white band or white with a brown head and brown markings are acceptable.

CARE REQUIRED
This breed does not need much attention to its coat. Brush the hair regularly and trim any excess hair between the pads of the feet.

Long-haired German Pointer

Occasionally it is necessary to pluck old (brown) hair. It is simple to recognize what hair to pluck as it will be lighter than the rest of the coat.

CHARACTER
These dogs are affectionate, lively, loyal to their family, gentle and equable, intelligent and eager to learn, and have a good scenting nose.

TRAINING
These dogs can learn and want to, making their training much easier. This makes them an ideal choice for those without much experience with dogs. They are outstanding all-round field sports dogs.

SOCIAL BEHAVIOR
This German Pointer is very sociable and gets on well with dogs and other animals. Most of them are very loving with children.

EXERCISE
This breed is first and foremost a hunting dog which likes to swim and search.

There is no greater pleasure you can give this dog than to take it on a hike through the countryside. They belong with a sporty family which likes to be outdoors.

When the Long-haired German Pointer gets sufficient exercise, it is quite calm when indoors.

SPECIAL REMARKS
The Long-haired German Pointer is highly regarded by field sports people who find it a very reliable working dog.
This dog also makes a first-class family pet provided it is kept active and gets enough exercise.

Epagneul Bleu de Picardie

COUNTRY OF ORIGIN
France.

SPECIAL SKILLS
Formerly mainly a field sports dog, today a family pet.

SIZE
The shoulder-height is 57 - 60cm (22½ - 23½in) for dogs and slightly less for bitches.

COAT
The medium-length hair forms a smooth or lightly waved coat. The black and white colors are so intermingled that the appearance is of a blue coat.

CARE REQUIRED
This breed does not need much attention to its coat. An occasional brushing, particularly in the areas where the coat is thickest, is sufficient to keep it in good condition.

Check the ear passages regularly to ensure they are clean.

CHARACTER
These dogs are gentle, sociable, intelligent and obedient, pliable, loyal, affectionate, friendly, and they have a good scenting nose.

TRAINING
These dogs learn quickly and easily. They react well to the voice and no firm correction should be necessary.
Because they like to please their handler, they are among the ideal choices for those without much experience of dogs.

SOCIAL BEHAVIOR
This breed is very adaptable and gets on well with dogs and other animals.
They are generally very loving and patient with children.

They will always announce the presence of strangers – and, if necessary, will protect their family.

EXERCISE

This former field sports dog can be very happy in its role as family pet but that does not mean it will be content with three little circuits of the neighborhood each day.

Take it on hikes regularly and give it the chance to run about and to play. These dogs love water and retrieving.

Epagneul Bleu de Picardie

Epagneul Breton, Brittany Spaniel

Epagneul Breton

COUNTRY OF ORIGIN
France.

SPECIAL SKILLS
Field sports dog and family pet.

SIZE
The shoulder-height is 48 - 50cm (18¾ - 19½in) for dogs and 47 - 49cm (18½ - 19¼in) for bitches.
They weigh about 15kg (33lb).

COAT

The coat consists of lightly or strongly waved fine hairs. The breed colors are white and orange, white and chestnut, white and black, three-colored, or a mixture of these colors. The most common color is white with reddish brown.

CARE REQUIRED

This breed does not need much attention to its coat. An occasional brushing, particularly in the areas where the coat is thickest, is sufficient to keep it in good condition. Check the ear passages regularly to ensure they are clean.

CHARACTER

These are lively, intelligent dogs that love to retrieve but which can have a mind of their own, rarely bark, are gentle, affectionate, and obedient. These outstanding and untiring field sports dogs are highly thought of by French hunters.

TRAINING

Epagneul Bretons are easily trained because they are intelligent, learn quickly, and are obedient. Remember that they are very sensitive and suffer from hard words and any undercurrents of unrest in the home.

SOCIAL BEHAVIOR

A well-trained Epagneul Breton is very loving with children, and gets on well with dogs and other animals. These dogs will bark if they sense danger.

EXERCISE

Although this dog fits into the role of family pet extremely well, it remains heart and soul a field sports dog.

It will not be content with three little walks around the block a day and it should be given the chance to run and work in a field, thereby satisfying both its need to exercise and its need to work. This dog enjoys agility skills trials or playing catch as well as swimming and retrieving.

Epagneul Français

COUNTRY OF ORIGIN
France.

SPECIAL SKILLS
Field sports dog and family pet.

Epagneul Français

SOCIAL BEHAVIOR
These dogs are friendly with everyone and anything, including other dogs, household animals, and children. They will bark if they sense danger.

EXERCISE
This is a field sports dog which can't live in a small apartment.
If you are unable or unwilling to work this dog in a large open field, you must find another form of exercise for them.
They greatly enjoy water sports, such as swimming, and retrieving for you.

Epagneul Français

Munsterlander (large)

COUNTRY OF ORIGIN
Germany.

SPECIAL SKILLS
Field sports dog and family pet.

SIZE
The shoulder-height is 60 - 65cm (23½ - 25½in) for dogs and 58 - 63cm (22¾ - 24¾in) for bitches.

COAT
The lank long-haired coat may be white with black patches and spots, but black is also permitted.

CARE REQUIRED
This breed needs little attention to its coat. Groom it regularly with brush and comb and check the ear passages well to ensure they are clean.

SIZE
The shoulder-height is 55 - 61cm (21½ - 24in) for dogs and 54 - 59cm (21¼ - 23¼in) for bitches.

COAT
The coat consists of medium-length lightly or strongly waved fine hairs. The color is always white with brown patches, with or without brown spots.

CARE REQUIRED
This breed needs to be groomed with brush and comb about once each week. Check the ear passages regularly to ensure they are clean and trim any excess hair between the pads of the feet.

CHARACTER
These are lovable and affectionate dogs that are obedient, eager to learn, energetic yet calm in the home. The Epagneul Français has considerable stamina, a good scenting nose, and doesn't bark very much.

TRAINING
These dogs need a soft-handed but consistent approach. They like to please their handler so training is not very difficult.

CHARACTER
These are intelligent, lovable, and affectionate dogs that are vigilant, brave, eager to work, that sometimes try to dominate. They have a good scenting nose and bond with their family.

TRAINING
Because they are so bright and keen, these dogs are easily trained. Munsterlanders may try to dominate so their handler should be an individual who can take positive control.

SOCIAL BEHAVIOR
This breed has no problems whatsoever with other dogs and household animals.

The majority of them are delightful and patient with children. They tend to be friendly with everyone although they will act as a watchdog when necessary.

EXERCISE
This dog is primarily a field sports dog but that does not mean that it cannot be a family pet. Provided the dog has enough opportunity for exercise it will be very content with you. Most of these dogs love water and enjoy retrieving.

Large Munsterlander

Large Munsterlanders

Heidewachtel

Heidewachtel, or small Munsterlander

COUNTRY OF ORIGIN
Germany.

SPECIAL SKILLS
Field sports dog and family pet.

SIZE
The shoulder-height is 50 - 56cm (19½ - 22in) for dogs and 52 - 56cm (20½ - 22in) for bitches. Variations of 2cm (¾in) are permitted.

COAT
The Heidewachtel (or small Munsterlander) has a long-haired coat that is lank or lightly waved. The color is usually brown with white but mixed brown is also permissible.

CARE REQUIRED
Check the ear passages regularly to ensure they are clean and remove any excess hair in the ears. Trim hair between the pads of the feet. The coat

should be groomed with brush and comb about twice a week. Occasionally light-brown hairs appear on the brown areas of the coat. These hairs should be plucked out. These dogs are not fully physically mature until they are three years old.

CHARACTER
The Heidewachtel loves to swim, is obedient, intelligent, cunning, gentle, cheerful, and fairly tough on itself.

TRAINING
These fine family pets want to please their handler. Train them with a gentle but consistent approach.

SOCIAL BEHAVIOR
Dogs of this breed are renowned for getting on well with children. They also mix well with other dogs and household pets without a problem.

EXERCISE
This is primarily a field sports dog with tremendous stamina.
If you are unable to work with them in the field, try to find alternatives such as agility skills trials

or playing catch, both of which are ideal for them.

Take this dog regularly to woods and open countryside and let it retrieve objects out of the water, which it enjoys doing very much.

Wire-haired Pointing Griffon

Head of a Wire-haired Pointing Griffon

Griffon (Wire-haired Pointing)

COUNTRY OF ORIGIN
France.

SPECIAL SKILLS
Field sports dog and family pet.

SIZE
The shoulder-height is 55 - 60cm (21½ - 23½in) for dogs and 50 - 55cm (19½ - 21½in) for bitches.

COAT
The hard and rough coat should never feel woolly. The undercoat is soft and dense. The most popular colors are blue-grey, grey with brown patches, and plain brown (often shot through with grey hairs). White with brown is also permissible.

CARE REQUIRED
The Wire-haired Pointing Griffon should be groomed regularly with brush and comb. Check during grooming that the ear passages are clean and trim excess hair from between the pads of the feet.

CHARACTER
These dogs are intelligent and eager to learn, affectionate, sociable and friendly, vigilant and protective, brave, tough on themselves, and have enormous stamina.

TRAINING
Dogs of this breed are not generally difficult to train, although the new owner needs to be consistent with them. The dog is intelligent enough to grasp quickly what is required of it.

SOCIAL BEHAVIOR
Generally these dogs get on well with children and also cause no problems with other dogs. Provided they are correctly socially trained, they will also put up with cats and other household animals.
Family friends will be heartily welcomed but they are very good at spotting people who are up to no good and will stop them in their tracks.

EXERCISE
This dog needs lots of exercise to keep it physically and mentally fit. It is a reliable all-round field sports dog but if it is not possible for you to work this dog in the classic manner in a field you must take it for long walks regularly.

Once fully grown, it enjoys running alongside a bicycle. Other favorite activities include retrieving and swimming.

Spinone Italiano

Spinone Italiano

COUNTRY OF ORIGIN
Italy.

SPECIAL SKILLS
Field sports dog and family pet.

SIZE
The shoulder-height is 60 - 70cm (23½ - 27½in) for dogs and 58 - 65cm (22¾ - 25½in) for bitches. The weight is 28 - 37kg (61¾ - 81½lb).

COAT
The rough, thick, wire-haired coat lies reasonably flat. The permissible colors are plain white, white with orange markings or flecks, white with brown markings or speckled brown – with and without larger brown markings.

Spinone Italiano, study of the head

This breed gets on well with its own kind and with other household animals, and they make outstanding playmates for children. Both wanted and unwanted visitors are likely to be treated to a warm welcome.

EXERCISE
The Spinone needs lots of exercise and also plenty of space so that it is not suitable for an apartment or a home in a densely crowded urban area.

They love to swim and once they are fully grown enjoy running alongside a bicycle. Consider exercising them in an open field where they can learn to follow your commands.

Braque de Bourbonnais

CARE REQUIRED
Groom the Spinone occasionally with a coarse comb. Trimming is strictly against breed society standards. Check that the ear passages are clean and trim excess hair from between the pads of the feet.

CHARACTER
These dogs are equable and friendly, very gentle and affectionate, but they can be stubborn if they don't want to do what you have in mind. They greatly enjoy water and are all-round field sports dogs with a very good scenting nose.

TRAINING
Do not expect miracles from this breed in terms of obedience.

However, they are gentle and affectionate enough to want to please you provided you do not expect too much. Remember that the Spinone is likely to follow its nose if it picks up an interesting scent. Make sure that your yard is well fenced and never let the dog run off the leash unless closely supervised.

French Braques (Pointers)

Breeds within the group of French Braques or Pointers include the Braque d'Auvergne, the Braque de Bourbonnais, the Braque Saint-Germain, and the Braque FranHais. These short-haired breeds are principally used for field sports in their country of origin. Depending upon the specific breed, the shoulder-height is 48 - 68cm (18¾ - 26¾in).
Few people know that these dogs make first class household pets. Their character is described as friendly, pliable, affectionate, intelligent, and obedient.
These quick-on-the-uptake pupils hate a harsh approach and are more successfully trained with a consistent and loving one. They get on fine with other dogs and are very friendly with children.
Introducing them early to cats and other household animals prevents problems. Generally speaking, all of these breeds need lots of exercise and activity.
Working with them as sporting dogs in the field

is something which they enjoy tremendously but don't worry if this isn't possible. As long as they have plenty of exercise and things to occupy them, they will adapt to home life perfectly.

Braque d'Auvergne

Braque d'Auvergne

Stabyhoun

COUNTRY OF ORIGIN
The Netherlands.

SPECIAL SKILLS
Field sports dog and family pet.

SIZE
The ideal shoulder-height is 53cm (20¾in) for dogs and 50cm (19½in) for bitches.

COAT
The coat consists of long lank hair. The most usual color is black and white but black roan, brown and white, and brown roan occur.

CARE REQUIRED
The Stabyhoun requires little grooming. Brush and comb these dogs regularly where tangles can occur, such as the chest, tail, and between the legs. Trim excess hair from between the pads of the feet.

CHARACTER
These dogs are affectionate, intelligent, and eager to learn, calm, have considerable stamina, and are vigilant. They can be somewhat obstinate at times.

Stabyhoun

TRAINING

This intelligent dog likes to do things for its handler but can have a mind of its own. During training, which must be very consistent in manner, it is essential to bear in mind that the dog reacts strongly to your voice.

Young dogs definitely benefit from attending obedience classes.

SOCIAL BEHAVIOR

Dogs of this breed generally get on extremely well with other dogs, other animals, and with children. At the hint of danger, they will warn you with full, loud barking.

EXERCISE

Stabyhouns are by origin working field sports dogs and they need lots of exercise. All of them like to go for long country walks and to have the chance to run and play off the leash. They also love to swim and retrieve things.

Provided they get enough exercise, they will be calm when indoors.

Young Stabyhoun

Vizsla, short-haired and wire-haired

COUNTRY OF ORIGIN

Hungary.

SPECIAL SKILLS

Hunting dog and family pet.

SIZE

For short-haired Vizslas the shoulder-height is 56 - 61cm (22 - 24in) for dogs and 52 - 57cm (20½ - 22½in) for bitches. Variations of up to 4cm (1½in) are permitted provided the dog looks correctly proportioned.

For wire-haired Vizslas the shoulder-height is 58 - 62cm (22¾ - 24½in) for dogs and 54 - 58cm (21¼ - 22¾in) for bitches.

Short-haired Vizsla

Variations of up to 3cm (1½in) are permitted provided the dog looks correctly proportioned.

COAT

The short-haired Vizsla is plain dark wheaten or dark gold. The wire-haired Vizsla is usually seen in shades of sandy-yellow. A small white patch on the breasts of both types is permissible.

CARE REQUIRED

The short-haired coat requires little grooming. When the dog is shedding remove loose and dead hairs with a rubber brush.

The wire-haired coat needs to be plucked from time to time – the old and dead hairs are removed by hand. Trim excess hair between the pads of the feet.

CHARACTER

These are equable, affectionate, loyal, and intelligent dogs which are eager to learn. They are sporty, like to retrieve, have a good scenting nose, and considerable stamina.

TRAINING

Generally these are not difficult dogs to train

because they like to please their handler. It is important to be consistent with them.

Wire-haired Vizsla

SOCIAL BEHAVIOR

The Vizsla gets on with its own kind, with other household animals and with children. These dogs will bark at strangers but that is usually all.

EXERCISE

This energetic breed needs lots of exercise and plenty to keep it occupied for it to feel both physically and mentally happy.

Consider hunting with them. If you do not want to do this, let them run and play off the leash at regular intervals. Most Vizslas like to retrieve and love water.

Weimaraner

Head of a Weimaraner

Weimaraner

COUNTRY OF ORIGIN
Germany.

SPECIAL SKILLS
Field sports dog and family pet.

SIZE
The ideal shoulder-height is 59 - 70cm (23¼ - 27½in) for dogs and 57 - 65cm (22½ - 25½in) for bitches.

COAT
There are two different types of coat: the short and the long-haired, both of which are silver/roe-deer or mouse-colored. Small white marks on the chest and feet are permitted.

CARE REQUIRED
The short-haired Weimaraner needs little attention for its coat.
Remove dead hairs occasionally with a rubber brush.
With the long-haired type it is best to brush the coat followed by combing. Check regularly to ensure that the ears are clean.

CHARACTER
These dogs are friendly, intelligent, keen to work, energetic with considerable stamina, vigilant, and protective. The Weimaraner is a good field sports dog.

TRAINING
Weimaraners are quick to learn, eager to please their handler, and intelligent enough to understand what is required of them. The handler needs to exude confidence because this breed can sometimes try to dominate.

Long-haired Weimaraners

SOCIAL BEHAVIOR

The dogs are usually very friendly with children and if they are properly socially trained when young, they can share companionship with cats and other animals without a problem. They also get on equally well with other dogs.

They are reasonably vigilant but not particularly unfriendly towards strangers, but if you need help the dog will be there for you.

EXERCISE

Consider working this dog at field sports. If this isn't possible take it for regular long walks – three little outings each day are definitely not sufficient. These dogs need lots of exercise and things to occupy them and make them feel content.

If they get sufficient exercise, they will be calm in the house. They like to retrieve and to swim and can happily be kept in an outdoor kennel provided they get that necessary attention and exercise.

Young long-haired Weimaraner bitch

English Setters

English Setters

Setters and Pointers

English Setter

COUNTRY OF ORIGIN
England.

SPECIAL SKILLS
Field sports dogs and family pets.

SIZE
The shoulder-height is 65 - 68cm
(25½ - 26¾in) for dogs and 61 - 65cm
(24 - 25½in) for bitches.

COAT
The coat is long, silk-like, and wavy. English Setter colors are white with blue-black, white with orange, white with lemon-yellow, and white with liver. There are also three colored English Setters.

CARE REQUIRED
From time to time the English Setter needs to have its extra, old hair clipped or trimmed.

If you intend to show this breed, then considerably more attention is required.

For household pets the coat can be kept in good condition between trims by clipping excess hair between the pads of the feet and also under the ears. This last point is important to let air reach the ears to prevent infections.

CHARACTER
The English Setter is a friendly, gentle, sensitive dog that bonds with its family. It is lively, intelligent, sociable, and cautious.

TRAINING
These dogs are not difficult to train but they do tend to have minds of their own and this needs to be taken into account.

They respond best to a consistent and loving approach. In some cases it is advisable to attend puppy obedience training courses with them.

SOCIAL BEHAVIOR
These dogs are naturally happy with other dogs and household animals.

Companionship with children will never lead to problems. These dogs are friendly to all people and will greet everyone as a friend.

EXERCISE
The English Setter needs quite a lot of exercise. Take it for regular long walks or, once it is fully grown, let it run alongside a bicycle. These dogs have a tendency to wander and you should make sure you have a good fence.

Gordon Setter

Gordon Setter

COUNTRY OF ORIGIN
Scotland.

SPECIAL SKILLS
Field sports dog and family pet.

SIZE
The shoulder-height is about 66cm (26in) for dogs and about 62cm (24½in) for bitches.

COAT
The coat, which must never be curly, consists of medium-length hair with feathering. The color is always black with warm chestnut markings. A small white patch on the chest is permissible.

CARE REQUIRED
Groom this dog regularly and check the ear passages to ensure they are clean.
The excess hair beneath the ear should be trimmed to let air reach the inner ear in order to avoid infections. The hair on the outside of the ear should never be clipped – something that is permitted with other Setters.
If you wish to show your dog, grooming will require considerably more attention.

CHARACTER
These are lovable, friendly, sociable, and intelligent dogs that are gentle and sensitive. These dogs do, however, often have minds of their own.

TRAINING
The training of this dog is certainly not difficult, provided you take account of the fact that it can be stubborn on occasion. They call for a handler who is both consistent and loving in approach. It is a good idea to attend a puppy obedience training course with your dog.

SOCIAL BEHAVIOR
It is necessary to introduce the young dog to all manner of situations and experiences with people, animals, and things. Only by doing so will you ensure the well-balanced development of this dog. In general they get on well with other dogs and with children because they are a friend to everyone.

Good early social training will also ensure they can get along with cats and other household animals. If strangers visit they adopt a wait-and-see attitude.

EXERCISE
This breed needs plenty of exercise. Running beside a bicycle is an ideal way to keep them fit but should not be started until the dog is fully grown.
A Gordon Setter that gets enough outdoor activity will be calm when indoors. They are apt to roam, so a good fence around your property is essential.

Irish Setter

Irish Setter

COUNTRY OF ORIGIN
Ireland.

SPECIAL SKILLS
Field sports dog and family pet.

SIZE
There are no standard dimensions. The shoulder-height is about 65cm (25½in) but there are many much larger specimens.

COAT
The coat is relatively long and flat, with as few curls or waves as possible. The color is rich chestnut without a trace of black. Markings such as white on the chest, throat, chin, or feet, or a

small star on the forehead and a white blaze are all undesirable. There is also a red-white Irish Setter which has a predominantly white coat with red markings.

CARE REQUIRED
The Irish Setter should be trimmed occasionally, removing excess hair. If you plan to show this dog much more elaborate grooming will be required. For dogs kept solely as pets, the coat can be kept in condition between trims by clipping excess hair between the pads of the feet and underneath the ears to prevent infections that can occur if the ear is not ventilated.

CHARACTER
These are lively, lovable, gentle, cheerful, and playful dogs that have minds of their own, and bond with their family. Generally Irish Setters do not bark much.

TRAINING
The training of these dogs is generally not difficult.
They are intelligent enough to understand quickly what is expected of them but they do have minds of their own, which calls for a handler who is both consistent and loving in approach. It can be a good idea in some cases to attend a puppy training course with the dog.

SOCIAL BEHAVIOR
Irish Setters are usually loving so that even unwanted visitors are enthusiastically welcomed.

They do however let you know of the arrival of visitors. With children they are friendly and patient and mix harmoniously with other dogs.

Mixing with other animals in the house will not be a problem if the young dog has learned to know them early in its life.

EXERCISE
Because this breed needs plenty of exercise you will need to take it on regular long walks. Letting the dog run beside a bicycle is an ideal form of exercise once the dog is fully grown.

Some Irish Setters follow their nose when they come across what they consider to be an interesting scent and will have a deaf ear to your calls.

Teach the young dog that it must come to you when you order it to do so.

Pointer

COUNTRY OF ORIGIN
England.

SPECIAL SKILLS
Pointer for game birds and family pet.

SIZE
The shoulder-height is 63 - 69cm (24¾ - 27¼in) for dogs and 61 - 66cm (24 - 26in) for bitches.

COAT
The topcoat is short while the undercoat is short and smooth. Pointers can have the following color combinations: white and yellow, white and liver, and white and black. Three colored varieties are also permissible.

CARE REQUIRED
The grooming of this breed is simple. All that is required is to use a rubber brush when the dog is shedding to remove dead and loose hairs.

CHARACTER
These are friendly, lovable, affectionate, and equable dogs which are intelligent, and obedient. They are first-class game pointers. (The dog stands absolutely still pointing towards wild game birds as it catches their scent on the wind.)

TRAINING
The Pointer is a reasonably quick learner because the dog is intelligent enough to understand what you want it to do.

SOCIAL BEHAVIOR
This breed get on well with their own kind and with other household animals. They are also generally loving and patient with children and they are friendly towards both known and unknown people.

They will get along fine with cats and other household animals if they have been introduced to them when young.

EXERCISE
Because Pointers are primarily field sports dogs, most owners are people who are involved in these activities.

They need lots of exercise so consider letting them work at field sports. If this is not possible, then it is essential that the dog gets at least half an hour every day to run about.

Head of a Pointer

Pointer working

8. Gundogs and retrievers

Retrievers

Chesapeake Bay Retriever

COUNTRY OF ORIGIN
United States.

SPECIAL SKILLS
Field sports dog and family pet.

SIZE
The shoulder-height is 58 - 66cm (22¾ - 26in) for dogs and 53 - 61cm (20¾ - 24in) for bitches. Greater consideration is given in the show ring to correct proportion than to height.

COAT
The Chesapeake's coat is its trade mark; thick and short with a dense woolly undercoat. The coat may be wavy in some places but never curly and it feels greasy to the touch.

The color is between yellow-brown, and dark brown. The darker coloring is more usual.

CARE REQUIRED
Grooming of this breed is fairly simple. Brush the dog to remove dead and loose hairs when it is shedding but take care not to harm the texture of the coat.
In order to keep the texture of the coat, avoid washing this dog.

CHARACTER
These are friendly, intelligent, and obedient dogs with a mind of their own. These dogs love swimming, tend to be a little boisterous, and are demanding of themselves. The males may try to dominate other dogs.

TRAINING
This breed is not recommended for the inexperienced new dog owner. The handler needs to be confident and to exude authority because these dogs like to have their own way. They are less gentle than, for example the Golden Retriever. A consistent but kind approach is the most successful way to handle these dogs. Attend an obedience class with this dog. They are usually slow to mature.

SOCIAL BEHAVIOR
This dog will get along perfectly well with a cat that is already present in the house, but may chase other cats. The dogs in particular can behave dominantly towards other males, although this may depend upon their social training.

Take the young dog out with you as often as possible and introduce it to other dogs so that it has the chance to feel relaxed with them.

Chesapeake Bay Retrievers get on extremely well with children but are somewhat reserved towards strangers.

EXERCISE
This breed needs lots of exercise. If they do not get it, they may become badly behaved from simple boredom.
Swimming and retrieving are two activities which they greatly enjoy. They also like field sports. They are, however, somewhat slow learners.

Chesapeake Bay Retriever

Golden Retriever

Curly Coated Retriever

Curly Coated Retriever

COUNTRY OF ORIGIN
England.

SPECIAL SKILLS
Field sports dog and family pet.

SIZE
The shoulder-height is about 68.5cm (27in) for dogs and 63.5cm (25in) for bitches.

COAT
The Curly Coated Retriever has a curly, waterproof coat. The hair on the head and on the legs is short and without curls. They are recognized in two colors: liver and black.

CARE REQUIRED
The coat of this breed should be brushed as little as possible to avoid changing its nature from the breed standard.
Grooming cannot be avoided, however, when the dog is shedding. Afterwards, the coat should be soaked with water by letting the dog swim or by sponging it down which will put the curl back into the coat. If the coat becomes too long, it can be trimmed with scissors.

CHARACTER
This is an intelligent, friendly, boisterous dog which can try to dominate. It is active, independent, vigilant, and has a good nose for scents. The Curly Coated Retriever likes to please its handler and learns commands fairly quickly. In spite of this, it has a mind of its own. The males are more dominant than the bitches.

TRAINING
This breed is intelligent enough to grasp what is expected of it. Make the training a challenge for this dog and vary the exercises because monotony will cause it to lose interest and, of course, always be consistent.

SOCIAL BEHAVIOR
In normal circumstances this breed usually gets on well with dogs and other household animals.

Provided children do not pester them, they are usually very patient with them. If strangers visit they may not pay much attention but if you are threatened they will stand by you.

EXERCISE
This retriever is first and foremost a working dog which likes to retrieve and to swim.

The dog can be trained for field sports but members of this breed have also become well known in other areas of dog sports. The most important thing is for the dog to get enough exercise and activity.

A Curly Coated Retriever that does not get enough exercise or work becomes extremely badly behaved.

Head of a Curly Coated Retriever

Flat Coated Retriever

COUNTRY OF ORIGIN
England.

SPECIAL SKILLS
Field sports dogs and family pets.

SIZE
The shoulder-height is 58 - 61cm (22¾ - 24in) for dogs and 55 - 58cm (21½ - 22¾in) for bitches.

COAT
The smooth, medium-length hair of the Flat Coated Retriever can be black or liver. Occasionally a blond example occurs but these are not recognized.

CARE REQUIRED
Groom them twice each week with a brush and comb, especially in those places where tangles occur. Check the ear passages at the same time to ensure they are clean and trim excess hair from between the pads of the feet. If necessary, the Flat Coated Retriever can be trimmed.

CHARACTER
These are intelligent, friendly dogs that are happy to work for their handler, pliable, and loyal. Most of them love swimming and have tremendous stamina, but they can sometimes be stubborn. Most of them are not particularly vigilant and they rarely bark.

TRAINING
This breed is reasonably easy to train. They learn fairly quickly and are intelligent enough to quickly grasp your instructions. They can be stubborn. Avoid letting the dog get the upper hand by being very consistent in your handling of them.

Flat Coated Retrievers

Flat Coated Retrievers

SOCIAL BEHAVIOR
Mixing with other dogs and animals never presents difficulties for these dogs and they are reliable playmates for children provided the children do not pester the dog. Strangers will be announced but that is all.

EXERCISE
This breed needs lots of exercise and these dogs find it enormous fun to swim and retrieve. If you miss a day of exercise with this dog it will accept it without a fuss but after one day they will start to become badly behaved. This is first and foremost a working dog.

Golden Retriever

COUNTRY OF ORIGIN
England.

SPECIAL SKILLS
Field sports dog and family pet.

SIZE
The shoulder-height is 56 - 61cm (22 - 24in) for dogs and 51 - 56cm (20 - 22in) for bitches.

COAT
The hair is smooth and wavy with a weather-resistant undercoat. The coat may be golden or cream. A single small white marking on the chest is permissible.

Golden Retriever

CARE REQUIRED
Groom regularly with brush and comb, trim excess hair between the pads of the feet, and check that the ears are clean at fixed intervals.

If necessary, the hair on the ears may be trimmed to create a well-groomed appearance.

CHARACTER
This is a lovable, intelligent, sociable, self-confident, sensitive dog with a good memory.

This dog adapts well to a variety of situations and is not given to barking very much.

TRAINING
The Golden Retriever learns quickly and remembers what it has learned for the rest of its life. Never treat these dogs harshly because they are very sensitive and you will harm their accommodating nature if you are too strict with them.

It is sensible to vary the training as much as possible and obedience classes are strongly recommended.

SOCIAL BEHAVIOR
Dogs of this breed get on fine with other dogs, animals, and children, although in some cases the dog might need protection from the children.

Most of these dogs become real friends with humans, although some can be very belligerent toward unknown visitors.

EXERCISE
The Golden Retriever will adapt itself to your family but do not forget they need more exercise than the average dog.
Once fully grown they can be exercised by running alongside a bicycle.

Most of them love to swim and retrieve things. They greatly enjoy participating in obedience competitions, catch, and agility skills trials.

SPECIAL REMARKS
The Golden Retriever is a very popular dog. Purchase a puppy only from very reputable breeders.

Labrador Retriever

COUNTRY OF ORIGIN
England.

SPECIAL SKILLS
Field sports dog, guide dog for the blind, drugs search dogs, and family pet among numerous roles.

SIZE
The shoulder-height is 56 - 57cm (22 - 22½in) for dogs and 54 - 56cm (21¼ - 22in) for bitches.

COAT
The coat is thick and dense with a weather-resistant undercoat. The Labrador's colors are plain black, yellow, or chocolate brown (liver). A small white marking on the chest is permissible.

CARE REQUIRED
The coat is not difficult to care for. Brush it once a week and give it more attention when the dog is shedding.

CHARACTER
This is a friendly, good-natured, intelligent dog that is keen to work, is obedient, sociable, affectionate, pliable, sensible, thoughtful, and loyal.

It has an outstanding scenting ability which is used in criminal investigation. Labradors mature quite late bodily and mentally.

Labrador Retriever

Training
The Labrador Retriever is an intelligent dog that is not difficult to train because it learns quickly and likes to work for its handler.

It is a great pity if such a dog can do nothing more than be a pet.

They are excellent field sports and search dogs, but they also excel in obedience competitions. If you take part in any of these activities, you will be very much aware of how much pleasure it gives this dog.

Social behavior
This breed usually gets on fine with other dogs and animals. These dogs are usually both patient and good-natured with children as they are true friends to humans. Don't count on them to be good watchdogs.

Exercise
They will adapt themselves completely to your family but do not forget they need quite a lot of exercise.

Take them for fairly long walks and give them the chance to run and play off the leash. They enjoy swimming and retrieving.

Head of a Nova Scotia Duck Tolling Retriever

Nova Scotia Duck Tolling Retriever

Country of origin
Canada.

Special skills
Field sports dog and family pet.

Nova Scotia Duck Tolling Retriever

Amerikaanse Cocker Spaniel

SIZE
The shoulder-height is 48 - 51cm (18¾ - 20in) for dogs and 45 - 48cm (17¾ - 18¾in) for bitches.

COAT
The Nova Scotia Duck Tolling Retriever has a double, water-resistant coat of medium-length hair with a softer undercoat. The color is between red and orange, usually with a blaze and a white marking on the tip of the tail, the feet, and the chest.

CARE REQUIRED
The coat does not call for much attention – a brushing once a week is sufficient. More attention will be needed, of course, when the dog is shedding.

CHARACTER
The Toller is a high-spirited, friendly, attentive, and intelligent dog that is obedient, lively, and sociable.

TRAINING
Training does not present much in the way of a problem because these dogs are fast learners and quickly remember new instructions. Since they also like to work for their handlers they are among the easiest of dogs to train.

SOCIAL BEHAVIOR
These are excellent family pets which get on well with other dogs and animals. They are very patient with children.
They bark when they sense danger but that is likely to be all.

EXERCISE
This breed needs quite a lot of exercise and likes to swim and retrieve, which are ideal activities for it.

With the right training they can do well in sports such as catch, agility skills trials, and obedience competitions.

Springers

American Cocker Spaniel

COUNTRY OF ORIGIN
United States.

SPECIAL SKILLS
Field sports dog by origin, mainly a family pet today.

SIZE
The shoulder-height is about 38cm (15in) for dogs and 35.5cm (14in) for bitches.

COAT
The hair on the head is short and fine while the body hair is medium length. There should be feathering of silken hair on the ears, chest, belly, and legs.
American Cocker Spaniels are recognized by this long hair. Almost any color is accepted, including black, deer red, light beige, black and tan, and multi-colored.

CARE REQUIRED
The grooming of the coat is very important. With this Spaniel it is necessary to brush and comb the hair every day. Additionally, if you want to keep the dog's appearance according to the breed standard, you will need to take it to a professional dog groomer about every four weeks. Of course, the ears should be examined regularly and excess hair between the pads of the

feet, under and inside the ear, should be trimmed.

If you do not have the time for the grooming required or cannot afford the cost of regular visits to a professional, avoid this breed.

CHARACTER
These are lovable, gentle, and playful dogs that are intelligent and obedient.

TRAINING
Training the American Cocker Spaniel rarely leads to any problems.

Train them with a gentle hand and bear in mind that they are sensitive to the tone of your voice and any upsets within the home.

SOCIAL BEHAVIOR
Dogs of this breed are very sociable and consequently they get along fine with their own kind and with other household pets.

Because they will meekly accept virtually anything, it is sensible to protect them from children's play which can become too rough.

EXERCISE
This Cocker Spaniel loves to play and frolic. Provided you bear this in mind, there is no reason why it cannot be kept in an apartment. A few of the breed are still used to find birds in hunting. Most of them greatly enjoy both swimming and retrieving.

SPECIAL REMARKS
In view of the popularity of this breed, it is advisable to purchase a puppy only from a recognized and reliable breeder.

Clumber Spaniel

COUNTRY OF ORIGIN
England.

SPECIAL SKILLS
Field sports dog and family pet.

WEIGHT
The weight is about 36kg (79lb) for dogs and 30kg (66lb) for bitches.

Clumber Spaniel

COAT

The Clumber Spaniel has a dense coat of medium-length silken hair. The color is usually white with lemon markings, although orange markings are also permissible.

CARE REQUIRED

The coat must be groomed regularly with brush and comb and the ear passages should be kept clean. Some of these dogs develop an irritation of the ear but there are special lotions which can provide relief for this. Occasionally it will become necessary to trim them back to breed standard, removing the unruly hairs which stick out, leaving the dog looking first class once more. If there is too much hair under the ears, clip it before the next overall trim.

CHARACTER

This is a gentle, equable, cheerful, brave, noble dog with a good memory, and considerable stamina. These dogs are calm indoors.

TRAINING

Because this dog has a good memory and likes to do things to please its handler it is a fairly easily taught pupil.

SOCIAL BEHAVIOR

Clumber Spaniels get on well with other dogs and that is true also for cats and other household animals. They are usually very trustworthy with children but they do not make friends easily with strangers. Don't expect these dogs to be friends with everybody.

EXERCISE

The Clumber Spaniel is primarily a field sports dog but it has no difficulty adapting its exercise needs to the family. If your dog does not get a good amount of exercise, watch its diet carefully as it gains weight easily.

Clumber Spaniel

English Cocker Spaniel

English Cocker Spaniel

COUNTRY OF ORIGIN
England.

SPECIAL SKILLS
Field sports dog and family pet.

SIZE
The shoulder-height is about 39 - 41cm (15¼ - 16½in) for dogs and 38 - 39cm (15- 15¼in) for bitches.
The weight is about 13kg (28½lb).

COAT
The hair is smooth, silken, and medium length. It should never be curly.
The most usual colors are russet brown, liver, black, black and tan, white with black, red, or liver patches (with or without tan markings), blue roan, orange roan, and liver roan (with or without tan markings).

CARE REQUIRED
The coat of Cocker Spaniels tangles easily, so it is necessary to brush and comb them thoroughly regularly. Do not overlook the hair between the front and back legs and the hair on the ears. The ears should be cleaned regularly and excess hair trimmed. Pluck out excessive hair on the top of the head, beneath the ears, and on the neck regularly by hand.

Depending upon the condition of the coat this should be done – by a dog professional if necessary – twice to four times a year.

CHARACTER
These are cheerful, lively, gentle, and affectionate dogs that are intelligent and easy to manage.

TRAINING

The Cocker Spaniel is a naturally willing dog which quickly understands what you want it to do.

Train these dogs with understanding and consistency as, if you are not consistent, the English Cocker Spaniel will try to take over your role.

SOCIAL BEHAVIOR

Dogs of this breed can usually get on well with pets, other dogs, and children. Make sure the children are not too rough with the dog because they will allow themselves to be used as toys.

EXERCISE

Cocker Spaniels are reasonably content with three walks a day but they also need regular opportunities to run freely in the countryside. Most of these dogs love to swim.

English Springer Spaniel

COUNTRY OF ORIGIN
England.

SPECIAL SKILLS
Field sports dog and family pet.

SIZE
The shoulder-height is about 51cm (20in).

COAT
The coat is dense, smooth, and water- and dirt-resistant.
The permitted color combinations are liver with white and black with white, which can include tan markings.

CARE REQUIRED
The coat of the English Springer Spaniel must be brushed regularly. Remove excess hair from the ear passages and also from beneath the ears so that they are adequately ventilated.

Do not forget to trim excess hair between the pads of the feet. An English Springer Spaniel needs to visit a professional dog groomer twice to four times each year.

CHARACTER
These are gentle, friendly, and sociable dogs that are intelligent and cunning, willing, obedient, equable, and very active.

TRAINING
The training of this breed is usually trouble-free. They are intelligent pupils anxious to please and to learn.

English Springer Spaniel

SOCIAL BEHAVIOR
Dogs of this breed are renowned for their friendly nature. They live in harmony with other dogs, pets, and children.

EXERCISE
Usually these dogs adapt effortlessly to the family situation but it is not fair to limit them to three

short outings a day – they need more exercise than that and should have chances to take long walks and run and play off the leash.

They love to retrieve and swim. These dogs perform very well in both agility skills trials and obedience competitions.

Field Spaniel

Field Spaniel

COUNTRY OF ORIGIN
England.

SPECIAL SKILLS
Field sports dog and family pet.

SIZE
The shoulder-height is about 46cm (18in).

COAT
The shiny and water-resistant coat is smooth with waves and has a silken texture. The most usual colors are liver, yellow-brown, mahogany, black, or a roan of one of these colors, sometimes including white or tan markings.

Field Spaniel

CARE REQUIRED
The Field Spaniel usually needs to visit a professional for grooming about four times a year. Dead hairs are removed by hand-plucking and hair on the ears, legs, and neck is also thinned out. Keep the ears clean.

CHARACTER
This breed is gentle, affectionate, and intelligent. It can be just a little bit stubborn, temperamental, and playful, but is very calm indoors. It is said that they have a tendency to become devoted to one member of a family and ignore the others.

TRAINING
These quick-learning pupils react very strongly to your voice. Train them with a kind but consistent manner.

Harsh words and a tough approach will disturb this dog's sensitive nature. These dogs need regular contact with people and become extremely neurotic if shut away in a kennel.

SOCIAL BEHAVIOR
These dogs are friendly with everyone. In general they are very patient with children but if play becomes too rough for them, they will become withdrawn. Make sure the dog is not pestered by children. Prevent problems later in the dog's life with other animals by introducing it to them when it is young.

EXERCISE
The Field Spaniel adapts effortlessly to the family situation but they are primarily a working field dog which means that it really needs lots of exercise and a sporty family suits it best. Because these dogs do have deeply-rooted hunting instincts, it is essential to have a good fence surrounding your property as otherwise they are likely to take off after any interesting scent.

Kooikerhondje or Dutch duck hunter's dog

The Netherlands.

SPECIAL SKILLS
Duck hunter's dog, vermin destroyer, and companion.

SIZE
The shoulder-height is 35 - 40cm (13¾ - 15¾in) and the weight is about 10kg (22lb).

COAT
The medium-length hair is lightly waved. The coat is predominantly white with orange patches and black ear tips – which are known as "earrings" within breed circles.

CARE REQUIRED
This breed needs little attention to its coat. Brush the dogs regularly and keep the ears clean. If necessary, trim excess hair from between the pads of the feet.

CHARACTER
This is a cheerful, friendly, and brave dog that is attentive and self-confident. It is intelligent enough to be somewhat wary with strangers. These dogs seldom bark. They bond closely with their own people and can be a good watchdog if called upon. The Kooikerhondje is so sensitive that it can be rather touchy and it is therefore not a suitable playmate for children.

TRAINING
In common with all breeds, the training of a Kooikerhondje has to be carried out consistently. These dogs are intelligent and eager to learn – properties which make them an easy dog to train – and they are also sensitive to the intonation of the voice so that a tough approach is absolutely unnecessary.
The handler must be firm because over-leniency will bring out the dog's tendency to try to dominate.

SOCIAL BEHAVIOR
They get on well with dogs and cats provided they meet them when they are young. This breed is not a friend-to-all and they are reserved towards strangers.
In contrast, familiar family friends will get an enthusiastic welcome.

EXERCISE
They like to run about and to frolic. Do not sentence them to three short outings a day. Most

of them like to swim and to retrieve. They perform well at obedience and agility skills trials and also shine at catch.

Kooikerhondje

Rhodesian Ridgeback

COUNTRY OF ORIGIN
Zimbabwe.

SPECIAL SKILLS
Hunting dog (principally for lions), and also watchdog, and family pet.

Rhodesian Ridgebacks

SIZE
The shoulder-height is 64-69cm (25¼ - 27¼in) for dogs and 61 - 62cm (24 - 24½in) for bitches.

COAT
The short-haired coat has its characteristic ridge along the back, which is a strip of hair in which the pile is opposite to the rest of the coat, making it appear darker.

The color is light to reddish wheaten with a dark mask. A small amount of white on the chest is permissible.

CARE
There is little to the grooming of a Ridgeback. Brush it and when it is shedding use a rubber brush to remove dead hairs.

CHARACTER
These are intelligent, cunning but straight-forward dogs that are loyal to the family, have something of a mind of their own, are brave, vigilant, reserved towards strangers, and possess considerable stamina.

TRAINING
They react best to an extremely consistent and equable approach to training. Ridgebacks are intelligent and learn quickly but they are also strong and a bit stubborn.

The handler needs to be confident and to exude natural authority.

SOCIAL BEHAVIOR

Provided this dog meets cats and other pets when it is young, any potential problems will be prevented.

They are usually kind with children but only so long as they are not pestered by them.

They mix satisfactorily with other dogs under most circumstances. They tend to be rather reserved towards strangers.

EXERCISE

This dog is a hunting dog by origin and it has tremendous stamina – meaning its exercise needs are also substantial.

Let them run beside a bicycle and take them for regular long walks.

Rhodesian Ridgeback

Sussex Spaniel

COUNTRY OF ORIGIN
England.

SPECIAL SKILLS
Field sports dog and family pet.

SIZE
The shoulder-height is about 30cm (11¾in) and the weight is 18 - 21kg (39½ - 46¼lb). For its height, the Sussex Spaniel is a heavy dog.

COAT
The Sussex Spaniel has soft medium-length hair which forms a smooth coat without curls. The color is only a golden-glistening shade of liver.

CARE REQUIRED
Groom them regularly with brush and comb and keep the ears clean. Trim excessive hair between

Head of a Sussex Spaniel

the pads on the bottom of the feet but leave the tufts growing between the toes on the upper part of the feet. If necessary, have the older and lighter hairs removed by plucking.

Too much hair beneath the ears should be trimmed at regular intervals.

Check when new teeth emerge that they do not push existing teeth aside, resulting in crooked teeth.

CHARACTER
This is a lovable, cunning, and affectionate dog that is cheerful, and likes to bark.

They make pleasant household companions. Some of them can be rather jealous and want to keep their handler to themselves.

TRAINING
These quick-learning pupils can have minds of their own. It is therefore important to be consistent with them.

Because they like to bark, it is sensible to teach them when they are young that one bark, for instance when the doorbell rings, is sufficient.

SOCIAL BEHAVIOR
These are very sociable dogs which usually get along with children, cats, and other dogs.

EXERCISE
The Sussex Spaniel will quickly put on weight if it gets too little exercise. It likes to be outdoors in fields and woods but bear in mind its tendency to follow its nose.

Swimming and retrieving are both activities which it enjoys.

SPECIAL REMARKS

This breed is fairly rare. If it interests you, visit one of the major international dog shows where you will usually find one or more examples.

It is difficult to find a first-class show dog because of the wide diversity within the breed.

Sussex Spaniel

CHARACTER

These are gentle, intelligent, sociable, and equable dogs that are pliable and obedient but a little bit stubborn.

The breed loves water and has an outstanding sense of smell.

TRAINING

These dogs are not difficult to train although they can have minds of their own. They learn fairly quickly.

Use your voice and praise them a lot but be consistent to achieve the best results. Keep in mind that these dogs have a strong desire to hunt so train your dog to come to your command at once.

SOCIAL BEHAVIOR

This breed is generally trouble-free in the company of other dogs and children and with cats and other household animals, especially if it was introduced to them when young. These dogs are always friendly with people.

EXERCISE

If these dogs are given the opportunity to enjoy themselves and run around outdoors they will be perfectly behaved indoors.

Welsh Springer Spaniel

Welsh Springer Spaniel

COUNTRY OF ORIGIN
Wales.

SPECIAL SKILLS
Field sports dog and family pet.

SIZE
The maximum shoulder-height is 48cm (18¾in) for dogs and 46cm (18in) for bitches.

COAT
The coat consists of medium-length silken and lank hair.
Curls are not permitted and the color is always red and white.

CARE REQUIRED
Regularly clip excess hair from the inner ear to prevent infections and also trim excessive hair between the pads of the feet.
Groom the coat at fixed intervals with brush and comb.

The Welsh Springer needs to visit a professional for grooming two to four times each year.

Water dogs

Barbet

COUNTRY OF ORIGIN
France.

SPECIAL SKILLS
Hunting dog and family pet.

SIZE
The shoulder-height is a minimum of 54cm (21¼in) for dogs and 50cm (19½in) for bitches.

COAT
The coat is water-resistant and long, soft, and wavy or curly. Permitted colors can be black, white, grey, or chestnut.

CARE REQUIRED
The coat must be regularly and thoroughly groomed with brush and comb to prevent tangles forming which can be difficult to remove.

CHARACTER
These are equable, pliable, and very affectionate dogs, which are loyal, lively, friendly, intelligent, and eager to learn.
They are also tough on themselves and straightforward by nature.

TRAINING
The Barbet learns quickly. This dog is very sensitive to its handler's voice and wants to please the handler.

Consistency during training is very important as otherwise the dog will not take commands seriously later.

SOCIAL BEHAVIOR
These dogs get on well with other dogs and other pets and usually present no problems in the

Head of a Barbet

company of children. They will certainly warn of danger but won't take any further action.

EXERCISE
These are working dogs by origin which love water and retrieving. They fit in perfectly as a family pet and like doing so.

They should not be shut away in a kennel as they will be extremely unhappy there.
Take this dog for regular long walks during which it can have get a chance to enjoy itself off the leash.

Barbet

Irish Water Spaniel

COUNTRY OF ORIGIN
Ireland.

SPECIAL SKILLS
Hunting dog and family pet.

SIZE
The shoulder-height is 53 - 59cm (20¾ - 23¼in) for dogs and 51 - 56cm (20 - 22in) for bitches.

COAT
The oily coat of the Irish Water Spaniel consists of dense, permanent curls which should never be fluffy. The only recognized color is a dark shade of liver.

CARE REQUIRED
Do not groom these dogs too much as otherwise the coat may become fluffy.
After a thorough brushing, the dog should be washed or allowed to swim to put the curl back in the coat. It is likely that the coat will require trimming from time to time to keep it in accordance with the breed standard. A major advantage of this coat is that loose hairs are not

shed, so that few will be found on the carpet. For showing they require more specialized grooming.

CHARACTER
This dog is lively and cheerful, with considerable stamina and drive, and a very good nose. It is intelligent, cunning, equable, and tough on itself. It can have something of a mind of its own.

TRAINING
Training needs to begin early with these dogs. They learn quickly but require consistent handling. If the handler lets them have their own way too much and are too forgiving in the dog's eyes, the dog will lose all respect for its handler and refuse to obey.

Bring as much variety as possible into training and make sure the dog enjoys it. These dogs can be very bad tempered. Do not expect them to perform consistently.

SOCIAL BEHAVIOR
This breed usually gets on well with children. There is no problem with the company of cats and other pets provided the dog has been socially trained when young.

They will bark to warn of danger but that is all. With strangers, they are rather cautious.

Irish Water Spaniel

EXERCISE
These are hunting dogs with tremendous stamina. They enjoy retrieving and swimming greatly.
These dogs are always ready for a good long walk.

Head of an Irish Water Spaniel

Perro de Agua Español

COUNTRY OF ORIGIN
Spain.

SPECIAL SKILLS
Water dog, herding dog, and family pet.

SIZE
The shoulder-height is 40 - 50cm (15¾ - 19½in) for dogs and 38 - 45cm (15 - 17¾in) for bitches.

COAT
The curly, woolly, and weather-protective coat should form cords when long.

The most usual colors are brown, black, white, black and white, or brown and white.

Head of a Perro de Agua Español

CARE REQUIRED
This dog needs little grooming. Unlike the Puli or Komondor which have similar coats, the cords form themselves. It is permissible to cut the cords short.

CHARACTER
This is an active, friendly, and intelligent dog that is eager to learn, playful, sociable, vigilant, and enterprising.

TRAINING
This breed learns quickly so that training should present no major problems.

SOCIAL BEHAVIOR
These dogs usually get along with other dogs and with children and other animals without problems.

They need to get to know cats so that the company of them will also cause no difficulties. They will warn of danger but little more.

EXERCISE
These are dogs that like and need exercise. They like to swim, enjoy retrieving, and usually perform well in both obedience competitions and at games of catch.

Perro de Agua Español

Portuguese Water Dog

COUNTRY OF ORIGIN
Portugal.

SPECIAL SKILLS
Fisherman's working dog and family pet.

SIZE
The shoulder-height is 50 - 57cm (19½ - 22½in) for dogs, but a height of 54cm (21¼in) is preferred, and 43 - 52cm (17 - 20½in) for bitches, with a preferred height for them of 46cm (18in).

COAT
The coat is dense and wavy or curly. The most usual colors and combinations are black, brown, white, black and white, and brown and white.

Portuguese Water Dog with wavy coat

CARE REQUIRED
The wavy-coated variety is usually closely clipped at the hindquarters and on the nose but the curly-coated dogs generally have a working retriever clip (especially in the United States) so that only the tail is close-clipped. Groom them regularly with brush and comb.

CHARACTER
These are high-spirited, friendly, obedient, and sociable dogs, which are keen to work, intelligent, and quick to understand instructions. They also have a good nose for scents.

TRAINING
Training these dogs is not difficult if you understand their character. They like to work hard, are intelligent, and understand quickly.

These dogs are very sensitive to the intonations in your voice. Alternate training and play and bear in mind that this extremely intelligent dog will take liberties if you think you can just fit a bit of training in when it suits you. Make sure you are consistent.

SOCIAL BEHAVIOR
The companionship of dogs and other animals will be accepted without difficulty and these dogs are very good with children.

Portuguese Water Dog puppy with curly coat

EXERCISE

The Portuguese Water Dog, as its name suggests, loves to swim.

There is no greater pleasure you can give it than to throw sticks or a ball for it to retrieve from water. They are suitable for agility skills trials and numerous other dog sports.

Wetterhoun

COUNTRY OF ORIGIN
The Netherlands.

SPECIAL SKILLS
Hunting dog, watchdog, farm dog, and family pet.

SIZE
The Wetterhoun's coat is curly and oily. It must not be woolly. Accepted colors are plain black, or brown, black and white, brown and white, or brown roan.

CARE REQUIRED
Little grooming is required for the Wetterhoun. Comb the coat occasionally and check that the ears are clean.

These dogs can live happily in an outdoor kennel provided they have sufficient contact with you and get their daily exercise.

CHARACTER
This dog is physically very demanding of itself and can be sensitive. It is an intelligent, somewhat independent dog, often with a mind of its own. It is brave, reliable, and very vigilant. The Wetterhoun likes swimming.

TRAINING
This is not a suitable dog for the beginner. These dogs are intelligent and learn quickly but they are independent-minded enough to refuse your commands.

A consistent but kind approach is absolutely essential. Depending upon the individual dog, corrective action may be appropriate.

SOCIAL BEHAVIOR
For its own people the Wetterhoun is a good-natured and friendly dog – and this includes the children, provided they treat him properly. It's another story with strangers. In the case of strangers this dog is always cautious and ready to protect your home.

Family friends, on the other hand, will get a hearty welcome. Other dogs and pets will be accepted without a murmur.

EXERCISE
The Wetterhoun needs lots of exercise. The ideal situation for this dog is to have a large piece of land that it can run around on freely and which it will protect vigorously.

This dog has no roaming instinct so it is unlikely to run away.

SPECIAL REMARKS
A Wetterhoun will pine away in an apartment in a busy urban area because these dogs are not suited to such a life.
They are rarely seen outside their country of origin.

Wetterhoun

Head of a brown Wetterhoun

9. Toy and other miniature dogs

Bichons

Bichon Frisé

COUNTRY OF ORIGIN
Belgium/France.

SPECIAL SKILLS
Family pet.

SIZE
The shoulder-height may not exceed 30cm (11¾in) and the weight should be about 4kg (8¾lb).

COAT
The silken coat consists of locks of spirally formed hairs. There is no undercoat and the color is always pure white.

CARE REQUIRED
The coat should be combed thoroughly every day. Occasionally, the coat of this dog will need a professional clipping. In common with other dogs with such coats, the Bichon Frisé is clipped to a specific style which can vary from country to country.
To keep the coat white, it will be necessary to wash the dog regularly with a recognized dog shampoo. Check at set intervals that the hairs around the eyes are not causing irritation and use the special lotion for this purpose to remove any tear stains.
Clip excess hair between the pads of the feet and remove loose hairs and any dirt from the ear passages.
This breed does not shed hair. Brush the dog regularly to remove dead hairs.

CHARACTER
These dogs bond very closely with their handler, though they can be left alone occasionally. They are also pliable, cheerful, active, playful, intelligent, sociable, and sensitive.

TRAINING
Since these are bright dogs which quickly catch

Maltese

on to what you want them to do, there is no real problem in training them.

SOCIAL BEHAVIOR
Bichons are naturally sociable dogs which are happiest when they are part of a family which takes them everywhere. This sociable trait also means that they are fine in the company of other dogs, pets, and children.

EXERCISE
This breed adapts itself entirely to the family circumstances.

SPECIAL REMARKS
These dogs need intensive grooming or they look unkempt. If this is a problem, another breed of dog should be considered.

Bichon Frisé

Bolognese

COUNTRY OF ORIGIN
Italy.

SPECIAL SKILLS
Family pet.

SIZE
The shoulder-height is 25 - 30cm (9¾ - 11¾in) and the weight is 2.5 - 4kg (5½ - 8¾lb).

Bolognese

SOCIAL BEHAVIOR
The Bolognese gets on well with other dogs, pets, and children.

They want to be with their family all the time so should not be considered by a family which would need to leave them alone. They are cautious towards strangers.

EXERCISE
These dogs are satisfied with an average amount of exercise but greatly enjoy long walks when those are offered.

SPECIAL REMARKS
If the intensive grooming required for this breed can't be provided, choose another breed with a coat that requires less attention.

Coton de Tuléar

COAT
The coat, which is always white, consists of a mass of long, erect locks. There is no undercoat.

CARE REQUIRED
Because the hair tangles easily, the coat should be combed out every day, especially on the belly, behind the ears, and between the legs.

These dogs need to be bathed regularly to keep the coat white.

One advantage of the coat is that it does not shed hair, but dead hairs should be removed by brushing.

Check the ears to ensure they are clean and free of any loose hairs.

When necessary, clip excess hair from between the pads of the feet.

CHARACTER
This is a cheerful, intelligent, and obedient dog that is very affectionate, calm, and vigilant.

TRAINING
Since these dogs are anxious to please and find it easy to learn they are usually easy to train.

Coton de Tuléar

COUNTRY OF ORIGIN
Madagascar.

SPECIAL SKILLS
Family pet.

SIZE
The shoulder-height is 25 - 32cm (9¾ - 12½in) for dogs and 22 - 28cm (8½ - 11in) for bitches.

COAT
The fine, long hairs create a curly coat with a cotton-like texture. There is no undercoat. The color is always white with a few yellow to dark grey patches, especially by the ears.

CARE REQUIRED
The coat needs grooming with brush and comb several times each week.

These dogs do not shed hair but the dead hairs should be brushed out.

Remove excess hair between the pads of the feet and in the inner ear. The Coton de Tuléar does not need a bath more than once or twice a year which will be adequate to keep the coat clean.

CHARACTER
These dogs are friendly, intelligent, vigilant, and playful. Occasionally, they can be a little bit obstinate.

TRAINING
The Coton de Tuléar learns quite quickly. Remember that although they are intelligent and eager to work they can have minds of their own. They do well in various areas of dog sports such as agility skills trials and catch.

SOCIAL BEHAVIOR
These are very sociable dogs that are happy to live in friendship with other dogs and animals. They are usually first-class playmates for children.

EXERCISE
The dogs of this breed adapt seamlessly to the family requirements. They like to swim and play ball games.

Coton de Tuléar

Havanese

COUNTRY OF ORIGIN
Cuba.

SPECIAL SKILLS
Family pet.

Havanese with puppies

Havanese

SIZE
The shoulder height is 22–29cm (8½–11½in).

COAT
This dog has a long-haired coat without an undercoat. Any color is accepted, with the exception of black which is not recognized by some countries.

CARE REQUIRED
The coat needs considerable grooming. These dogs need to be thoroughly brushed and combed at least twice a week with a coarse comb. There is a lotion available to prevent the hair from splitting. Clip excess hair from between the pads of the feet. The feet themselves may be clipped to a round form.
This breed does not shed hair and dead hairs should be removed with a brush. Check the eyes regularly.

CHARACTER
These are cheerful, very affectionate, playful, gentle dogs which are highly intelligent, sociable, and sensitive.

TRAINING
The Havanese learns quickly and enjoys doing things for you which is why this breed has a long reputation as a circus dog. It is very sensitive to the intonation of your voice and harsh words will achieve very little except to upset the dog unnecessarily.
Some of them tend to bark more than necessary, so it is best to teach this dog when young not to do so before it becomes a habit.

SOCIAL BEHAVIOR
The Havanese gets along well with everyone including dogs and cats or other pets, and they can be fine too with children but they do not like to be pestered by them. If they are pestered, the dog may become withdrawn for quite some time.

EXERCISE
They have only an average need for exercise and three outings a day will keep them happy.

Löwchen (Little Lion Dog)

COUNTRY OF ORIGIN
France.

SPECIAL SKILLS
Family pet.

SIZE
The shoulder-height is 20 - 35cm (7¾ - 13¾in).

Löwchen or Little Lion Dog

Löwchen or Little Lion Dog

COAT

The coat is long and wavy but should not curl. Löwchen do not have undercoats. Any color is acceptable.

CARE REQUIRED

Brush and comb the coat regularly to prevent tangles forming. This dog is usually clipped out in the breed style regardless of whether they are to be shown. The hindquarters, the section of the tail closest to the body, and part of the front legs are close-clipped. The dog does not shed hairs. Remove any dead hairs by brushing.

CHARACTER

This is a cheerful, playful, and companionable dog that is intelligent, eager to learn, gentle, and sensitive.

TRAINING

These dogs usually learn quickly and present little difficulty in their training.

SOCIAL BEHAVIOR

The company of children and other household animals causes no problems of any kind.

EXERCISE

These dogs have average needs in terms of exercise and normally will adapt to your circumstances although when you want to go for a long walk, this dog will be happy to go along.

Maltezer

Maltese

Maltese puppy

COUNTRY OF ORIGIN

Italy/Malta.

SPECIAL SKILLS

Family pet.

SIZE

The shoulder-height is 21 - 25cm (8½ - 9¾in) for dogs and 20 - 23cm (7¾ - 9in) for bitches.

COAT

The Maltese has a white coat of long silken hair without an undercoat. The coat is always parted down the center of the back.

CARE REQUIRED

Grooming requirements for this breed are substantial, including daily brushing and combing and regular washing. There is a special lotion to remove the ugly "tear" stains that some dogs get.

Hairs can grow in the corner of the eyes which cause irritation and should be removed. As these dogs do not shed hair, the dead hairs should be brushed out. The coat is supposed to be long, reaching the ground.

The hair in front of the eyes is usually held together with a hair band or bow. Keeping the coat in show condition requires considerable effort.

Owners of show dogs oil the hair and wind the hair in curling papers to prevent it from splitting.

CHARACTER

These are friendly, lovable, and playful dogs which are sociable and eager to learn but very sensitive.

They can get along very well with children and bond very closely with their handler.

TRAINING

Training these dogs is relatively easy because they like to be with their family and will adapt to almost any circumstance.

They are very sensitive to harsh words and

should always be trained with encouragement, rather than harsh words.

SOCIAL BEHAVIOR
The Maltese likes to avoid causing any problems and therefore usually gets on well with other dogs, household animals, and children.
The breed causes no difficulties with visitors.

EXERCISE
It is not necessary to take this dog for lots of long walks but if you like doing so it will enjoy them.

Poodles

Poodles

Toy and Miniature Poodles

COUNTRY OF ORIGIN
France.

SPECIAL SKILLS
Family pet.

SIZE
The minimum shoulder height for the Toy Poodle is 25cm (9¾in) and should not be more than 28cm (11in).
The shoulder-height for the Miniature Poodle is 28 - 35cm (11 - 13¾in).

COAT
The coat consists of fine, woolly, frizzy hair. Acceptable colors are monotone white, black, apricot, brown, and grey.
Poodles that form corded coats are very unusual.

CARE REQUIRED
Show dogs have to be clipped out according to the breed style. This requires considerable skill

and knowledge and is best left to a professional. Keeping a dog in this condition requires not only considerable time but also costs a great deal of money.

The Poodle is regarded as one of the most difficult breed standard patterns to achieve, if not the most difficult. There is tremendous competition at shows.

Poodles that are kept as pets are usually closely trimmed, leaving longer hair on the head, the ears, and the legs. The grooming requirements for these household pets is considerably easier than with show dogs. Poodles do not shed. Check the teeth regularly for tartar and clean the ears regularly. Poodles can be washed quite often.

CHARACTER
These are lively, playful dogs that are intelligent, and keen to learn but very sensitive. They bond closely with their owner and family.

TRAINING
Miniature and Toy Poodles are very intelligent dogs, which if handled properly, quickly learn what is required of them.

The best results are achieved with a gentle but consistent approach.

SOCIAL BEHAVIOR
These are generally trouble-free dogs in terms of getting along with other dogs and pets. They announce visitors but that is all.

EXERCISE
Although these Poodles can happily live in an apartment it is important to give them as much exercise as possible.

Brown Toy Poodle

Giant Poodle

COUNTRY OF ORIGIN
France.

SPECIAL SKILLS
Hunting dog by origin, now a family pet.

SIZE
The shoulder-height is 45 - 58cm (17¾ - 22¾in).

COAT
The coat consists of fine, woolly, frizzy hair. Acceptable colors are monotone white, black, apricot, brown, and grey.
Poodles that form corded coats are rare.

Black Giant Poodle with corded coat

CARE REQUIRED
See Miniature and Toy Poodles.

CHARACTER
These are high-spirited and highly intelligent dogs that are sporty, companionable, loyal, pliable, active, careful, curious, and vigilant. They are eager to learn and so easy to train.

TRAINING
The Giant Poodle learns quite quickly and training should be easy. Be clear with them and make sure that you are always consistent.

Poodles are very sensitive to the intonation of your voice.

SOCIAL BEHAVIOR
These are sociable animals by nature and they get on well with dogs and other pets as well as with children.
The dogs are vigilant but not unfriendly towards strangers.

EXERCISE
Giant Poodles need fairly substantial amounts of exercise. Play ball with them in the yard or take them for long walks to keep them in shape. They do well at such things as catch, activity skills trials, and obedience competitions. The Giant Poodle is one of the most intelligent dog breeds in the world.

Grey Standard Poodle

Standard Poodle

COUNTRY OF ORIGIN
France.

SPECIAL SKILLS
Hunting dog by origin but now a family pet.

SIZE
The shoulder-height is 35 - 45cm (13¾ - 17¾in).

COAT
The coat consists of fine, woolly, frizzy hair. Acceptable colors are monotone white, black, apricot, brown, and grey. Poodles that form corded coats after a time are rare.

CARE REQUIRED
See Miniature and Toy Poodles.

CHARACTER
These are extremely intelligent, high-spirited dogs which are lively, affectionate, and sociable with other dogs.

They are very loyal to their handler. Most of them love to swim.

TRAINING
This breed is fairly easy to train because they learn so quickly. They tend to do very well in such games as catch, and agility skills trials.

SOCIAL BEHAVIOR
These dogs get on well with their own kind and with other household pets as well as with children. You will always be warned of visitors.

EXERCISE
This Poodle needs fairly large amounts of exercise. Most of them like to swim and to retrieve.

Belgian Griffons

Griffon Bruxellois, Belgian Griffon and Petit Brabançon

COUNTRY OF ORIGIN
Belgium.

SPECIAL SKILLS
Family pets.

WEIGHT
These dogs weigh about 5kg (11lb).

COAT
The Griffon Bruxellois and the Belgian Griffon are rough-haired The Griffon Bruxellois is reddish pink, perhaps with black on its nose and chin.
The Belgian Griffon is completely black, black

Griffons and Petit Brabançons

Belgian Griffon (Griffon Belge)

and tan, or red. The Petit Brabançon is short-haired and is accepted in the same colors as the other Griffons.

CARE REQUIRED
The rough-haired Griffons are usually plucked by hand at regular intervals, leaving the beard, moustache, and other facial hair features alone. Comb the beard frequently as food can get caught in it and it tangles easily.

The hairs in the corners of the eye must be removed if necessary to prevent them pricking the eyeball and causing irritation.

CHARACTER
These are curious, mischievous dogs that are playful, straightforward, calm, and eager to learn. They are also good with children. They watch their surroundings closely and like to be near their handler.

TRAINING
Training should run smoothly because these are very intelligent dogs that are anxious to learn. They do well in many areas of dog sports.

Griffon Bruxellois (Brussels Griffon)

Petit Brabançon

SOCIAL BEHAVIOR
The dogs of these breeds get on well with children, dogs, and cats because they are naturally sociable and enjoy company.

EXERCISE
Although Griffons can be perfectly happily kept in an apartment, they do like to be taken to the woods and other country places.

This is important to keep these dogs really happy even though they adapt so well to town life.

Hairless dogs

Chinese Crested

COUNTRY OF ORIGIN
China.

SPECIAL SKILLS
Companionship dog.

SIZE
The shoulder-height is 28 - 33cm (11 - 13in) for dogs and 23 - 30cm (9 - 11¾in) for bitches.

COAT
There are two sorts of Chinese Crested. One only has hair on its head, ears, the tip of the tail, and a few on the feet. The hairless body feels soft to the touch.
The other type is known as the Powder Puff. This type has an undercoat and a veil-like topcoat of silken hair.

Any color is acceptable. These two varieties are interbred with each other.

CARE REQUIRED
The skin of the Chinese Crested requires careful attention. Those with show dogs wash the skin regularly with skin exfoliating creams made for humans to remove the dead cells and to soften the skin. The important point is for the skin to be supple and smooth and protected against becoming dry. There are excellent lotions and creams for this purpose. The unpigmented areas of the dog's skin are especially sensitive to the sun and it is advisable to either keep the dog out of the sun entirely or to use a good quality sunscreen on it. The Powder Puff should be brushed now and then and washed frequently. Usually these dogs have the hair on the face

Chinese Crested Powder Puff

clipped to form downward-facing points to achieve the typical style of this type of dog.

CHARACTER
These are high-spirited, cunning, and playful dogs that are sensitive, vigilant, very lively, and active. They are cautious with people they do not know.

TRAINING
The Chinese Crested is not difficult to train because this dog is intelligent and quick to grasp what is required of it.

SOCIAL BEHAVIOR
Provided children do not disturb the dog in what it considers its own territory, they will have no problems with this dog. These dogs also rarely cause problems with other dogs and pets.

EXERCISE
They adapt to the family circumstances in terms of their exercise needs. If you can give them lots of exercise they will enjoy that but if you can't they will be content with their three walks around the block.

SPECIAL REMARKS
Skin wounds hardly show up on dogs with hair but the opposite is the case with the Chinese

Crested. An advantage of these dogs is that they are very clean and there are no loose hairs to litter the carpet.

Chinese Crested

Head of a Chinese Crested

Mexican Hairless or Xoloitzcuintli

Mexican Hairless or Xoloitzcuintli

COUNTRY OF ORIGIN
Mexico.

SPECIAL SKILLS
Watchdog and family pet.

SIZE
The Mexican Hairless is bred in two sizes: one has a shoulder-height of 25 - 33cm (9¾ - 13in), the other is 33 - 56cm (13 - 22in).

COAT
This breed has no hair except for a tuft of short straight hairs on the forehead and longer hair on the tip of the tail.

The skin is a variety of colors including black, elephant grey, dark bronze, and grey-black.

CARE REQUIRED
The fact that this breed has no hair does not mean that its skin requires no care. The skin must be protected as much as possible from the sun to prevent sunburn. Use a good sunscreen on it if the dog will be in the sun.

People who show these dogs scrub them regularly to remove dead skin and to keep the skin soft, using special exfoliating creams intended for use by humans.

It is most important to keep the skin supple and smooth and to prevent it becoming dry by using a lotion or cream or, sometimes, rubbing it with oil.

CHARACTER
These dogs are affectionate towards their own people and get on well with children.

They are also intelligent, peaceful, and noble, and are extremely adaptable. They cannot bark but let out a sound like a howl.

TRAINING
The Mexican Hairless is not difficult to train.

SOCIAL BEHAVIOR
These highly noticeable dogs generally get on with other dogs, all household animals, and with children.

EXERCISE
This breed does not require much exercise. If you let them romp and play regularly, they will be

Mexican Hairless or Xoloitzcuintli

quite contented. They are happy to walk on the leash everywhere their handler goes.

SPECIAL REMARKS
The Mexican Hairless or Xoloitzcuintli is an extremely rare and special dog. These breed is in danger of dying out from lack of interest in it, which would be unfortunate.

Tibetan breeds

Lhasa Apso

COUNTRY OF ORIGIN
Tibet.

SPECIAL SKILLS
Family pet.

SIZE
The shoulder-height is about 25cm (9¾in).

COAT
The very long topcoat has no curls and is quite hard. The undercoat is medium-length and somewhat softer. Almost any color is acceptable,

including blue, black, all manner of shades of beige, red, grey, white, brown, and multi-colored.

CARE REQUIRED
Groom this dog thoroughly with brush and comb every week, paying attention not only to the topcoat but also removing and preventing tangles in the undercoat.

Do not pull too hard during combing to keep the hairs from breaking. If necessary, use a special lotion to keep the hair from becoming brittle. Check the eyes regularly for dirt and for any irritant hair, clip excess hair from between the pads of the feet, and keep the ear passages clean. Getting the coat into show condition and then keeping it so requires much attention.

Dogs kept as pets are often clipped short, and although breed enthusiasts will frown at this, it is preferable to a long-haired dog going through life with its coat full of tangles.

CHARACTER
These are calm, loyal, lovable dogs, which are equable, cheerful, and independent. They are distrustful of strangers. The Lhasa Apso likes company but it will not cling to you.

TRAINING

In common with other Eastern breeds, the Lhasa Apso is somewhat obstinate. Do not expect any tricks from it and lead its character in the right direction by rewarding it when it does well.

Harsh words will deeply upset these dogs, causing them to feel insulted, be disconcerted and grow withdrawn. They are intelligent enough to understand your rules.

SOCIAL BEHAVIOR

The Lhaso Apso gets on well with other dogs and other household pets and children. They are rather cautious towards strangers.

EXERCISE

These dogs have normal exercise needs. The dogs are quite happy indoors and there is no need to go for long walks on their account.

SPECIAL REMARKS

Provided you do not regard grooming as an unimportant little job to be fitted in when you can, the Lhasa Apso is an excellent dog for a family.

Shih Tzu

Shih Tzu

Shih Tzus

Shih Tzu

COUNTRY OF ORIGIN
Tibet.

SPECIAL SKILLS
Family pet.

SIZE
The shoulder-height is about 25cm (9¾in) and the weight is 5 - 6kg (11 - 13¼lb).

COAT
The long-haired coat is accepted in any color, including beige, black, and red, often with white.

CARE REQUIRED
A Shih Tzu requires a lot of grooming. Comb the coat thoroughly every day to prevent tangles. A hair bow or something similar is essential to keep the hair out of the dog's eyes. These dogs have very sensitive eyes so be sure they are kept clean.
Use the special eye drops prepared for this purpose. Clean the ear passages regularly, too. If

you do not have the time to keep the coat in good condition, you will need to take the dog to a professional about every two months to be clipped.

CHARACTER
These are intelligent, lovable, affectionate, cheerful, and sociable dogs that are also independent. They are not the kind of dogs that consider everyone a friend. The Shih Tzu rarely barks.

TRAINING
If you approach this somewhat obstinate breed with plenty of patience and remain consistent at all times, it is possible to achieve a reasonable level of training.

SOCIAL BEHAVIOR
Dogs of this breed usually get on well with other household animals and children. They always behave with dignity.

EXERCISE
The Shih Tzu is content with short walks.

SPECIAL REMARKS
The true beauty of this breed is only fully appreciated when the coat is immaculately groomed.
It is difficult to attain and maintain the level of condition required for showing.

Tibetan Spaniel

Tibetan Spaniel

COUNTRY OF ORIGIN
Tibet.

SPECIAL SKILLS
Family pet.

SIZE
The shoulder-height is about 25cm (9¾cm) and the weight is 4 - 6.5kg (8¾ - 14½lb).

COAT
The Tibetan Spaniel has a double, long, silken-haired coat. Any color is acceptable but the most common color is golden.

CARE REQUIRED
The coat is fairly easy to care for. Brush the dog regularly and keep the ear passages clean.

CHARACTER
These self-assured dogs are brave, vigilant, and cautious with strangers but they are not the kind of dog that barks a lot and jumps all over a stranger. They are also blessed with a strong constitution and intelligence.

TRAINING
Tibetan Spaniels are quite easily trained because they quickly grasp what you intend.

Always be consistent with them because they can sometimes be obstinate.

SOCIAL BEHAVIOR
These dogs are very good at living with children and can also get on well with other dogs and cats provided they have met them when they were young.
They always warn of danger.

EXERCISE
These dogs do not need much exercise to keep them in good condition.

It is sufficient to take them for three short walks each day and then to let them run and play off the leash in your yard.

Tibetan Terriers

Tibetan Terriers

COUNTRY OF ORIGIN
Tibet.

SPECIAL SKILLS
Family pet.

SIZE
The shoulder-height is 35.5 - 43cm (14 - 17in) for dogs. The bitches are slightly smaller.

COAT
Tibetan Terriers have a double coat: the topcoat is long, luxuriant, fine, and either straight or wavy while the undercoat is dense and woolly. The colors of these dogs can be black, white, various shades of beige or grey, and multi-colored.

CARE REQUIRED
Brush this dog every day to prevent tangles and remove loose hair. Do not overlook those places where tangles form most readily, such as beneath the leg joints, the beard, and the hindquarters. Give this dog regular baths and remove excess hair from the ear passages. Clip any build-up of hair between the pads of the feet.

CHARACTER
Beneath its cuddly appearance on the outside is a tough, brave dog, that is lively, vigilant, equable, intelligent, noble, and cheerful.

These dogs are dedicated to their handler and somewhat cautious with strangers, and try to dominate other dogs. They are unhappy when left alone.

TRAINING
Train these dogs in a calm, equable manner. They are sensitive by nature and react very well to the intonation of your voice.

SOCIAL BEHAVIOR
When these dogs are with other dogs, they can try to dominate.

They need to be socially trained when young with cats and other household animals if they are to live in harmony with them.
They are good with children if the children do not pester them.

EXERCISE
This breed has lots of energy and the dog must have regular opportunities to enjoy itself. Agility skills trials and games of catch are suitable activities for them.

Tibetan Terrier

Chihuahua

Chihuahua

COUNTRY OF ORIGIN
Mexico.

SPECIAL SKILLS
Family pet.

SIZE
The Chihuahua is the world's smallest dog, weighing between 500 - 2,500g (1 - 5½lb).

COAT
There are long-coat and short-coat Chihuahuas. Their colors include black, white, blue, red, or wheaten, with or without dark or white markings.

CARE REQUIRED
The long-haired type of Chihuahua should be groomed normally with brush and comb while

Short-coat Chihuahua

Long-coat Chihuahua

the short-haired ones should be groomed occasionally with a rubber brush. Administer eye-drops regularly to prevent "tear" stains, and check the teeth frequently for tartar and to ensure with young dogs that the new teeth are forming properly. Keep the claws trimmed.

CHARACTER
These are intelligent, brave little dogs but sometimes they are too brave for their own good. They can be stubborn, and can also be sensitive, and playful. Chihuahuas usually bond with one person.

Long-coat Chihuahua

TRAINING
Because these little dogs can do little damage, they are usually not trained. This is a shame because the Chihuahua is an eager pupil.

SOCIAL BEHAVIOR
Chihuahuas are sociable animals so that living together with dogs and cats does not usually cause any difficulty.

Do not forget that they are so small that they can easily be trampled underfoot by larger dogs. They are not suitable for small children who will tend to regard the dog as a toy.

EXERCISE
Because these dogs are so small, they usually get sufficient exercise indoors.

If taught to do so, they can use a cat litter tray for their toilet. They feel the cold, damp, and draughts, and they need to wear a coat when they go outside in cold or rainy weather.

The Chihuahua is a perfect choice for people who do not have much space in their home. You can easily take them with you everywhere and they are inexpensive to feed.

It is a shame that this little creature is regarded as a toy. Try not to forget that this animal is a real dog, in spite of its size, complete with the needs of all dogs.

Short-coat Chihuahua puppies

Dwarf English Spaniels

Cavalier King Charles Spaniel

Cavalier King Charles Spaniels

Cavalier King Charles Spaniel

COUNTRY OF ORIGIN
England.

SPECIAL SKILLS
Family pet.

SIZE
The weight is 5.4 - 8.1kg (11¾- 17¾lb).

COAT
The coat consists of light to firmly waved soft hair.
The recognized colors are black and tan, ruby, and Blenheim (chestnut markings on a pearl white ground).

There is also a three-colored coat (black and white with russet brown markings).

CARE REQUIRED
Comb the coat regularly with particular care

given to the chest, ears, and between the legs. Check the ears frequently for dirt or loose hairs.

CHARACTER
These are lovable engaging dogs that are high-spirited and active, intelligent, obedient, gentle, sociable, and very adaptable.

TRAINING
Since these dogs want to learn and are intelligent enough to understand what you want, they are usually easy to train.

SOCIAL BEHAVIOR
These are uncomplicated household companions that happily get along with children, other dogs, and any other animals you may have.

EXERCISE
The Cavalier King Charles Spaniel will adapt itself to your family circumstances.

Cavalier King Charles Spaniel

King Charles Spaniel

Head of a King Charles Spaniel

King Charles Spaniel

COUNTRY OF ORIGIN
England.

SPECIAL SKILLS
Family pet.

SIZE
The shoulder-height is 25 - 30cm (9¾ - 11¾cm) and the weight is about 5kg (11lb).

COAT
The coat consists of lightly waved, long, soft hair. The colors are black and tan, ruby, and Blenheim (chestnut markings on a pearl white ground).
There is also a three-colored coat (black and white with reddish brown markings).

CARE REQUIRED
Take care of the folds of the face from time to time with a special lotion for this purpose and brush the coat well twice each week, with particular attention to the hair on the chest, behind the ears, and between the legs.
Remove any dirt or loose hairs from the ear passages.

CHARACTER
These dogs like to be with the family and to receive lots of attention. They are playful, intelligent, cheerful, and are also very adaptable. They rarely bark.

TRAINING
Training these dogs is usually very easy because they are intelligent enough to quickly grasp what is expected of them.

King Charles Spaniels

SOCIAL BEHAVIOR

The dogs of this breed are almost exclusively sociable animals which usually get on with other dogs and household pets.

Children which approach calmly will not have any problems.

EXERCISE

They adapt themselves for their exercise needs to the family of which they form a part.

Japanese Chin and Pekingese

Japanese Chin (Japanese Spaniel)

COUNTRY OF ORIGIN

China.

SPECIAL SKILLS

Family pet.

SIZE

The shoulder-height is 20 - 25cm (7¾ - 9¾in), although the dogs may be slightly taller. The weight is 2.5 - 3kg (5½ - 6½lb).

COAT

The silken coat consists of soft, long hair which should not be curly. The accepted colors are black with white or red with white.

The red with white combination is permitted to vary from lemon to dark red. The most usual coloring is black with white.

There are also three colored dogs and sable and white but these are not recognized in every country.

CARE REQUIRED

The beautiful coat fortunately does not easily tangle so that grooming twice per week with a brush and comb is sufficient.

To keep the beautiful white of the coat, it will be necessary to wash the dog from time to time. Keep the ear passages clean and clean the facial creases with acid-free petroleum jelly, to prevent dark stains.

CHARACTER

These engaging dogs are affectionate, and playful, but also calm, straightforward and cheerful. They can have minds of their own and they like to be the center of attention. They do not bark often. They like to be close to their handler.

Japanese Chin or Japanese Spaniel

TRAINING

Provided you make allowances for a slight obstinate streak, there should be few problems in training this dog. It is usually quickly house broken.

SOCIAL BEHAVIOR

These are not difficult dogs and they usually get on extremely well with children, cats, and other dogs. A dog of this size cannot, of course, cope with rough handling by larger dogs or children. These dogs will not readily bite.

EXERCISE

Running, romping, and playing are the activities this breed enjoys. Some people insist they can also climb.

They will be perfectly happy in an apartment and they can be taught to use a cat litter tray. In such cases make sure they do get sufficient exercise and fresh air.

Japanese Chin

Japanese Chins

Pekingese

Pekingese

COUNTRY OF ORIGIN

China.

SPECIAL SKILLS

Companion dog.

SIZE

The shoulder-height is about 20cm (7¾in) and these dogs weigh 4 - 5kg (8¾ - 11lb).

COAT

The abundant long-haired coat has a copious undercoat.

A wide range of colors are known for the breed with the most usual being black and beige, sometimes combined with white. There are no albino or liver-colored Pekingese.

CARE REQUIRED

This breed requires intensive grooming of its coat. Teach the dog when it is young to regard grooming as something enjoyable, as otherwise you will end up in a wrestling match every time you use a brush and comb later. Pay special attention to the hair under the leg joints, on the belly, and the legs, where tangles form most readily. Before, during, and after grooming you can use talcum powder or dry shampoo. Give attention to the facial creases where infections are otherwise likely to occur. Clip the excess hair from between the pads of the feet.

CHARACTER

These are affectionate, noble dogs that possess a winning way. They can be both self-centered and stubborn, but they are intelligent, brave, and not particularly fond of strangers. They choose who will be their "boss".

TRAINING

Although a Pekingese will not let you be overly bossy with it, you must teach it some basic principles if you do not want to be saddled with a bad-tempered dog that wants its own way all the time.

Praise it when it does something well but do not punish too harshly when it gets it wrong – this is the best way to achieve anything. A Pekingese that has been punished will withdraw, feeling very hurt and affronted.

SOCIAL BEHAVIOR
Pekingese do not generally have problems in mixing with other animals although this has a lot to do with the extent to which they have been socially trained. Since they do not like to be disturbed when they are resting, they are not really suitable for a household with young children.

EXERCISE
These dogs are not really suitable for long walks because of their physique.

Since they have relatively small demands for exercise, they are ideal dogs for those living in towns or for people who don't like exercise themselves.

SPECIAL REMARKS
Careful grooming is an essential part of caring for this dog.

Continental Dwarf Spaniels

Papillon and Epagneul Phalene

COUNTRY OF ORIGIN
Belgium/France.

SPECIAL SKILLS
Family pet.

SIZE
The shoulder-height for both breeds is about 28cm (11in).

COAT
The long-haired coat is usually white with colored patches. A white blaze on the head is desirable.

CARE REQUIRED
Brush regularly and thoroughly and remove loose hairs from the ear passages.

Papillon

CHARACTER
These are affectionate, lovable, lively little dogs that are playful, intelligent, and keen to learn. They can be jealous of and withdrawn with strangers.

TRAINING
Be gentle when training this dog. It is always eager to learn which means it is fairly easy to teach. Vary basic instruction by playing ball or with some reward.

These are very intelligent and obedient dogs that with the right training can perform outstandingly in obedience and agility skills trials, or at catch.

SOCIAL BEHAVIOR
Some of these dogs can be jealous if their owner's attention is directed elsewhere but this does not apply to every dog and is largely dependent upon the way their social training was carried out. In general they get on well with other pets and children.

Epagneul Phalene

Dwarf Mastiffs

Boston Terrier

COUNTRY OF ORIGIN
England/United States.

SPECIAL SKILLS
Family pet.

SIZE
Boston Terriers are bred in a variety of sizes. The largest of them should not weigh more than 11kg (24lb).

COAT
The short-haired coat can be a black roan or black with white markings. The preference is for the roan.

CARE REQUIRED
These dogs do not require much grooming. Run a smooth glove or brush across the coat.

Keep the ears clean and the claws trimmed. Attend to the facial creases occasionally with a special lotion made for this purpose.

CHARACTER
These are intelligent, enthusiastic, occasionally boisterous dogs, that have a sense of humor, are playful, self-confident, and affectionate.

They make good watchdogs without barking unnecessarily.

TRAINING
The breed is not difficult to train because they like to learn and their intelligence ensures they pick things up quickly. They are very sensitive to the intonation of your voice.

Boston Terriers

SOCIAL BEHAVIOR
Generally these dogs can get along very well with other dogs and pets and also with children.

EXERCISE
This Terrier has no desire for long walks but does like to go everywhere you go. They are fairly lightweight and often can easily be carried. They love to play.

French Bulldog

COUNTRY OF ORIGIN
France.

SPECIAL SKILLS
Family pet.

SIZE
The shoulder-height is about 30cm (11¾in) and the weight is 8 - 13kg (17½ - 28½lb).

COAT
The coat is made up of short, shiny hairs which lie one upon another to form a dense layer. They can be a roan but fawn and white with streaked patches is the most usual combination.

CARE REQUIRED
There is little to the grooming of this breed. Brush them occasionally with a rubber brush and keep the ear passages clean – do not use cotton swabs as they tend to push the wax and debris into the ear.

Clip the claws to keep them short and treat the facial creases with a special lotion occasionally. Petroleum jelly can also be used.

CHARACTER
These are intelligent, very affectionate, lovable dogs that are tolerant of children, and also playful, cheerful, sensitive, sometimes boisterous, with a strongly developed sense of humor.

They are persistent, tough on themselves, and sometimes can be obstinate. French Bulldogs can be jealous if their owner's attention is directed elsewhere. They like to be part of the family and hate being left alone.

TRAINING
This breed is not difficult to train because they are bright and learn quickly. Always be consistent with them.

They are not only sensitive to the intonation of your voice but will pick up on any bad atmosphere in your house.

SOCIAL BEHAVIOR
It is often said that these dogs adore children but actually it is more the case that children adore these dogs. Some of these dogs can try to dominate other dogs, although there are never problems with other household pets provided these dogs have met them when they were young and grown up with them.

Most of them are fond of people and visitors are generally enthusiastically welcomed, although some of the dogs can be quite antagonistic toward strangers.

EXERCISE
Provided these dogs get enough attention they don't require much exercise.

In hot weather avoid exercise because of their short noses. They usually are content with three walks around the block if they also have a chance to run and play in the yard. They are ideal dogs for apartment living.

SPECIAL REMARKS
The French Bulldog likes to be part of the family and can be taken everywhere with you. They do not belong in a kennel.

Pug

COUNTRY OF ORIGIN
England.

SPECIAL SKILLS
Family pet.

SIZE
The shoulder-height is about 35cm (13¾in) and the weight is about 7kg (15½lb).

Pug

COAT

The short-haired coat can be black, silver, or beige, all with a black mask.

CARE REQUIRED

Attend to the facial creases now and then with the special lotion intended for this purpose. Loose hair can be easily removed with a rubber brush. When necessary, apply drops to the eyes.

CHARACTER

These straightforward pliable dogs are calm indoors, sociable, sensitive, have a well-developed sense of humor, are very affectionate and intelligent, and they are physically demanding of themselves. Most of them snore.

TRAINING

Train them with a gentle-handed approach. They are sensitive to the tone of your voice so harsh punishment is unnecessary.

SOCIAL BEHAVIOR

Pugs get on well with other dogs and pets, and they behave impeccably with both children and visitors.

Do not forget, though, that they require lots of attention and become jealous if their owner ignores them.

EXERCISE

When the weather is good these dogs love to romp and play outdoors.

If it is very hot, do not leave them outside for long and make sure they have a cool shady place to spend most of the day.

The expressive face of a Pug.

Pug

Most French Bulldogs are gentle with children.

10. Sighthounds

Breeds with feathering or long coats

Afghan Hound

COUNTRY OF ORIGIN
Afghanistan/England.

SPECIAL SKILLS
Hunter by sight of large and small wild game, also watchdog, racing dog, and companion.

SIZE
The shoulder-height is 68 - 74cm (26¾ - 29¼in) for dogs and 63 - 69cm (24¾ - 27¼in) for bitches.

COAT
The Afghan Hound has a very long, fine coat. The hair on the face is short.

Any color is accepted but the most common colors are red through to shades of beige, often with a darker mask.

CARE REQUIRED
The grooming of the coat of these dogs requires a full hour, twice a week. The best method is to comb each handful of hair from the skin outwards so that no tangles can be overlooked, being careful not to break any of the hairs. Keep the ear passages clean.

Afghans should be bathed about every two months, using a good quality dog shampoo which does not dry the skin. Grooming is so basic to the care of an Afghan Hound that no one should consider owning one who doesn't have the time to do it.

CHARACTER
These are independent, proud, and noble dogs that are calm indoors but very active and fast outdoors.

These intelligent animals are not slavishly obedient. They are brave, and vigilant, not noisy, and cautious with strangers. By instinct, they will chase anything that moves quickly. The males can try to dominate.

Afghan Hound

TRAINING
These dogs are not suitable for inexperienced people.
Their independent nature makes them difficult to train and they will never be totally and consistently obedient.

Hitting or shouting at them lowers their respect for their handler. The best way to achieve anything with these dogs is to use a firm yet soft hand with them.

SOCIAL BEHAVIOR
The dogs can be rather dominant towards other males.
They get along fine with children provided the dog is not pestered by them and is left alone in its own territory.

They are probably better for a family with older children. An existing cat will be accepted. Remember it is in their blood to chase anything that runs quickly.

EXERCISE
The Afghan Hound needs lots of exercise. Try bicycling with the dog every day to give it the chance to get rid of its energy, but do not forget their hunting instinct.

Only allow an Afghan to run freely off the leash where it cannot run off.

Afghan Hound

A well groomed Afghan Hound is a marvelous sight and the dog knows it. This is a dog for the real enthusiast; you must appreciate its independent and sometimes unfathomable character.

Borzoi

Borzoi

COUNTRY OF ORIGIN
Russia.

SPECIAL SKILLS
Hunting by sight of large and small game, companion.

SIZE
The shoulder-height is 70 - 82cm (27½ - 32¼in) for dogs, and about 5cm (2in) shorter for bitches.

COAT
The coat consists of soft, medium-length wavy hair.
Accepted colors are white, gold, red, grey, black, black roan, and patched.

CARE REQUIRED
The coat needs regular grooming. Trim excess hair from between the pads of the feet. During the growing stage, these dogs need a highly nutritional diet.

CHARACTER
These are proud and self-aware dogs that are loyal to their family. They are also good-natured, equable, calm when indoors, and somewhat independent.

The Borzoi may be difficult to understand. When necessary, these dogs will protect your home.

TRAINING
The training of this breed has to be based upon mutual respect.
They really are not very obedient dogs but they can learn the basic requirements for living with you.

SOCIAL BEHAVIOR
These dogs do not like intrusive strangers. They are noble animals that get on fairly well with children but they are certainly not playmates.

They prize their rest and do not like rough play. They are usually fine with like-minded dogs. It is advisable to train them socially with cats and other pets as young as possible but they will always be hunters that and will race after a fleeing animal.

Borzoi

EXERCISE
Indoors the Borzoi can be so peaceful it might escape notice but outdoors it needs lots of space to walk and run.

In some countries it is forbidden to allow all the dogs in this fleet-footed hunting category off the leash. They usually enjoy running alongside a bicycle but beware – a Borzoi is quite likely to shoot off after any prey it catches sight of. You will need to react very quickly if this happens.

SPECIAL REMARKS

These majestic dogs are at their best with an owner who has a large area of fenced ground in which they can run all day to their heart's content.

Indoors they like to be close to the family and are fond of rest and comfort, making them unsuitable for life in a kennel.

Head of a Saluki

Saluki

COUNTRY OF ORIGIN
Iran.

SPECIAL SKILLS
Hunter by sight of large and small game, and a companion.

SIZE
The shoulder-height is 58 - 71cm (22¾ - 28in) for dogs, and slightly less for the bitches.

COAT
The coat is smooth and silken. The hair on the tail, ears, and rear of the legs should be feather-like and longer.
Salukis are white, cream, sandy, golden, red, grey with grey, three-colored (black, brown, and white), black with brown, and variations of these colorings.

CARE REQUIRED
The coat is kept in condition with an occasional thorough brushing, especially of the longer haired parts of the dog. Check the ear passages to make sure they are clean.

CHARACTER
These are independent dogs with minds of their own but they are noble, peaceful, and need the company of their owner. They are cautious with strangers and have strong hunting instincts.

TRAINING
A degree of care is needed in the rearing of a young Saluki.

This breed will never be perfectly obedient so do not set your sights too high. With much patience and insight you can get the dog to be fond of you and not an embarrassment to you.

SOCIAL BEHAVIOR
Salukis can get along perfectly well with like-minded dogs and it is possible to put them together with children.

Other animals are better kept well away from them, because their hunting instincts are very strong.
With a few exceptions it has proven impossible to train these dogs not to hunt.

EXERCISE
Salukis hunt on sight which means that they may not be let off the leash in some countries. They will pay no attention to their handler's calls if they are chasing something.

Trotting alongside a bicycle is an excellent ways for them to get rid of their energy.

Saluki

Rough-haired breeds

Deerhound

COUNTRY OF ORIGIN
Great Britain.

SPECIAL SKILLS
Hunter by sight of large game and family pet.

SIZE
The shoulder-height is a minimum of 76cm (30in) for dogs and 71cm (28in) for bitches.

COAT
The rough, medium-length coat should not feel woolly. The most common and the most prized color is a dark blue-grey.
Yellow, sandy red, light grey, and roans of these colors are also possible, with dark mask and ears. A small amount of white on the tip of the tail, chest, and feet is acceptable.

CARE REQUIRED
The coat should be brushed thoroughly on a regular basis. Pluck excess hair from the ear passages from time to time and remove surplus hair between the pads of the feet.
The coat may require plucking by hand once or twice per year depending on its condition.

CHARACTER
These are friendly, gentle, sensible, and straightforward dogs that are noble, intelligent, kind to children, and not particularly vigilant.

They rarely bark but are rather hard on themselves physically. Most of them have very strong hunting instincts.

Deerhound

TRAINING
The Deerhound learns quite quickly providing the handler and dog understand each other. A friendly request is often all that is needed to get the dog to do what you want.

SOCIAL BEHAVIOR
With dogs similar to it the Deerhound can get along fine and there are few difficulties with children.
Some of the dogs of this breed have stronger hunting instincts than others and this will have to be remembered if you have cats and other animals.

EXERCISE
This dog needs lots of exercise. Once you have seen how much enjoyment they get when allowed to run freely you will understand that these dogs cannot be limited to three trips around the block a day.

Trotting alongside a bicycle will keep them both mentally and physically fit.

Irish Wolfhound

COUNTRY OF ORIGIN
Ireland.

SPECIAL SKILLS
Hunter by sight of large game and family pet.

SIZE
The shoulder-height is a minimum of 79cm (31¼in) for dogs and 71cm (28in) for bitches.

COAT
The coat consists of rough, coarse, hard, and rather unkempt-looking hair. They can be grey, grey roan, red, black, roe deer colored, and plain white. Grey is the most common color.

CARE REQUIRED
Regular and thorough grooming with brush and comb will keep the coat in good condition. About once or twice a year pluck the coat to remove excess dead hair.

CHARACTER
These are friendly, gentle dogs that are kind to children, unconditionally loyal to their owner and family, pliable though not slavishly so, and calm.

TRAINING

The Irish Wolfhound is relatively easy to train. A gentle approach with plenty of understanding will go a long way because this dog quickly grasps what you intend.

Make sure that the young dog is given as much self-confidence as possible and that you are always consistent with it, so that it grows into an equable, confident dog.

Teach it not to pull on its leash before it gets too strong. These dogs grow rapidly and high-quality food is essential. Let the dog decide for itself how much exercise it wants.

Forced exercise and long-distance walks are too taxing for this dog's body when it is young. It takes two whole years before these dogs are fully grown.

SOCIAL BEHAVIOR

This breed normally gets on well with children and there should be no difficulty with other dogs.

This is also true for other animals if the dog has got to know them when it was young. They need to be at the center of a family and will be very unhappy in a kennel.

They tend to greet everyone as a friend, so don't count on them as watchdogs.

EXERCISE

These dogs adapt to your family circumstances and will not misbehave if the odd week passes with fewer chances to enjoy exercise, but that does not mean they do not enjoy being taken for long walks in the country.

Smooth-haired breeds

Azawakh

COUNTRY OF ORIGIN
Mali.

SPECIAL SKILLS
Hunter by sight of small and large game.

SIZE
The shoulder-height is 64 - 72cm (25¼ - 28½in) for dogs and 61 - 71cm (24 - 28in) for bitches.

COAT
The Azawakh has a short-haired coat which is sandy, red, or a roan of these colors. A white blaze and some white on the chest are acceptable, and white feet are a breed requirement.

CARE REQUIRED
The coat of this breed does not require much attention, only brushing now and then. Keep the dog's claws trimmed, the ears clean, and check from time to time to see if there is tartar on the teeth.

CHARACTER
These are temperamental, lively, independent, and proud dogs, that have considerable stamina, and are vigilant. These dogs only let people they like see their affectionate and gentle nature. Because their original natural behavior has not been bred out of them, these dogs will defend their own people if they are threatened.

Head of an Azawakh

TRAINING
It is not easy to train this dog. The most success is achieved with lots of patience and much insight into the dog's character. Corporal punishment will not force the dog to respect you – quite the opposite. Nevertheless, make sure the dog doesn't take liberties with you.

SOCIAL BEHAVIOR
The company of similar dogs is not a problem, and this dog also gets along well with children, as long as they respect the dog.
In view of their strong hunting instincts, these dogs should not be trusted with cats and other household animals. They are usually rather distrustful of strangers.

EXERCISE
This breed cannot be restricted to a daily trot around the block.
They must be able to run in order to get rid of their tremendous energy. This is an ideal dog for the really keen cyclist since they can cover considerable distances without tiring. In some countries it is forbidden to let dogs which hunt by sight such as the Azawakh to run freely off the leash.

Azawakh

Galgo Español

COUNTRY OF ORIGIN
Spain.

SPECIAL SKILLS
Hunting of small game by sight and family pet.

SIZE
The shoulder-height is 65 - 70cm (25½ - 27½in) for dogs and 60 - 68cm (23½ - 26¾in) for bitches.

Galgo Español

Head of a Galgo Español

COAT
This breed has both a short and rough-haired version. The majority of dogs are black, sandy, white, red, brown, yellow, or a roan.

CARE REQUIRED
Little grooming is required. In common with other dogs, the ears should be checked regularly and the claws kept short.

CHARACTER
These are intelligent, curious, and affectionate dogs which are kind to children and very loyal to their handler and family. If necessary they will protect their family.

TRAINING
With a very consistent approach and much patience and insight, these relatively untamed dogs can be basically trained in the basics. Direct the dog's natural character in the desired direction but do not try to create a perfectly responsive machine because this is the wrong dog for that.

It is extremely important that the young dog becomes acquainted with a variety of people and situations.

SOCIAL BEHAVIOR
These dogs will rarely cause any problems with children because they are still close to nature and instinctively know that small persons need care.

They like to play with other dogs and enjoy showing off their speed. They are not, however, a good ideal choice of dog if you have cats or other small animals because they have strong hunting instincts which make them chase anything which suddenly moves and they cannot resist that instinct.

EXERCISE
If these dogs have the freedom of a fair-sized piece of ground which is well fenced in, an outing twice a week with the bicycle for a change of background will be sufficient.
If not, they will need a considerable amount of more formal exercise.
If this is not available the dog is likely to become very frustrated and to make this obvious.

Greyhound

Greyhound

COUNTRY OF ORIGIN
England.

SPECIAL SKILLS
Racing dog, hunter by sight of large and small game, and family pet.

255

SIZE
The shoulder-height is 71 - 76cm (28 - 30in) for dogs and 68 - 71cm (26¾ - 28in) for bitches.

COAT
Greyhounds have a smooth, close coat of short hairs most commonly seen in black, white, fawn, orange, and roans of these colors or with other white markings.

CARE REQUIRED
It is sufficient to groom the Greyhound occasionally with a soft brush. However, the ears should be checked regularly and the claws kept trimmed. These dogs are suitable for living in an outdoor kennel because they are reasonably resistant to the cold. Make sure that where they sleep is dry and draught-free.

CHARACTER
These dogs are calm and sociable indoors, to the point where they can even be considered lazy. These dogs are intelligent, sensitive, bond strongly with their own people, have tremendous stamina, and do not bark much. Greyhounds are not particularly vigilant.

TRAINING
Compared with the other fleet-footed keen-eyed hunters, the Greyhound is reasonably easy to train.
They can learn almost all commands and are fairly obedient except when they have set their eyes on a prey. Then they will ignore all your commands.

In some countries dogs of this entire group are not allowed out unless they remain on a leash,

Greyhounds are suitable for dog racing.

not just because of the danger they could present for wild animals but also the danger to themselves and road-users.

SOCIAL BEHAVIOR
It is instinctive for these dogs to chase anything that moves quickly, which means that they are not really suitable companions for people with one or more cats.
They seldom present difficulties with other dogs and are normally good with children. With strangers, they tend to be rather cautious.

EXERCISE
The dogs of this breed want to cover long distances running and walking. Consider joining a Greyhound racing association because the dogs can really express their natural selves on a race track.
Trotting alongside a bicycle is a good alternative for working off the dog's energy. It does not really matter how the dog gets its exercise provided it gets enough.

SPECIAL REMARKS
Greyhounds which race differ quite a bit from those which must do well in the show ring. They are a very healthy breed and can live quite long.

Italian Greyhound

COUNTRY OF ORIGIN
Italy/Egypt.

SPECIAL SKILLS
Hunter by sight of rabbits and other game; also a family pet.

SIZE
The shoulder-height is 32 - 38cm (12½ - 15in).

COAT
The coat is fine and short. The color of this breed is frequently a greyish yellow, black, or slate, perhaps with white on the chest and feet. Flecked versions also exist but are not accepted in all countries.

CARE REQUIRED
These dogs need little grooming. It is usually sufficient to wipe the dog with a cloth to make the coat shine. It is necessary to check the teeth regularly because tartar is prevalent with this breed. The adult dog is certainly not delicate but until they are about eighteen-months old their bones are quite fragile and they can break a leg rather easily.

Italian Greyhound

Italian Greyhounds

CHARACTER
These are gentle, affectionate, and cheerful dogs that are quick and active, intelligent, and compliant.

TRAINING
Generally these are not difficult dogs to train provided their handler is consistent with them. They are often naughty and are aware that they are.

It is important that you can see the funny side when things go wrong but this does not mean allowing them to take advantage of you.

SOCIAL BEHAVIOR
These dogs get on well with other dogs and cats and they normally also get on well with children, but do not let children treat the dog as a toy.

They are not good companions for Rottweilers. Italian Greyhounds usually get on well with each other and it is recommended that you have more than one of them.

EXERCISE
This active breed likes to run. If possible, let your Italian Greyhound run freely on an enclosed patch of land.

Sloughi

COUNTRY OF ORIGIN
Morocco.

SPECIAL SKILLS
Hunter by sight of large and small game, and companion.

SIZE
The shoulder-height is 66 - 72cm (26 - 28½in) for dogs and 61 - 68cm (24 - 26¾in) for bitches. The ideal height is 70cm (27½in) for dogs and 65cm (25½in) for bitches.

COAT
The Sloughi has a soft, short, coat, usually seen in various shades of sandy colorings or a roan, with or without a darker mask.

CARE REQUIRED
These dogs require little grooming. An occasional brushing is adequate.
Keep the claws trimmed and check the teeth for tartar.

CHARACTER
These are proud, temperamental, and somewhat obstinate dogs with considerable stamina.

They are vigilant, and cautious with strangers. They only show affection towards people they truly like.

Sloughi

This independent-minded dog is not easy to train, but that does not mean it cannot be taught anything.

A handler with sufficient insight into the dog's character and lots of patience can teach the Sloughi much, creating a bond of mutual respect between them.

SOCIAL BEHAVIOR
It is necessary to introduce this breed when quite young to all manner of situations, different people and animals.

Properly trained, it is possible for a Sloughi to live together with one or more cats.

EXERCISE
This breed has an enormous desire for exercise.

In some countries breeds such as this that hunt by sight are not allowed to run freely off the leash and when this is the case the race track is the only place where they can rid themselves of their energy.
These dogs have tremendous stamina.

Whippet

COUNTRY OF ORIGIN
England.

SPECIAL SKILLS
Racing dog and family pet.

SIZE
The shoulder-height is 47 - 51cm (18½ - 20in) for dogs and 44 - 47cm (17¼- 18½in) for bitches.

COAT
The short coat is fine and dense. It comes in many colors but the most common are white with streaked or yellow patches, black, black with white, blue, roan, or beige with darker mask.

CARE REQUIRED
Little grooming is required for these dogs. It is sufficient to brush them from time to time to remove dead and loose hairs. Some examples have a predisposition for tartar on their teeth but this can be kept in check by regularly giving them something to chew. Keep the claws trimmed short.

Head of a Sloughi

Whippet

CHARACTER
These dogs are affectionate, cuddly, and lovely with children. They are also intelligent but not particularly obedient, cheerful, peaceable, playful, a touch obstinate, and sometimes also vigilant.

TRAINING
Introduce plenty of variety into a Whippet's training. The best results are achieved by interspersing games and running but remember that you will never achieve perfect obedience from this dog.

SOCIAL BEHAVIOR
Whippets are usually very good with children but they tend not to be too fond of strangers. They will invariably warn you of visitors. They are very tolerant of other dogs and there is rarely any difficulty. The tendency to chase everything that moves quickly is inborn in them. The household cat, to which the dog has grown accustomed, will be left alone.

EXERCISE
The Whippet is a small Greyhound, meaning that its entire body is built for racing and hunting. Understandably, therefore, Whippets need plenty of exercise. In some countries they may not be allowed to run freely off the leash, in common with other dogs that hunt by sight. In these circumstances bicycle with the dog or join an organization that races Whippets so that you can let the dog live its life fully on the race track.

Whippets

11. Breeds that are not recognized

American-Canadian White Shepherd

COUNTRY OF ORIGIN
United States/Canada/Europe.

SPECIAL SKILLS
Family pet.

SIZE
The shoulder-height is 60 - 65cm (23½ - 25½n) for dogs and 55 - 60cm (21½ - 23½in) for bitches.

Variation of 2cm (¾in) on these dimensions is permitted provided the overall proportions of the dog are correct.

COAT
This breed has stiff, long stiff, or long-haired coats. The long-haired types do not have an undercoat. The color is always white.

CARE REQUIRED
Brush and comb these dogs every day when they are shedding. Check the ears regularly and keep the claws trimmed short.

CHARACTER
These are friendly, intelligent, attentive, and loyal dogs that are eager to work. They like to be close to their handler.

TRAINING
These dogs are easy to train because they like to work for their handler and they learn quite quickly. It is very important that the young dog has lots of positive encounters with many different animals, people, things, and situations to help it grow up to be a well-balanced animal.

SOCIAL BEHAVIOR
These dogs generally get on well with other dogs and children. If they have the chance to get to know them when they are young, they will also get along with cats and other pets.

EXERCISE
This breed has an average demand for

American-Canadian White Shepherd

exercise, but three trips around the block a day is not adequate exercise and the dog would quickly become bored with this routine. These dogs are very suitable for various sporting activities such as obedience, catch, and agility skills trials.

American-Canadian White Shepherd

Short-legged Jack Russell

Short-legged Jack Russell

COUNTRY OF ORIGIN
England.

SPECIAL SKILLS
Hunting dog and family pet.

SIZE
The shoulder-height is 25 - 30cm (9¾ - 11¾in).

COAT

There are two types of coat: the rough and the smooth-haired. With both types the hair is wiry, close, and dense.

The color is either all white or marked with tan, lemon, or black markings, or with all three. The markings are preferably restricted to the root of the tail and the head.

CARE REQUIRED

This Jack Russell needs little grooming. Brush occasionally to keep the coat in good condition.

CHARACTER

These are animated, very brave and temperamental dogs, that are vigilant, lively, enterprising, intelligent, and playful. They can also be hard on themselves, have minds of their own, try to dominate, and be independent.

TRAINING

This healthy breed is not difficult to train for handlers who are kind, very consistent, and confident of themselves. They are brimming with self-confidence and if you and your family let them, they will do what they want rather than what you want.

SOCIAL BEHAVIOR

Provided they are socially trained when they are young, there should be no difficulties with other dogs and pets. These dogs are independent hunting dogs by nature, which accept a cat that lives in its own house but will chase any others. They are normally good with children and can accept a little roughousing.

EXERCISE

These dogs have tremendous energy and they like to work. Not surprisingly, they are not content to be hurried through three walks a day. They want to run and play, and they love to dig. They are first-class destroyers of vermin, making them ideal dogs to live on a farm. They can be quite impressive in sports such as catch.

Short-legged Jack Russells

Important addresses

For all questions regarding breeds in general you can contact your national dog institution.

In the United States this is:
The American Kennel Club
51 Madison Avenue
New York NY 10010

In Canada this is:
The Canadian Kennel Club
89 Skyway Ave., Unit 100
Etobicoke, ON M9W GR4

Photograph acknowledgements and thanks

All the photographs were taken by Esther J.J. Verhoef-Verhallen. Additional material was provided by:
Sandra Arts; H. Settelaar: R. van Riet; C.C. Asselbergs; A. Christiansen; Archief Pystykorva; Joenpolvi; J.W.A. Snel; Lochs-Romans; Reina Jansen; Willemien Dubislav-Tol; Henk and Ine Hartgers-Wagener.

The publishers and author would like to thank the following owners for making their dogs available:

2. Sheepdogs and cattle herders
The Avontuur family, F.H.M. Backx, the Beenen-Sluijters family, Mascha Bollen, the van Boven family, Bea and Gerrit Enthoven, P.B.T. Gerritsen, J. de Gids, D. Griffin, H. ten Haaf, the De Haas family, T. van der Heijden, W.L. van der Hoek, C.A. Keizer, the Klein family, D. van Klingeren, H.M. Luijken, Yvonne Maas, Jacky Marks, M. and J. van Mook, Mr Van de Meijden senior, M.A. van Mierlo, Laura van den Nieuwenhuijzen, A. van Noorda, M.E. Spiering, M. Olsthoorn, the Van Ooijen family, R. Peschier, the Prins family, Bert Reintjes, T.A. Scherbeyn, Yvonne Schultz, H. Settelaar, H. Smits, R. and A. Tetteroo, H.P.P. Verbakel, Jet Vermeulen, the Welvering family, Nancy Wijnhoven.

3. Pinscher, Schnauzer, Molossian, Mastiff, and Swiss Sennenhunds breeds
J.M.W. van de Berg, J. Bouland-Planken, Arie and JosJ den Dekker-Bragt, M. van Deursen, the Gest family, M.I.J. van Goethem-Jagt, H. and I. Hartgers-Wagener, P. Hendriks, Louis Hillebrand, the Hoendervanger family, J.C.G. van der Kant, Frans Kappe, G. Kemps, J. and E. Kloosterhof, E. Kluijs, H.T.J. van Laar, M.C. Langendoen, L.J. Lodders, J. Luyks, B. Martens, the van de Mierden family, the Nettenbreijer family, the Oudendijk family, the Plattje family, Pranger, the Reijnen-Labee family, J .Rutten, Schellekens, J.M. Stramer, Joke and Jan Verberkt, E. Verhoef, the J. Westerhoven family, A. van Wijk, F. and L. van Wijk, G. van Wijk, Annette Wijnsouw, C. Zuydeweg-Roxs.

3. Terriers
J.H. Albers, Atilla and Nancy, Marianne Baas-Becking, R. Bomers, Laurens and Sandra van de Burgt, J. Dekker and J. Roskam, Charlotte Froon, A. Hartmann-Tibbe, A. van Hoorn, Peter Jaspers, Colette de Jong, R. and I. Kelleter, E. Lahaye, B. and P. Langemaat-Oudkerk, J. van Lieshout, G.H.J. Lustigheid, C. Meijer, W. Pul, W. de Reus and R. Bomers, Irma de Roo-Strous, R.P. Snip and J. Bourret, Marga Steenvoorden, C.C.E. Thomas, P. Koolen, W. Tijsse-Claase, T. Hoffman-Winkels, Jet Vermeulen, Th. and W. van Vessem, Lily Weber, the De Wolf family.

4. Dachshunds
Mrs Blom, Jeanine van de Heuvel, P. van Leeuwen, the van Oers family.

5. Spitz and other primitive breeds
J.A. van de Berkmortel, A.W. Bruynzeel, Michel Cayol, M. van Deursen, Chris Eizenga, R. and M. Fisher, Jennifer Gielisse, Sandra van de Graaf, Cornelis Koot, Marjo van Oers-van Mimpen, Ronny van Riet, H. Vrieze, J.W.A. Snel, A.M.M. Konijnenburg, Jet Vermeulen, the De Wolf family.

6. Hounds
Thea Bouman, M. van de Broek, N. Horsten, H. and F. Huikeshoven, Mrs De Jong-Van Wijngaarden, G.M. Koenraadt, B. and P.

Langemaat-Oudkerk, R. Morgans, the Rust family, R. Smits.

7. Pointers
J.F.H. Brocken, Anneke Cornelissen, A. Dekker, Lianne Eekman-Lampio, Margriet Gijsen-van de Bosch, Jan van Haren, A. Harduin, N. Hoogervorst-Hazenoot, J. Kamsteeg, G. Kemps, R. Key, Marianne Krans, B.G.A.W. Maton, M.B. Melchior, I. Nannings-Balvert, the Roks family, the Van Son family, A. Vorstenbosch, M.J.A.H.M. van Wanrooij, J. van Dommelen, Annette Wijnsouw.

7. Gundogs and retrievers
A. Cat, Jolanda van Gils, A. de Goede-van den Burg, Ellen Hagendijk, M. Hoogendorp, Hazel Huybregts-Kingham, A.T. Kramer, the Knol family, Ge and Ria Kleynen, H. Konings, R. Lochs-Romans, J. Luyks, R. Notenboom, J-P and V. Perennec, the Smits-Steenbakkers's, Van der Linden-Steenbakkers, J. Tresoor-Homan, Marc Wynn, Ton and Louise van Zoom, C. Zuydeweg-Roxs.

1. Toy and other miniature dogs
Hans Bleeker, Jan den Otter, M.W.A.H. Cooymans, A.M. and T. van Dongen-Ribberink, Willemien Dubislav-Tol, A.P.M. van de Horst, H.R. Jacobs, Reina Jansen, Wim and Ria Jansen, Reina Janssen-Spits, M. Kavelaars, J. and E. Kloosterhof, T.J. Koster, T.J. Koster and A. Leliveld, J. van Lieshout, H.M. Luijken, Erwin Manders, Jo and Majorie Nelissen, B. and Chr. Schiltman, J. Tekelenburg, J. Timmers, H. Verhees, the De Wit-Meemen's, F. Voogt, R. Rullens.

2. Sighthounds
The Ferber-Llinares family, Anita, M.T.H Gielisse, Jennifer Gielisse, Sandra van de Graaf, E. van de Have-van Dipten, Annemie and Jo Hoffman, Phil Morgan, the Oudendijk family, Sonja van Rij-van Baarle.

3. Breeds that are not recognized
B. Klerken, H.L. Noordhoek.

The author particularly wishes to thank C.C. and T.J. Asselbergs for the information they provided regarding the Scandinavian breeds.

Thanks are also due to all the breed societies, breed specialist, breeders, owners, and enthusiasts not named above who made equally important contributions to ensure accurate descriptions of the breeds in question.

Index

Labrador Retriever

Grand Basset Griffon Vendéen

Glen of Imaal Terrier

Tervueren Belgian Sheperd